Essential Italian

Edited by

Laura Riggio and Giulia Bencini

LIVING LANGUAGE®

Content in this program has been modified and enhanced from *Starting Out in Italian*, published in 2008.

Published in the United States by Living Language, an imprint of Random House, Inc.

www.livinglanguage.com

Editor: Laura Riggio
Production Editor: Ciara Robinson
Production Manager: Tom Marshall
Interior Design: Sophie Chin
Illustrations: Sophie Chin

First Edition

Library of Congress Cataloging-in-Publication Data

Essential Italian / edited by Laura Riggio and Giulia Bencini. — 1st ed.
    p. cm.
  ISBN 978-0-307-97156-2
  1. Italian language—Textbooks for foreign speakers—English. 2. Italian language—Grammar.
  3. Italian language—Spoken Italian. I. Riggio, Laura. II. Bencini, Giulia.
  PC1129.E5E88 2011
  458.2'421—dc23
                        2011021873

This book is available at special discounts for bulk purchases for sales promotions or premiums. Special editions, including personalized covers, excerpts of existing books, and corporate imprints, can be created in large quantities for special needs. For more information, write to Special Markets/ Premium Sales, 1745 Broadway, MD 3-1, New York, New York 10019 or e-mail specialmarkets@ randomhouse.com.
PRINTED IN THE UNITED STATES OF AMERICA
20 19 18 17 16 15

Acknowledgments

Thanks to the Living Language team: Amanda D'Acierno, Christopher Warnasch, Suzanne McQuade, Laura Riggio, Erin Quirk, Amanda Munoz, Fabrizio LaRocca, Siobhan O'Hare, Sophie Chin, Sue Daulton, Alison Skrabek, Carolyn Roth, Ciara Robinson, and Tom Marshall.

How to Use This Course **6**

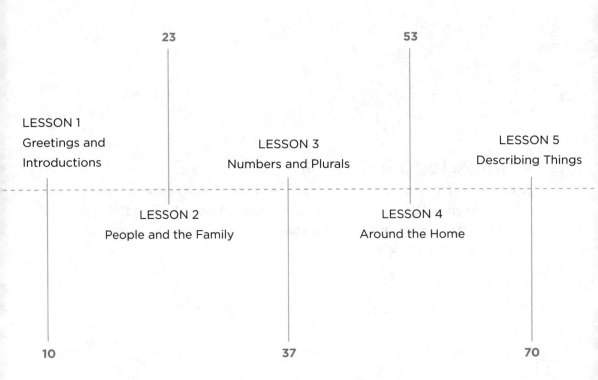

23

53

LESSON 1
Greetings and
Introductions

LESSON 3
Numbers and Plurals

LESSON 5
Describing Things

LESSON 2
People and the Family

LESSON 4
Around the Home

10

37

70

C O U R S E

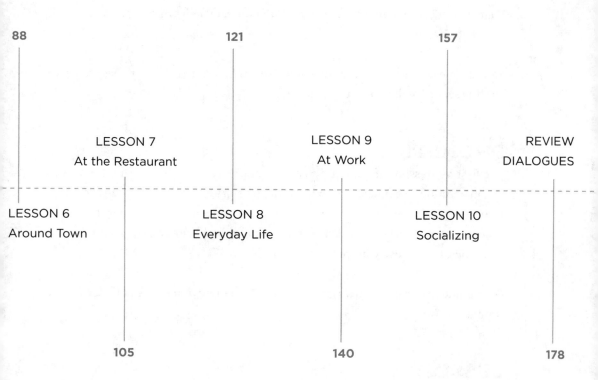

88

121

157

LESSON 7
At the Restaurant

LESSON 9
At Work

REVIEW
DIALOGUES

LESSON 6
Around Town

LESSON 8
Everyday Life

LESSON 10
Socializing

105

140

178

Quiz 1 85
Quiz 2 175
Pronunciation Guide 194
Grammar Summary 198
Glossary 228

OUTLINE

How to Use This Course

Ciao!

Welcome to *Living Language Essential Italian*! Ready to learn how to speak, read, and write Italian?

Before we begin, let's go over what you'll see in this course. It's very easy to use, but this section will help you get started.

PHONETICS

The first five lessons of this course contain phonetics (in other words, [broo-SKEH-tah] in addition to **bruschetta**) to help you get started with Italian pronunciation. However, please keep in mind that phonetics are not exact—they are just a general approximation of sounds—and you should rely most on the audio, *not* the phonetics, to improve your pronunciation skills.

For a guide to our phonetics system, see the Pronunciation Guide at the end of the course.

LESSONS

There are 10 lessons in this course. Each lesson is divided into three parts and has the following components:

Welcome at the beginning outlining what you will cover in each of the three parts of the lesson.

PART 1

- **Vocabulary Builder 1** listing the key words and phrases for that lesson.

- **Vocabulary Practice 1** to practice what you learned in Vocabulary Builder 1.

- **Grammar Builder 1** to guide you through the structure of the Italian language (how to form sentences, questions, and so on).

PART 2

- **Vocabulary Builder 2** listing more key words and phrases.

- **Vocabulary Practice 2** to practice what you learned in Vocabulary Builder 2.

- **Grammar Builder 2** for more information on language structure.

- **Work Out 1** for a comprehensive practice of what you've learned so far.

PART 3

- **Bring It All Together** to put what you've learned in a conversational context through a dialogue, monologue, description, or other similar text.

- **Work Out 2** for another helpful practice exercise.

- **Drive It Home** to ingrain an important point of Italian structure for the long term.

- **Parting Words** outlining what you learned in the lesson.

TAKE IT FURTHER

- **Take It Further** sections scattered throughout the lesson to provide extra information about the new vocabulary you just saw, expand on some grammar points, or introduce additional words and phrases.

WORD RECALL

Word Recall sections appear in between lessons. They review important vocabulary and grammar from previous lessons, including the one you just finished. These sections will reinforce what you've learned so far in the course, and help you retain the information for the long term.

QUIZZES

This course contains two quizzes: **Quiz 1** is halfway through the course (after Lesson 5), and **Quiz 2** appears after the last lesson (Lesson 10). The quizzes are self-graded so it's easy for you to test your progress and see if you should go back and review.

REVIEW DIALOGUES

There are five **Review Dialogues** at the end of the course, after Quiz 2. These everyday dialogues review what you learned in Lessons 1-10, introduce some new vocabulary and structures, and allow you to become more familiar with conversational Italian. Each dialogue is followed by comprehension questions that serve as the course's final review.

PROGRESS BAR

You will see a **Progress Bar** on almost every page that has course material. It indicates your current position in the course and lets you know how much progress you're making. Each line in the bar represents a lesson, with the final line representing the Review Dialogues.

AUDIO

Look for this symbol ▶ to help guide you through the audio as you're reading the book. It will tell you which track to listen to for each section that has audio. When you see the symbol, select the indicated track and start listening! If you don't see the symbol, then there isn't any audio for that section. You'll also see ⏸, which will tell you where that track ends.

The audio can be used on its own—in other words, without the book—when you're on the go. Whether in your car or at the gym, you can listen to the audio to brush up on your pronunciation, review what you've learned in the book, or even use it as a standalone course.

PRONUNCIATION GUIDE, GRAMMAR SUMMARY, GLOSSARY

At the back of this book you will find a **Pronunciation Guide**, **Grammar Summary**, and **Glossary**. The Pronunciation Guide provides information on Italian pronunciation and the phonetics system used in this course. The Grammar Summary contains a helpful, brief overview of key points in the Italian grammar system. It also includes a **Grammar Index**, which lists the principal grammar topics covered in this course and where to find them in the book. The Glossary (Italian-English and English-Italian) includes all of the essential words from the ten lessons, as well as additional key vocabulary.

FREE ONLINE TOOLS

Go to **www.livinglanguage.com/languagelab** to access your free online tools. The tools are organized around lessons in this course, with audiovisual flash cards, as well as interactive games and quizzes for each lesson. These tools will help you review and practice the vocabulary and grammar that you've seen in the lessons, as well as provide some extra words and phrases related to the lesson's topic.

Lesson 1:
Greetings and Introductions

Prima Lezione: Saluti e presentazioni

PREE-mah leh-TSYOH-neh: sah-LOO-tee eh preh-zen-tah-TSYOH-nee

Ciao! [chow] *Hello!* In this lesson, you'll learn some basic expressions and other useful words and phrases to get you started speaking Italian. You'll learn how to:

☐ say *hello* and *good-bye*

☐ greet people at different times of the day

☐ introduce yourself and give your name

☐ ask other people's names, and find out how they're doing

☐ put it all together in a simple conversation

Let's get started with some simple greetings. Ready?

Remember to look for this symbol ⊙ to help guide you through the audio as you're reading the book. It will tell you which track to listen to for each section that has audio. When you see the symbol, select the indicated track and start listening. If you don't see the symbol, there isn't any audio for that section. You'll also see ⊚, which will tell you where the track ends. Finally, keep in mind that the audio can be used on its own for review and practice on the go!

Vocabulary Builder 1

▶ 1B Vocabulary Builder 1 (CD 1, Track 2)

hi, hello, good-bye	**ciao**	chow
hello	**salve**	SAHL-veh
good morning	**buon giorno**	bwohn JOHR-noh
good afternoon	**buon pomeriggio**	bwohn poh-meh-REE-jyoh
good evening	**buona sera**	BWOH-nah SEH-rah
good night	**buona notte**	BWOH-nah NOH-teh
have a good day	**buona giornata**	BWOH-nah JOHR-nah-tah
have a good evening	**buona serata**	BWOH-nah seh-RAH-tah
good-bye (infml.)	**arrivederci**	ah-ree-veh-DEHR-chee
good-bye (fml.)	**arrivederLa**	ah-ree-veh-DEHR-lah
see you soon	**a presto**	ah PREH-stoh
see you later	**a dopo**	ah DOH-poh

⏸

✎ Vocabulary Practice 1

Let's practice the vocabulary you've learned. Match the Italian in the left column with the English equivalent in the right.

1. **ciao**   a. *good-bye (infml.)*

2. **buon giorno**   b. *see you later*

3. **buon pomeriggio**   c. *good evening*

4. **buona sera**   d. *good-bye (fml.)*

5. **buona notte**   e. *hi, hello*

6. **buona giornata**   f. *see you soon*

7. **arrivederci**   g. *good morning*

8. **arrivederLa**   h. *good night*

9. a presto

10. a dopo

i. *good afternoon*

j. *have a good day*

ANSWER KEY
1. e; 2. g; 3. i; 4. c; 5. h; 6. j; 7. a; 8. d; 9. f; 10. b.

Grammar Builder 1

▶ 1C Grammar Builder 1 (CD 1, Track 3)

Okay, let's stop for a moment. You just learned how to say:

hello	ciao, salve
good morning	buon giorno
good afternoon	buon pomeriggio
good evening	buona sera
good night	buona notte
have a good day	buona giornata
have a good evening	buona serata
see you soon	a presto
see you later	a dopo

Did you notice that there are two expressions for *good-bye*, either **arrivederci** or **arrivederLa**? That's because the first (**arrivederci**) is informal, and the second (**arrivederLa**) is formal. You'll use **arrivederci** with family and friends, and **arrivederLa** in any other context. However, very often people tend to use **arrivederci** in formal contexts, too.

Also keep in mind that another informal—and very common—way to say good-bye is **ciao**, better if repeated twice: **ciao ciao!** (*bye-bye!*)

Now that you know how to greet people, let's move on to some vocabulary and expressions you can use to introduce yourself and make someone's acquaintance.

Take It Further

You've probably noticed the capital L in **arriverderLa**. It's not a typo. It's actually a pronoun that corresponds to the formal form of *you*. You'll learn more about pronouns later, but for now keep in mind that there are several different ways of saying *you* in Italian, depending on whether you're being polite or familiar, and whether you're speaking to one person or more. The word **arrivederLa** literally means something like "until I see you again," and the **-La** means that the *you* is a polite form.

The **-ci** in **arriverderci** is also a pronoun, but it means *us* or *each other*. So, **arrivederci** literally means something like "until we see each other again."

Vocabulary Builder 2

▶ 1D Vocabulary Builder 2 (CD 1, Track 4)

My name is …	**Mi chiamo …**	mee KYAH-moh
I am from …	**Sono di …**	SOH-noh dee
… and you (infml.)?	**… e tu?**	eh too
… and you (fml.)?	**… e Lei?**	eh lay
Pleased to meet you.	**Piacere.**	pyah-CHEH-reh
Pleased to meet you, too.	**Piacere mio.**	pyah-CHEH-reh MEE-oh
How are you doing (infml.)?	**Come stai?**	KOH-meh STAH-ee
How are you doing (fml.)?	**Come sta?**	KOH-meh stah
Very well, thanks.	**Molto bene, grazie.**	MOHL-toh BEH-neh GRAH-tsyeh

(I am) Fine, thanks.	(Sto) Bene, grazie.	stoh BEH-neh GRAH-tsyeh
So so, not bad.	Così, così.	koh-ZEE koh-ZEE
Thank you.	Grazie.	GRAH-tsyeh
Thanks a lot.	Grazie mille.	GRAH-tsyeh MEEL-leh
You're welcome.	Prego.	PREH-goh
Don't mention it.	Non c'è di che.	nohn cheh dee keh

✎ Vocabulary Practice 2

Now let's practice the new vocabulary. Fill in the missing words in each of the following expressions.

1. _____ chiamo … (My name is …)

2. Molto _____, grazie. (Very well, thanks.)

3. _____ mille. (Thanks a lot.)

4. Come _____? (How are you doing? (fml.))

5. E____? (And you? (infml.))

6. _____ di (I am from …)

ANSWER KEY
1. Mi; 2. bene; 3. Grazie; 4. sta; 5. tu; 6. Sono

Grammar Builder 2

▶ 1E Grammar Builder 2 (CD 1, Track 5)

Let's pause there for a moment and focus on a very important distinction. In Italian, there is a formal and an informal way to introduce yourself and make someone's acquaintance. If you're meeting someone in a casual context you'll say:

Ciao, mi chiamo … e tu?
Hi, my name is … , and you?

While in a more formal context you'll say:

Salve (Buon giorno/Buona sera/ …), mi chiamo … e Lei?
Hello, my name is … , and you?

Again, you have two options to ask someone how he or she is doing:

Come stai?
How are you? (infml.)

Come sta?
How are you? (fml.)

Keep in mind that the formal *you* (**Lei**) is always capitalized in writing to avoid confusion with the feminine pronoun **lei**, meaning *she*.

⨀

✎ Work Out 1

Let's practice some of what you've heard in a listening comprehension exercise.
Listen to the audio, and fill in the blanks with the words that you hear.

▶ 1F Work Out 1 (CD 1, Track 6)

1. *My name is Mario, and you?*

   Mi _____ Mario, e tu?

2. *Good evening Mario, my name is Carla. How are you?*

   Buona _____ Mario, mi chiamo Carla. Come _____?

3. *Very well, thanks.*

   _____ bene, grazie.

4. *Pleased to meet you!*

   _____!

5. *Pleased to meet you, too!*

   Piacere _____!

6. *Have a good day.*

   _____ giornata.

7. *See you later.*

   _____.

ⓘ

ANSWER KEY
1. chiamo; 2. sera, stai; 3. Molto; 4. Piacere; 5. mio; 6. Buona; 7. A dopo

🅰 Bring It All Together

▶ 1G Bring It All Together (CD 1, Track 7)

Now let's bring it all together, and add a little bit more vocabulary and structure.

Good morning, my name is Paul Bennet. I'm from Boston, and you (fml.)?
Buon giorno, mi chiamo Paul Bennet. Io sono di Boston e Lei?
bwohn JOHR-noh, mee KYAH-moh paul bennet. EE-oh SOH-noh dee boston. eh lay?

My name is Carla Betti and I'm from Milan. Very pleased to meet you!
Mi chiamo Carla Betti e io sono di Milano. Molto piacere!
mee KYAH-moh KAHr-lah BET-tee eh EE-oh SOH-noh dee mee-LAH-noh. MOHL-toh
pyah-CHEH-reh!

Pleased to meet you, too.
Piacere mio.
pyah-CHEH-reh MEE-oh.

How's it going, Mr. Bennet?
Come va signor Bennet?
KOH-meh vah see-NYOHR bennet?

Fine, thanks. And how are you doing?
Bene, grazie. E Lei come sta?
BEH-neh, GRAH-tsyeh. Eh lay KOH-meh stah?

So so.
Così, così.
koh-ZEE, koh-ZEE

Good-bye, Mr. Bennet.

ArrivederLa signor Bennet.

ah-ree-veh-DEHR-lah, see-NYOHR bennet.

Have a good day!

Buona giornata!

BWOH-nah JOHR-nah-tah!

Take It Further

 1H Take It Further (CD 1, Track 8)

Okay, let's focus on a couple of new words and expressions you just heard in the dialogue. Did you notice that **(io) sono di** means *I am from*? This is a very useful expression to use when you want to say what city you come from:

Sono di Milano.	*I'm from Milan.*
Sono di Boston.	*I'm from Boston.*
Sono di New York.	*I'm from New York.*

You already know how to ask someone how he or she is doing using the informal **come stai?** and the formal **come sta?**. You just learned a new expression that you can use in both formal and informal contexts: **come va?**, which literally means *how's it going?*

✎ Work Out 2

Let's go back and take a second look at the conversation you heard in the **Bring It All Together** section. Can you fill in the blanks? If you need to, go back and listen to the dialogue one more time.

1. Buon _____, mi _____ Paul Bennet. Io sono ____ Boston, e Lei?

2. Mi chiamo Carla Betti e io _____ di Milano. Molto _____!

3. Piacere _____.

4. _____ va signor Bennet?

5. Bene, _____. E Lei come _____?

6. Così _____.

7. _____ signor Bennet.

8. _____ giornata!

ANSWER KEY
1. giorno, chiamo, di; 2. sono, piacere; 3. mio; 4. Come; 5. grazie, sta; 6. così; 7. ArrivederLa 8. Buona

▶ 1I Work Out 2 (CD 1, Track 9)

Now listen to the audio for some more audio-only practice. This will help you master the material you've learned so far!

⏸

✎ Drive It Home

Throughout this course you'll see **Drive It Home** sections that include practices on key grammar and constructions you've learned. At first glance, these exercises may seem simple and repetitive, so you may be tempted to skip them. But don't! These exercises are designed to help make the structures that you learn more automatic, and to move them into your long-term memory. So take the time to do each exercise completely, writing out all the answers, and speaking them aloud to yourself. This will really help you retain the information.

A. First, let's start with something simple. Fill in the blanks of each greeting, according to the time of day given in parentheses. Then speak the whole sentence aloud.

1. Buon _____, Paolo. Come stai? *(morning)*

2. Buon _____, Lucia. Come stai? *(afternoon)*

3. Buona _____, Riccardo. Come stai? *(evening)*

4. Buona _____, Alessandro! *(night)*

B. Now, fill in each blank with the Italian for *I am from*. Don't use the pronoun, so your answer should have just two words. Say each sentence aloud after you've written out the answer.

1. _____ Milano.

2. _____ Roma.

3. _____ Venezia.

4. _____ Napoli.

5. _____ Firenze.

ANSWER KEY
A. 1. giorno; 2. pomeriggio; 3. sera; 4. notte
B. Sono di …

Parting Words

Molto bene! *Well done!* You just finished your first lesson of *Essential Italian*. How did you do? You should now be able to:

☐ say *hello* and *good-bye*. (Still unsure? Go back to page 11.)

☐ greet people at different times of the day. (Still unsure? Go back to page 12.)

☐ introduce yourself and give your name. (Still unsure? Go back to page 13.)

☐ ask other people's names, and find out how they're doing. (Still unsure? Go back to page 15.)

☐ put it all together in a simple conversation. (Still unsure? Go back to page 17.)

Don't forget to practice and reinforce what you've learned by visiting **www.livinglanguage.com/ languagelab** for flashcards, games, and quizzes for Lesson One!

Take It Further

 1J Take It Further (CD 1, Track 10)

You learned a lot of essential greetings in this first lesson. As you can probably guess, **buon pomeriggio** (*good afternoon*) is used to greet people between 1 pm and 6 pm. **Buona notte** (*good night*) is used when parting late at night, or before going to bed. Another useful expression to know is **a presto!** [ah PREH-stoh], which means *see you soon!*

Word Recall

You will see this section between each lesson. It gives you the chance to review key vocabulary from all of the previous lessons up to that point, not only the lesson you've just completed. This will reinforce the vocabulary, as well as some of the structures that you've learned so far in the course, so that you can retain them in your long-term memory. For now, though, we'll only review the key vocabulary you learned in Lesson One. Match the Italian in the left column with the English equivalent in the right.

1. Grazie mille   a. *How are you (infml.)*

2. Mi chiamo   b. *I am from*

3. Come va?   c. *Pleased to meet you too*

4. Non c'è di che   d. *And you (fml.)*

5. Così, così.   e. *Hello*

6. Come sta?   f. *My name is*

7. Prego   g. *How are you/How's it going*

8. Piacere mio   h. *Thanks a lot*

9. Come stai?   i. *How are you (fml.)*

10. E Lei?   j. *So so*

11. Salve   k. *Don't mention it*

12. Sono di   l. *You're welcome*

ANSWER KEY
1. h; 2. f; 3. g; 4. k; 5. j; 6. i; 7. l; 8. c; 9. a; 10. d; 11. e; 12 b.

Lesson 2: People and the Family

Seconda Lezione: Le persone e la famiglia

seh-KOHN-dah leh-TSYOH-neh: leh pehr-SOH-neh eh lah
fah-MEE-lyah

Benvenuto! [BEHN-veh-noo-toh] *Welcome!* In your second lesson, you'll continue to build your basic vocabulary and learn some key structures in Italian. In this lesson you'll learn:

☐ basic vocabulary related to people

☐ about gender in Italian, and how to say *a*

☐ basic vocabulary related to the family

☐ how to say *the, there is,* and *there are*

☐ how to have a simple conversation about your family

Let's get started with some vocabulary first!

Vocabulary Builder 1

▶ 2B Vocabulary Builder 1 (CD 1, Track 12)

a person	una persona	OO-nah pehr-SOH-nah
a woman	una donna	OO-nah DOHN-nah
Here is …	Ecco …	EHK-koh …
Here is a woman.	Ecco una donna.	EHK-koh OO-nah DOHN-nah
a man	un uomo	oon oo-OH-moh
a girl	una ragazza	OO-nah rah-GAH-tsah
a boy	un ragazzo	oon rah-GAH-tsoh
a child (boy)	un bambino	oon bahm-BEE-noh
a child (girl)	una bambina	OO-nah bahm-BEE-nah

Vocabulary Practice 1

Find the translations of the following words.

1. girl

2. person

3. here is …

4. child (boy)

5. man

6. woman

7. boy

8. a (as in a man)

9. a (as in a woman)

B	A	M	D	O	N	N	A
U	B	R	R	U	O	M	P
R	A	G	A	Z	Z	A	E
A	M	C	G	B	U	M	R
G	B	C	A	A	N	E	S
A	I	U	Z	E	C	C	O
Z	N	O	Z	D	O	N	N
U	O	M	O	A	U	N	A

ANSWER KEY

1. ragazza; 2. persona; 3. ecco; 4. bambino; 5. uomo; 6. donna; 7. ragazzo; 8. un; 9. una

Grammar Builder 1

▶ 2C Grammar Builder 1 (CD 1, Track 13)

Okay, let's stop there. You learned how to say *a person* (**una persona**), *a woman* (**una donna**), *a man* (**un uomo**), *a girl* (**una ragazza**), *a boy* (**un ragazzo**), and *a child* (**un bambino/una bambina**).

Did you notice that there are two words for *a*, either **un** or **una**? That's because all Italian nouns are either masculine or feminine.

GENDER	INDEFINITE ARTICLE (A/AN)	EXAMPLES
feminine	una	una donna (*a woman*) una ragazza (*a girl*) una bambina (*a child*)
masculine	un	un uomo (*a man*) un ragazzo (*a boy*) un bambino (*a child*)

It's easy to remember the gender of nouns like *man, woman, girl,* or *boy,* but in Italian, all nouns have gender. Sometimes it's illogical; the word for *a person* is feminine: **una persona**, but can refer to both male and female individuals. Sometimes it's impossible to tell—would you ever guess that *a stone* is feminine (**una pietra**) while *a river* is masculine (**un fiume**)? It's best not to overthink it! Just memorize the gender of each new noun you learn.

⏸

Take It Further

Even though you have to memorize the gender of each new noun that you learn in Italian, there are some endings that are typically masculine or typically feminine. Most nouns that end in -o are masculine, and most nouns that end in -a are feminine. You can see that from the few nouns you've learned already:

MASCULINE (-O)	FEMININE (-A)
un giorno (*a day*)	una sera (*an evening*)
un pomeriggio (*an afternoon*)	una giornata (*a day*)
un uomo (*a man*)	una donna (*a woman*)
un ragazzo (*a boy*)	una ragazza (*a girl*)
un bambino (*a child*)	una bambina (*a child*)

With nouns that end in -e, though, you usually can't be sure whether you're dealing with a feminine noun or a masculine noun: **una notte** (*a night*), but **un fiume** (*a river*). But two common endings with -e are easier. Nouns that end in -ione are usually feminine, and nouns that end in -ore are usually masculine.

FEMININE (-IONE)	MASCULINE (-ORE)
una stazione (*a station*)	un signore (*a gentleman*)
una televisione (*a television*)	un dottore (*a male doctor*)

Vocabulary Builder 2

▶ 2D Vocabulary Builder 2 (CD 1, Track 14)

Here is a family.	Ecco una famiglia.	EHK-koh OO-nah fah-MEEL-lyah
There is …	C'è …	cheh
There are …	Ci sono …	chee SOH-noh
There's the father.	C'è il padre.	cheh eel PAH-dreh

There's the mother.	C'è la madre.	cheh lah MAH-dreh
There are the father and the mother.	Ci sono il padre e la madre.	chee SOH-noh eel PAH-dreh eh lah MAH-dreh
There's the son.	C'è il figlio.	cheh eel FEE-lyoh
There's the daughter.	C'è la figlia.	cheh lah FEE-lyah
There are the son and daughter.	Ci sono il figlio e la figlia.	chee SOH-noh eel FEE-lyoh eh lah FEE-lyah
There's the brother.	C'è il fratello.	cheh eel frah-TEHL-loh
There's the sister.	C'è la sorella.	cheh lah soh-REHL-lah
There are the brother and sister.	Ci sono il fratello e la sorella.	chee SOH-noh eel frah-TEHL-loh eh lah soh-REHL-lah

✎ Vocabulary Practice 2

Fill in the following family tree with the correct Italian word for each member of the family.

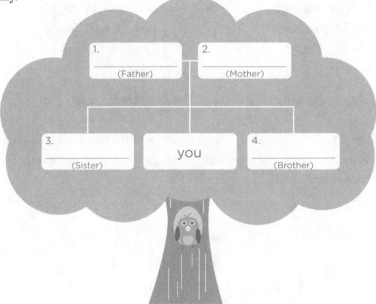

1. _____ (Father)

2. _____ (Mother)

3. _____ (Sister)

you

4. _____ (Brother)

ANSWER KEY
1. il padre; 2. la madre; 3. la sorella; 4. il fratello

Grammar Builder 2

▶ 2E Grammar Builder 2 (CD 1, Track 15)

Let's pause there for a moment. You just learned a few important things. First you learned how to say *there is* (**c'è**) and *there are* (**ci sono**) in Italian. These are important expressions that you're likely to use a lot, so be sure to practice them: **C'è … Ci sono …**

You also learned how to say *a* or *an* in Italian, **un** for masculine nouns, and **una** for feminine nouns. Now you just heard how to say *the*, also known as the definite article. Again, gender is important. The masculine form is **il**, and the feminine form is **la**.

FEMININE NOUNS	MASCULINE NOUNS
la famiglia (the family)	il padre (the father)
la madre (the mother)	il figlio (the son)
la figlia (the daughter)	il ragazzo (the boy)
la sorella (the sister)	il fratello (the brother)
la persona (the person)	il bambino (the child)

In Italian you usually have to repeat the article before each noun:

Ci sono il padre e la madre, il fratello e la sorella, il figlio e la figlia.
There are the father and (the) mother, the brother and (the) sister, the son and (the) daughter.

⏸

✎ Work Out 1

Let's practice some of what you've learned again with a listening comprehension exercise. Listen to the audio, and fill in the blanks with the words that you hear.

▶ 2F Work Out 1 (CD 1, Track 16)

1. *Here is the Belli family.*

   Ecco la _____ Belli.

2. *Mrs. Belli is a woman.*

   La signora Belli è una _____.

3. *Mr. Belli is a man.*

   Il signor Belli è un _____.

4. *Francesco is a boy.*

   Francesco è un _____.

5. *Maria is a girl.*

   Maria è una _____.

6. *Mrs. Belli is the mother.*

   La signora Belli è la _____.

7. *Mr. Belli is the father.*

   Il signor Belli è il _____.

8. *Maria is the daughter.*

   Maria è la _____.

9. *Francesco is the son.*

   Francesco è il _____.

ANSWER KEY
1. famiglia; 2. donna; 3. uomo; 4. ragazzo; 5. ragazza; 6. madre; 7. padre; 8. figlia; 9. figlio

Bring It All Together
▶ 2G Bring It All Together (CD 1, Track 17)

Now let's bring it all together in a brief monologue, and add a little bit more vocabulary and structure.

I'm Francesco.
Io sono Francesco.
ee-oh SOH-noh frahn-CHEH-skoh

I'm Italian.
Sono italiano.
SOH-noh ee-tah-LYAH-noh

I have a small family.
Io ho una famiglia piccola.
ee-oh oh OO-nah fah-MEE-lya PEEK-koh-lah

I have a father.
Ho un padre.
oh oon PAH-dreh

He's a policeman.
Lui è un poliziotto.
loo-ee eh oon poh-lee-TSYOHT-toh

And I have a mother.
E ho una madre.
eh oh OO-nah MAH-dreh

She's a teacher.
Lei è una professoressa.
lay eh OO-nah proh-fehs-soh-REHS-sah

And I have a sister.
E ho una sorella.
eh oh OO-nah soh-REHL-lah

She's a student.
Lei è una studentessa.
lay eh OO-nah stoo-dehn-TEHS-sah

And me, too, I'm a student.
E anche io sono uno studente.
eh AHN-keh EE-oh SOH-noh OO-noh stoo-DEHN-teh

Take It Further

▶ 2H Take It Further (CD 1, Track 18)

You probably knew already that **italiano** means *Italian*. Did you remember that **io sono** means *I am*? **Io** is the pronoun *I*, and **sono** is a form of the verb **essere** (*to be*), which you'll learn more about later. Francesco drops the pronoun **io**, when he says **sono italiano**, because the pronoun isn't always necessary; you can tell the subject of the sentence by the verb form.

You heard two other pronouns, **lui** (*he*), and **lei** (*she*), used with **essere**:

lui è	he is
lei è	she is

Francesco used another useful verb: **io ho ...**, meaning *I have*, as in:

Io ho una famiglia piccola.	I have a small family.

Finally, you heard Francesco say that his father is **un poliziotto**, or *a policeman*, his mother is **una professoressa**, or *a teacher*, and both he and his sister are students, **studentessa** in the feminine, and **studente** in the masculine.

Did you notice that the article before **studente** is **uno** and not **un**? That's because **uno** is the form of the indefinite article that comes before masculine nouns beginning with the letter **s** followed by a consonant, or before the letter **z**. We'll come back to that later.

uno studente	a (male) student
uno zio	an uncle

Ⓘ

✎ Work Out 2

Fill in each blank with the Italian for *a* or *the*. Say each sentence aloud after you've written out the answer.

1. Ecco _____ signora Belli.

2. Lei è _____ studentessa.

3. Io ho _____ fratello.

4. Lui è _____ studente.

5. Ecco _____ signor Belli.

6. Io ho _____ nonno.

7. Lei ha _____ sorella.

8. Lei è _____ madre.

ANSWER KEY
1. la; 2. una; 3. un; 4; uno; 5. il; 6. un; 7. una; 8. la

▶ 2I Work Out 2 (CD 1, Track 19)

Now listen to the audio for some more audio-only practice.

⏸

✎ Drive It Home

A. Now let's do one final practice dealing with some key grammar you learned in this lesson. As we mentioned in Lesson One, although this exercise may seem repetitive, it is very important that you complete each question carefully. Write out the answers, and speak them aloud to yourself a few times. This will help you retain the information in the long term. First, fill in each blank with **c'è** and **ci sono**, and don't forget to read out each sentence aloud. Ready?

1. _____ una ragazza.

2. _____ la famiglia.

3. _____ il fratello e la sorella.

4. _____ il padre.

5. _____ la madre e il padre.

B. Now, fill in each blank with the Italian for *there is*. Say each sentence aloud after you've written out the answer.

1. _____ la signora.

2. _____ lo zio.

3. _____ la cugina.

4. _____ lo studente.

5. _____ Francesco.

C. Now, fill in each blank with the Italian for *there are*. Say each sentence aloud after you've written out the answer.

1. _____ il padre e la madre.

2. _____ il fratello e la sorella.

3. _____ il signore e la signora Belli.

4. _____ il ragazzo e la ragazza.

5. _____ il nonno e la nonna.

ANSWER KEY
A. 1. C'è; 2. C'è; 3. Ci sono; 4.C'è; 5. Ci sono
B. 1-5. C'è
C. 1-5. Ci sono

Parting Words

Complimenti! [kohm-plee-MEHN-tee] *Congratulations!* You just finished your second lesson, and you've learned:

☐ basic vocabulary related to people. (Still unsure? Go back to page 24.)

☐ about gender in Italian, and how to say *a*. (Still unsure? Go back to page 25.)

☐ basic vocabulary related to the family. (Still unsure? Go back to page 26.)

☐ how to say *the, there is,* and *there are.* (Still unsure? Go back to page 28.)

☐ how to have a simple conversation about your family.
(Still unsure? Go back to page 30.)

Don't forget to practice and reinforce what you've learned by visiting **www.livinglanguage.com/ languagelab** for flashcards, games, and quizzes for Lesson Two!

Take It Further

▶ 2J Take It Further (CD 1, Track 20)

You may of course want to extend the discussion a bit, and talk about your:

zio	*uncle*	DZEE-oh
zia	*aunt*	DZEE-ah
cugina	*female cousin*	koo-JEE-nah
cugino	*male cousin*	koo-JEE-noh
nonna	*grandmother*	NOHN-nah
nonno	*grandfather*	NOHN-noh
un nipote	*a nephew*	oon nee-POH-teh
una nipote	*a niece*	OO-nah nee-POH-teh

One last note: although it may sound a bit strange to you, keep in mind that in Italian il nipote/la nipote means both *the nephew* or *the niece* and *the grandson* or *the granddaughter*.

⑪

Word Recall

Match the Italian in the left column with the English in the right.

1. a presto	a. *here's a family*
2. ci sono	b. *good-bye (fml.)*
3. una ragazza	c. *good morning*
4. buon giorno	e. *the mother*
5. lui è	f. *I have*
6. una persona	g. *there is*
7. io ho	h. *a person*
8. la madre	i. *there are*
9. arrivederLa	j. *see you soon*
10. la figlia	k. *the father*
11. ecco una famiglia	l. *he is*
12. lei è	m. *a girl*
13. arrivederci	n. *the daughter*
14. c'è	o. *she is*
15. il padre	p. *good-bye (infml.)*

ANSWER KEY
1. j; 2. i; 3. m; 4. c; 5. l; 6. h; 7. f; 8. e; 9. b; 10. n; 11. a; 12. o; 13. p; 14. g; 15. k.

Lesson 3: Numbers and Plurals

Terza Lezione: I numeri e i plurali

TEHR-tsah leh-TSYOH-neh: ee NOO-meh-ree eh ee ploo-RAH-lee

Bentornato! [BEHN-tohr-nah-toh] *Welcome back!* In this lesson, you'll continue to build on your Italian with some very important vocabulary and new structures. You'll learn how to:

☐ use numbers

☐ form plurals in Italian

☐ use the verb **avere** (*to have*)

☐ use **avere** in some very common expressions

☐ put it all together in a short conversation

As usual, let's start with some vocabulary. Ready?

Vocabulary Builder 1

▶ 3B Vocabulary Builder 1 (CD 1, Track 22)

There is one student.	**C'è uno studente.**	che OO-noh stoo-DEHN-teh
There are two students.	**Ci sono due studenti.**	chee SOH-noh DOO-eh stoo-DEHN-tee
There are three sisters and four brothers.	**Ci sono tre sorelle e quattro fratelli.**	chee SOH-noh treh soh-REHL-leh eh KWAHT-troh frah-TEHL-lee
There are five boys and six girls.	**Ci sono cinque ragazzi e sei ragazze.**	chee SOH-noh CHEEN-kweh rah-GAH-tsee eh say rah-GAH-tseh
Here are seven families.	**Ecco sette famiglie.**	EHK-koh SEHT-teh fah-MEE-lyeh
Here are eight children (boys).	**Ecco otto bambini.**	EHK-koh OHT-toh bahm-BEE-nee
Here are nine children (girls).	**Ecco nove bambine.**	EHK-koh NOH-veh bahm-BEE-neh
Here are ten men and eleven women.	**Ecco dieci uomini e undici donne.**	EHK-koh DYEH-chee oo-OH-mee-nee eh OON-dee-chee DOHN-neh
Here are twelve people.	**Ecco dodici persone.**	EHK-koh DOH-dee-chee pehr-SOH-neh

Ⅱ

✎ Vocabulary Practice 1

Let's practice the vocabulary you've learned. Match the Italian in the left column with the English equivalent in the right.

1. cinque persone	a. *four boys*
2. ci sono sei studenti	b. *there's a woman*
3. sei ragazze	c. *twelve children*
4. quattro ragazzi	d. *eleven (female) students*
5. tre uomini	e. *five people*
6. ecco due donne	f. *there are seven girls*
7. c'è una donna	g. *here are two women*
8. dodici bambini	h. *three men*
9. undici studentesse	i. *there are six students*
10. ci sono sette bambine	j. *six girls*

ANSWER KEY

1. e; 2. i; 3. j; 4. a; 5. h; 6. g; 7. b; 8. c; 9. d; 10. f.

Grammar Builder 1

▷ 3C Grammar Builder 1 (CD 1, Track 23)

Okay, let's take a short break. You just learned how to say:

one, two, three	uno, due, tre
four, five, six	quattro, cinque, sei
seven, eight, nine	sette, otto, nove
ten, eleven, twelve	dieci, undici, dodici

You also heard some of the same words from Lesson Two used with them, only this time they had a different ending, and that ending changes them from singular nouns into plural nouns.

SINGULAR ENDING	EXAMPLES	PLURAL ENDING	EXAMPLES
-o or -e	(un) bambino (uno) studente	-i	otto bambini due studenti
-a	(una) bambina	-e	sei bambine

There are a few exceptions. The plural **uomini** (*men*) is irregular: you say **uomo** (*man*) in the singular and **uomini** in the plural. There are more words with irregular plurals, but you will learn them as they come up in your vocabulary.

Now let's move on to a different topic, the verb **avere** (*to have*).

 Take It Further

Let's take a closer look at forming plurals in Italian. The regular rules are quite simple. The singular ending -o changes to -i, which covers most masculine nouns. The singular ending -a changes to -e, which covers most feminine nouns. But don't forget that some singular nouns end in -e, and they can be either masculine or feminine. In both cases, they form their plurals with the ending -i. Here are some more examples:

ENDINGS	SINGULAR EXAMPLES	PLURAL EXAMPLES
o → i	un giorno (*one/a day*) un ragazzo (*a boy*) un fratello (*a brother*) un poliziotto (*a policeman*)	due giorni (*two days*) due ragazzi (*two boys*) tre fratelli (*three brothers*) cinque poliziotti (*five policemen*)

ENDINGS	SINGULAR EXAMPLES	PLURAL EXAMPLES
a → e	una donna (*one/a woman*)	quattro donne (*four women*)
	una sera (*an evening*)	due sere (*two evenings*)
	una ragazza (*a girl*)	tre ragazze (*three girls*)
	una sorella (*a sister*)	due sorelle (*two sisters*)
e → i	un padre (*a father*)	due padri (*two fathers*)
	una madre (*a mother*)	due madri (*two mothers*)
	un signore (*a gentleman*)	tre signori (*three gentlemen*)
	una stazione (*a station*)	quattro stazioni (*four stations*)

Vocabulary Builder 2

▶ 3D Vocabulary Builder 2 (CD 1, Track 24)

to have	**avere**	ah-VEH-reh
I have	**io ho**	ee-oh oh
you have (sg., infml.)	**tu hai**	too ah-ee
you have (sg., fml.)	**Lei ha**	lay ah
he has	**lui ha**	loo-ee ah
she has	**lei ha**	lay ah
we have	**noi abbiamo**	noy ahb-BYAH-moh
you have (pl.)	**voi avete**	voh-ee ah-VEH-teh
they have	**loro hanno**	LOH-roh AHN-noh
I am hungry.	**(Io) ho fame.**	ee-oh oh FAH-meh
You (sg., infml.) are thirsty.	**(Tu) hai sete.**	too eye SEH-teh
He is sleepy.	**(Lui) ha sonno.**	loo-ee ah SOHN-noh
We are cold.	**(Noi) abbiamo freddo.**	noh-ee ahb-BYA-moh FREHD-doh
They are in a hurry.	**(Loro) hanno fretta.**	LOH-roh ahn-noh FREHT-tah

Ⅱ

✎ Vocabulary Practice 2

Translate the following sentences using the words you know as well as the new words from the following word bank:

not	non	nohn
to be afraid	avere paura	ah-VEH-reh POW-rah
I am afraid.	(Io) ho paura.	ee-oh oh POW-rah
I am not afraid.	(Io) non ho paura.	ee-oh nohn oh POW-rah

1. *I am thirsty.* _____

2. *She is hungry.* _____

3. *He is cold.* _____

4. *You (pl.) are in a hurry.* _____

5. *You (sg., fml.) are hungry.* _____

6. *They are sleepy.* _____

7. *You (sg., infml.) are afraid.* _____

8. *We are not afraid.* _____

ANSWER KEY

1. (Io) ho sete.; 2. (Lei) ha fame.; 3. (Lui) ha freddo.; 4. (Voi) avete fretta.; 5. (Lei) ha fame.; 6. (Loro) hanno sonno.; 7. (Tu) hai paura.; 8. (Noi) non abbiamo paura.

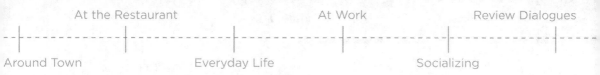

Grammar Builder 2

▶ 3E Grammar Builder 2 (CD 1, Track 25)

Let's pause for a moment and make a few comments on the verb *avere*. Have you seen how many useful expressions you can form with *avere* by combining it with the following words?

fame	FAH-meh	*hunger*
sete	SEH-teh	*thirst*
sonno	SOHN-noh	*sleep*
caldo	KAHL-doh	*heat*
freddo	FREHD-doh	*cold*
paura	POW-rah	*fear*
ragione	rah-JOH-neh	*reason*
fretta	FREHT-tah	*hurry*

All these expressions are translated in English using the verb *to be* followed by an adjective. In Italian, on the other hand, you will use the verb *avere* (*to have*), followed by a noun to create these expressions:

avere fame	*to be hungry*
avere sete	*to be thirsty*
avere sonno	*to be sleepy*
avere caldo	*to be hot*
avere freddo	*to be cold*
avere paura	*to be afraid*
avere ragione	*to be right*
avere fretta	*to be in a hurry*

While repeating the conjugation of the verb **avere**, you also had the opportunity to learn the Italian subject pronouns:

io (*I*)	noi (*we*)
tu (*you, sg., infml.*)	voi (*you, pl.*)
Lei (*you, sg., fml.*) lui (*he*) lei (*she*)	loro (*they*)

Don't forget that the formal *you* (the **Lei** form), is always capitalized in writing to distinguish it from the third person singular **lei** (*she*). Also remember that subject pronouns are usually omitted in Italian. They're usually used only when you want to give more emphasis to your statements. Compare:

Ho bisogno di un caffè.	*I need a coffee.*
Io ho bisogno di un caffè.	*I do need a coffee!*

⓿

✎ Work Out 1

Let's practice what you've learned so far in a listening comprehension exercise. Listen to the audio, and fill in the blanks with the words that you hear.

▶ 3F Work Out 1 (CD 1, Track 26)

1. *Here are three families.*

   Ecco tre _____.

2. *There are ten men and nine women.*

   Ci sono dieci _____ **e nove** _____.

3. *You (sg., infml.) have two sisters and five brothers.*

   Tu _____ **due sorelle e cinque** _____.

4. *She has eight uncles and six cousins.*

   Lei _____ **otto zii e sei** _____.

5. *We have four grandparents and seven nephews.*

   Noi _____ **quattro nonni e sette nipoti.**

6. *They have nine aunts and ten nieces.*

   Loro _____ **nove zie e dieci nipoti.**

7. *Mario is hungry.*

   Mario _____.

8. *Carla is thirsty.*

   Carla ha _____.

9. *You (pl.) are in a hurry.*

   Voi _____ **fretta.**

10. *They are in a hurry, too.*

   Anche loro _____.

⓫

ANSWER KEY
1. **famiglie**; 2. **uomini, donne**; 3. **hai, fratelli**; 4. **ha, cugini**; 5. **abbiamo**; 6. **hanno**; 7. **ha fame**; 8. **sete**;
9. **avete**; 10. **hanno fretta**

▣ Bring It All Together

▶ 3G Bring It All Together (CD 1, Track 27)

Now let's bring it all together, and add a little bit more vocabulary and structure.

Here are my friends.
Ecco i miei amici.
EHK-koh ee MYAY-ee ah-MEE-chee

There are three boys and five girls.
Ci sono quattro ragazzi e cinque ragazze.
chee SOH-noh KWAHT-troh rah-GAH-tsee eh CHEEN-kweh rah-GAH-tseh

Matteo is always hungry.
Matteo ha sempre fame.
maht-TEH-oh ah SEHM-preh FAH-meh

He feels like having a sandwich.
Lui ha voglia di un panino.
loo-ee ah VOH-lyah dee oon pah-NEE-noh

Maria is always cold.
Maria ha sempre freddo.
mah-REE-ah ah SEHM-preh FREHD-doh

She needs a scarf.
Lei ha bisogno di una sciarpa.
lay ah bee-SOH-nyoh dee OO-nah SHAHR-pah

Giorgio and Pete are always sleepy.
Giorgio e Pete hanno sempre sonno.
JYOHR-jyoh eh Pete AHN-noh SEHM-preh SOHN-noh

They feel like having a coffee.

Loro hanno voglia di un caffè.

LOH-roh AHN-noh VOH-lyah dee oon KAHF-feh

Kate and I are always hot.

Io e Kate abbiamo sempre caldo.

EE-oh eh Kate ahb-BYAH-moh SEHM-preh KAHL-doh

We need a fan.

Noi abbiamo bisogno di un ventilatore.

NOH-ee ahb-BYAH-moh bee-SOH-nyoh dee oon vehn-tee-lah-TOH-reh

Betty and Rose are always in a hurry.

Betty e Rose hanno sempre fretta.

Betty eh Rose AHN-noh SEHM-preh FREHT-tah

I am always in a hurry, too.

Anche io ho sempre fretta.

AHN-keh ee-oh oh SEHM-preh FREHT-tah

Take It Further

▶ 3H Take It Further (CD 1, Track 28)

Okay, let's focus for a moment on the new words you just heard:

panino (*sandwich*)	sciarpa (*scarf*)
caffè (*coffee*)	ventilatore (*fan*)

You also heard the word amici, or *friends*, which, in this case, includes both male and female friends. In the singular, you will make a distinction between a *male friend* (**amico**), and a *female friend* (**amica**). The same happens with many words you've already learned for describing people, such as:

MALE	FEMALE
studente	studentessa
ragazzo	ragazza

You can say **ragazzi** or **studenti**, to refer either to a group of males, or to a group that includes both males and females. Of course, if you want to refer to a group of female friends, students, or girls, you'll say **amiche**, **studentesse**, and **ragazze**.

Finally, did you catch the new expressions?

avere bisogno di	*to need*
avere voglia di	*to feel like something*

They are two very useful expressions to remember. Keep in mind that they can be followed either by a noun, as in the many examples you've heard, or by the infinitive of a verb, as you'll see later on.

Ⓜ

✎ Work Out 2

Let's practice what you've learned so far; we'll focus on plurals and the verb **avere**. First, convert the following singulars to plurals.

1. **studente** → _____

2. **ragazza** → _____

3. **fratello** → _____

4. **sorella** → _____

5. madre → _____

6. padre → _____

7. ragazzo → _____

8. studentessa → _____

ANSWER KEY
1. studenti; 2. ragazze; 3. fratelli; 4. sorelle; 5. madri; 6. padri; 7. ragazzi; 8. studentesse

Now fill in the table with the appropriate pronoun and form of avere, *to have.*

io ...	1.	noi ...	4.
tu ...	2.	voi ...	5.
lui/lei/Lei ...	3.	loro ...	6.

ANSWER KEY
1. ho; 2. hai; 3. ha; 4. abbiamo; 5. avete; 6. hanno

▶ 3I Work Out 2 (CD 1, Track 29)

Now listen to the audio for some audio-only practice with the vocabulary and grammar that you've learned in this lesson.

⏸

✎ Drive It Home

Now let's do one final practice dealing with some key grammar you learned in this lesson. As we mentioned in Lessons 1 and 2, although this exercise may seem repetitive, it is very important that you complete each question carefully. Write out the answers, and speak them aloud to yourself a few times.

First, change the sentences below following the model:

Io ho un fratello. → Io ho due fratelli.

Ready?

1. Io ho una sorella. → Io ho due _____.

2. Io ho una nonna. → Io ho due _____.

3. Io ho una zia. → Io ho due _____.

4. Io ho una cugina. → Io ho due _____.

5. Io ho un bambino. → Io ho due _____.

6. Io ho una bambina. → Io ho due _____.

7. Io ho un figlio. → Io ho due _____.

8. Io ho una nipote. → Io ho due _____.

ANSWER KEY

1. sorelle; 2. nonne; 3. zie; 4. cugine; 5. bambini; 6. bambine; 7. figli; 8. nipoti

Now fill in the blank with the appropriate form of avere. Don't forget to read out each sentence aloud. Ready?

1. Io _____ due sorelle.

2. Tu _____ due sorelle.

3. Lei _____ due sorelle.

4. Lui _____ due sorelle.

5. Marta _____ due sorelle.

6. Carlo _____ due sorelle.

7. Noi _____ due sorelle.

8. Voi _____ due sorelle.

Essential Italian

9. Loro _____ due sorelle.

ANSWER KEY
1. ho; 2. hai; 3. ha; 4. ha; 5. ha; 6. ha; 7. abbiamo; 8. avete; 9. hanno

Parting Words

Perfetto! *Great!* You just finished your third lesson, which means that you know how to:

☐ use numbers. (Still unsure? Go back to page 38.)

☐ form plurals in Italian. (Still unsure? Go back to page 39.)

☐ use the verb **avere** (*to have*). (Still unsure? Go back to page 41.)

☐ use **avere** in some very common expressions. (Still unsure? Go back to page 43.)

☐ put it all together in a short conversation. (Still unsure? Go back to page 46.)

Don't forget to practice and reinforce what you've learned by visiting **www.livinglanguage.com/ languagelab** for flashcards, games, and quizzes for Lesson Three!

Word Recall

Match the Italian in the left column with the English in the right.

1. (Tu) hai una cugina.   a. *to need*

2. quattro giorni   b. *You (infml.) are in a hurry.*

3. Lei ha sempre ragione.   c. *There are seven families.*

4. avere caldo   e. *You (infml.) have a (female) cousin.*

5. Hanno sonno.   f. *You (infml.) are not thirsty.*

6. Loro hanno cinque figli.   g. *two nights*

7. avere bisogno   h. *She is always right.*

8. Ci sono cinque studentesse.   i. *to be hot*

9. Ho voglia di un caffè.   j. *I am thirsty.*

10. (Tu) hai fretta.   k. *They are sleepy.*

11. Ho sete.   l. *They have five children.*

12. Lui ha sempre fame.   m. *four days*

13. due notti   n. *He is always hungry.*

14. Ci sono sette famiglie.   o. *There are five (female) students.*

15. Tu non hai sete.   p. *I feel like having a coffee.*

ANSWER KEY
1. e; 2. m; 3. h; 4. i; 5. k; 6. l; 7. a; 8. o; 9. p; 10. b; 11. j; 12. n; 13. g; 14. c; 15. f.

Lesson 4: Around the Home

Quarta Lezione: In giro per la casa

KWAHR-tah leh-TSYOH-neh: een JEE-roh pehr lah KAH-sah

Rieccoci! [Ree- EHK-koh-chee] *Here we are again!* In this lesson you'll continue to learn more vocabulary and grammar, and build your skills in Italian. You'll learn how to:

☐ use common vocabulary for around the house

☐ say *the* in the plural

☐ use the very important verb **essere** (*to be*)

☐ talk about possession with the word **di** (*of*)

☐ put it all together in a conversation about the home

But first, we'll start with some key vocabulary.

Vocabulary Builder 1

▶ 4B Vocabulary Builder 1 (CD 1, Track 31)

In the kitchen there is the table.	**In cucina c'è il tavolo.**	een koo-CHEE-nah cheh eel TAH-voh-loh
in the kitchen there are …	**in cucina ci sono …**	een koo-CHEE-nah chee SOH-noh
the pans	**le pentole**	leh pehn-TOH-leh
the dishes	**i piatti**	ee PYAT-tee
in the bedroom there is …	**in camera (da letto) c'è …**	een KAH-meh-rah (dah LEHT-toh) cheh …
the bed	**il letto**	eel LEHT-toh
the closet	**l'armadio**	lahr-MAH-dyoh
In the bedroom there are the pillows.	**In camera ci sono i cuscini.**	een KAH-meh-rah chee SOH-noh ee koo-SHEE-nee
in the living room there is …	**in soggiorno c'è …**	een sohj-JOHR-noh cheh …
the couch	**il divano**	eel dee-VAH-noh
the rug	**il tappeto**	eel TAHP-peh-toh
In the living room there are the chairs.	**In soggiorno ci sono le sedie.**	een sohj-JOHR-noh chee SOH-noh leh SEH-dyeh
in the bathroom there is …	**in bagno c'è …**	een BAH-nyoh cheh …
the washing machine	**la lavatrice**	lah lah-vah-TREE-cheh
the mirror	**lo specchio**	loh SPEHK-kyoh
In the bathroom there are the towels.	**In bagno ci sono gli asciugamani.**	een BAH-nyoh chee SOH-noh lyee ah-SHOO-gah-MAH-nee

✏ Vocabulary Practice 1

Find the translations of the following words below:

1. *towels*

2. *bathroom*

3. *chairs*

4. *bed*

5. *plates*

6. *bedroom*

7. *wardrobe*

8. *kitchen*

9. *pans*

B	P	L	R	A	A	R	T
A	E	E	U	S	C	A	A
G	N	T	L	C	U	N	V
N	T	T	A	I	G	E	O
E	O	O	T	U	D	I	L
C	L	B	A	G	N	O	O
U	E	P	I	A	T	T	I
C	E	C	A	M	E	R	A
I	A	R	M	A	D	I	O
N	P	E	N	N	O	L	E
A	S	E	D	I	E	I	O

ANSWER KEY

1. asciugamani; 2. bagno; 3. sedie; 4. letto; 5. piatti; 6. camera; 7. armadio;
8. cucina; 9. pentole

Grammar Builder 1

▶ 4C Grammar Builder 1 (CD 1, Track 32)

Okay, let's pause for a moment and look closer at what you just heard. You just learned how to say:

(la) cucina	kitchen
(la) camera da letto or camera	bedroom
(il) soggiorno	living room
(il) bagno	bathroom
(la) stanza	room
in cucina	in the kitchen
il tavolo	the table
le pentole	the pans
i piatti	the dishes
in camera (da letto)	in the bedroom
il letto	the bed
l'armadio	the closet
i cuscini	the pillows
in soggiorno	in the living room
il divano	the couch
il tappeto	the carpet
le sedie	the chairs
in bagno	in the bathroom
la lavatrice	the washing machine
lo specchio	the mirror
gli asciugamani	the towels

Did you notice how many different definite articles were used in the examples? You already learned **il** and **la** in Lesson Two. Let's look at some more of them, starting with the masculine. In the singular you have these options:

ARTICLE:	USED BEFORE:	EXAMPLES
il	most nouns beginning with a consonant	il tavolo (*the table*) il letto (*the bed*)
lo	(1) words beginning with the letter s followed by a consonant (sp, st, sc, etc.)	lo specchio (*the mirror*)
lo	(2) words beginning with the letter z	lo zio (*the uncle*)
l'	before all vowels	l'armadio (*the closet*) l'uomo (*the man*) l'amico (*the friend, m.*)

In the plural:

il → i	i piatti (*the dishes*) i cuscini (*the pillows*)
lo and l' → gli	gli asciugamani (*the towels*)

Let's look at the feminine forms.

ARTICLE:	USED BEFORE:	EXAMPLES
la	singular nouns	la lavatrice (*the washing machine*)
le	all plural nouns	le pentole (*the pans*) le sedie (*the chairs*) le amiche (*the friends*)
l'	before singular nouns that begin with vowels	l'amica (*the friend, f.*)

Next we'll learn more about the verb **essere** (*to be*).

Ⅱ

Vocabulary Builder 2

▶ 4D Vocabulary Builder 2 (CD 1, Track 33)

to be	essere	EHS-seh-reh
I am	io sono	ee-oh SOH-noh
you are (sg., infml.)	tu sei	too SEH-ee
you are (sg., fml.)	Lei è	lay eh
he is	lui è	loo-ee eh
she is	lei è	lay eh
we are	noi siamo	noh-ee SYAH-moh
you are (pl.)	voi siete	voh-ee SYEH-teh
they are	loro sono	loh-roh SOH-noh
I am at home.	Io sono a casa.	ee-oh SOH-noh ah KAH-zah
You (sg., infml.) are in the kitchen.	Tu sei in cucina.	too say een koo-CHEE-nah
He is in the bathroom.	Lui è in bagno.	loo-ee eh een BAH-nyoh
We are in the bedroom.	Noi siamo in camera da letto.	noh-ee SYAH-moh een KAH-meh-rah dah LEHT-toh
They are in the living room.	Loro sono in soggiorno.	loh-roh SOH-noh een sohj-JOHR-noh

⏸

✎ Vocabulary Practice 2

Let's practice the vocabulary you've learned. Match the Italian in the left column with the English equivalent in the right.

1. lei è in bagno

2. in soggiorno

3. noi siamo a casa

a. *they are*

b. *in the kitchen*

c. *at home*

4. camera da letto	d. *she is in the bathroom*
5. a casa	e. *in the bedroom*
6. io sono	f. *you (pl.) are*
7. loro sono	g. *in the living room*
8. in cucina	h. *bedroom*
9. voi siete	i. *we are at home*
10. in camera	j. *I am*

ANSWER KEY

1. d; 2. g; 3. i; 4. h; 5. c; 6. j; 7. a; 8. b; 9. f; 10. e.

Grammar Builder 2

▶ 4E Grammar Builder 2 (CD 1, Track 34)

Let's pause for a moment and make a few comments on the verb essere. You already learned in Lesson One that essere di, followed by the name of a town or city, is used to express someone's hometown:

Io sono di Firenze.
I'm from Florence.

Tu sei di Filadelfia.
You're from Philadelphia.

Paolo è di Milano.
Paolo is from Milan.

Essere di followed by the name of a person is also used to express possession.

I piatti sono di Nicola.
The dishes belong to Nicola./The dishes are Nicola's.

La lavatrice è di Ann.
The washing machine belongs to Ann./The washing machine is Ann's.

To ask who owns something, say **di chi è?** (when referring to a single object), and **di chi sono?** (when referring to more than one object).

Whose washing machine is it?
Di chi è la lavatrice?

It's Ann's.
È di Ann.

Whose dishes are they?
Di chi sono i piatti?

They are Nicola's.
Sono di Nicola.

Of course, if you just want to express the possessive of a noun, you'll say:

la lavatrice di Ann
Ann's washing machine

i piatti di Nicola
Nicola's dishes

✎ Work Out 1

Now let's do a listening comprehension exercise. Fill in each blank with the word you hear on the audio.

▶ 4F Work Out 1 (CD 1, Track 35)

1. *I am in the kitchen.*

   Io _____ in cucina.

2. *In the kitchen there are the cups, the dishes, and the table.*

   In cucina ci sono _____ tazze, _____ piatti e _____ tavolo.

3. *The cups are Michael's.*

   Le tazze _____ Michael.

4. *You are in the living room.*

   Tu _____ in soggiorno.

5. *She is in the bathroom.*

   Lei _____ in bagno.

6. *In the bedroom there are the pillows, the closet, and the bed.*

   In _____ da letto ci _____ i cuscini, l'armadio e il letto.

7. *The pillows are Paolo's.*

   _____ cuscini sono _____ Paolo.

ⅠⅠ

ANSWER KEY
1. sono; 2. le, i, il; 3. sono di; 4. sei; 5. è; 6. camera, sono; 7. I, di

🔊 Bring It All Together

▶ 4G Bring It All Together (CD 1, Track 36)

Now let's bring it all together, and add a little bit more vocabulary and structure.

This is Paolo and Marta's house.
Questa è la casa di Paolo e Marta.
QUEH-stah eh lah KAH-zah dee PAH-oh-loh eh MAHR-tah

Paolo and Marta are at home.
Paolo e Marta sono in casa.
PAH-oh-loh eh MAHR-tah SOH-noh een KAH-sah

Paolo is in the bedroom.
Paolo è in camera da letto.
PAH-oh-loh eh een KAH-meh-rah dah LEHT-toh

In the bedroom there is the double bed.
In camera da letto c'è il letto matrimoniale.
een KAH-meh-rah dah LEHT-toh cheh eel LEHT-toh mah-tree-moh-nee-AH-leh

Paolo's cups are in the kitchen.
Le tazze di Paolo sono in cucina.
leh TAHZ-zeh dee PAH-oh-loh SOH-noh een koo-CHEE-nah

Marta is in the garden.
Marta è in giardino.
MAHR-tah eh een jahr-DEE-noh

In the garden there are the flowers.
In giardino ci sono i fiori.
een jahr-DEE-noh chee SOH-noh ee FYOH-ree

Marta's books are in the living room.
I libri di Marta sono in soggiorno.
ee LEE-bree dee MAHR-tah SOH-noh een sohj-JOHR-noh

Paolo and Marta have a daughter: Anna.
Paolo e Marta hanno una figlia: Anna.
PAH-oh-loh eh MAHR-tah AHN-noh OO-nah FEE-lyah: AHN-nah

Anna is in the bathroom.
Anna è in bagno.
AHN-nah eh een BAHN-yoh

In the bathroom there is the shower.
In bagno c'è la doccia.
een BAHN-yoh cheh lah DOHCH-chah

Anna's desk is in her room.
La scrivania di Anna è in camera sua.
lah scree-vah-NEE-ah dee AHN-nah eh een KAH-meh-rah SOO-ah

⏸

Take It Further

▶ 4H Take It Further (CD 1, Track 37)

You probably noticed some new words:

il giardino	the garden
i fiori	the flowers
i libri	the books
il letto matrimoniale	the double bed
la doccia	the shower
la scrivania	the desk

You also heard that Paolo and Marta are in casa (*at home*). That's another useful expression to remember. Finally, in the sentence la scrivania di Anna è in camera sua, you heard one of the possessive adjectives: sua (*her*) for the first time. Keep this in mind; you will be working on possessive adjectives in your next lesson.

Ⅱ

✎ Work Out 2

Let's practice what you've learned so far; we'll focus on the verb essere. First, change the verb to the appropriate form of essere, following the model. Remember to read each sentence out loud.

Io sono a casa. → Tu sei a casa.

1. Io sono a casa. → Loro _____ a casa.

2. Tu sei a casa. → Voi _____ a casa.

3. Tu sei a casa. → Io _____ casa.

4. **Lui è a casa. → Noi** _____ **a casa.**

5. **Lui è a casa. → Lei** _____ **casa.**

6. **Io sono in cucina. → Noi** _____ **in cucina.**

7. **Io sono in cucina. → Voi** _____ **in cucina.**

8. **Tu sei in cucina. → Lei** _____ **in cucina.**

9. **Lei è in cucina. → Loro** _____ **in cucina.**

10. **Loro sono in cucina. → Io** _____ **in cucina.**

ANSWER KEY
1. sono; 2. siete; 3. sono; 4. siamo; 5. è; 6. siamo; 7. siete; 8. è; 9. sono; 10. sono

▶ 4I Work Out 2 (CD 1, Track 38)

Now listen to the audio for additional practice with definite articles and essere.

⃝

✎ Drive It Home

Let's do one final practice dealing with some key grammar you learned in this lesson. Write out the answers, and speak them aloud to yourself a few times. We will focus on essere and the plural. Let's start with essere.

First, fill in the following table with the appropriate pronoun and form of essere.

1.	I am	4.	we are
2.	you are (infml.)	5.	you are (pl.)
3.	he/she is	6.	they are

ANSWER KEY
1. io sono; 2. tu sei; 3. lui/lei è; 4. noi siamo; 5. voi siete; 6. loro sono

Let's do one more practice with essere. Fill in the blanks with the appropriate form of essere.

1. Io _____ di Firenze.

2. Carlo _____ di Firenze.

3. Noi _____ di Firenze.

4. Voi _____ di Firenze.

5. La madre _____ di Roma.

6. Le ragazze _____ di Roma.

7. La ragazza _____ di Roma.

8. I ragazzi _____ di Roma.

ANSWER KEY
1. sono; 2. è; 3. siamo; 4. siete; 5. è; 6. sono; 7. è; 8. sono

Now let's do an exercise with the plural form for articles and nouns. We'll start with masculine nouns. Fill in the blanks following the model: amico → l'amico → gli amici.

1. padre → _____ → _____

2. ragazzo → _____ → _____

3. studente → _____ → _____

4. zio → _____ → _____

5. bambino → _____ → _____

6. tavolo → _____ → _____

7. armadio → _____ → _____

8. specchio → _____ → _____

ANSWER KEY

1. il padre, i padri; 2. il ragazzo, i ragazzi; 3. lo studente, gli studenti; 4. lo zio, gli zii; 5. il bambino, i bambini; 6. il tavolo, i tavoli; 7. l'armadio, gli armadi; 8. lo specchio, gli specchi

Now let's do the same with feminine nouns.

1. madre → _____ → _____

2. ragazza → _____ → _____

3. studentessa → _____ → _____

4. zia → _____ → _____

5. bambina → _____ → _____

6. casa → _____ → _____

7. camera → _____ → _____

8. cucina → _____ → _____

ANSWER KEY

1. la madre, le madri; 2. la ragazza, le ragazze; 3. la studentessa, le studentesse; 4. la zia, le zie; 5. la bambina, le bambine; 6. la casa, le case; 7. la camera, le camere; 8. la cucina, le cucine

Parting Words

Benissimo! [beh-NEES-see-moh] *Great!* You just finished Lesson Four, and you've learned how to:

☐ use common vocabulary for around the house. (Still unsure? Go back to page 54.)

☐ say *the* in the plural. (Still unsure? Go back to page 56.)

☐ use the very important verb **essere** (*to be*). (Still unsure? Go back to page 58.)

☐ talk about possession with the word **di** (*of*). (Still unsure? Go back to page 59.)

☐ put it all together in a conversation about the home. (Still unsure? Go back to page 62.)

Don't forget to practice and reinforce what you've learned by visiting **www.livinglanguage.com/languagelab** for flashcards, games, and quizzes for Lesson Four!

Take It Further

▶ 4J Take It Further (CD 1, Track 39)

Now that you've learned the important verb **essere**, let's look at a few common and useful expressions that use this verb:

essere d'accordo	*to agree*
essere in orario	*to be on time*
essere puntuale	*to be on time*
essere in ritardo	*to be late*
Sei d'accordo?	*Do you agree?*

⏸

Word Recall

Match the Italian in the left column with the English equivalent in the right.

1. Il professore è sempre puntuale.

2. Gli amici sono in soggiorno.

3. I nonni sono in camera da letto.

4. Ho fretta.

5. La figlia è in camera.

6. Sei in ritardo.

7. Le bambine hanno fame.

8. Le sedie sono in cucina.

9. In cucina ci sono i piatti e le tazze.

10. Loro sono in giardino.

11. Io sono di Roma, e Lei?

12. I libri sono sul tavolo.

13. Il padre è di Venezia.

14. In bagno c'è uno specchio.

15. Lei è d'accordo?

a. *The chairs are in the kitchen.*

b. *Do you (fml.) agree?*

c. *The girls are hungry.*

e. *In the kitchen there are plates and cups.*

f. *In the bathroom there is a mirror.*

g. *The professor is always on time.*

h. *I am from Rome, and you (fml.)?*

i. *You (infml.) are late.*

j. *The books are on the table.*

k. *The father is from Venice.*

l. *The daughter is in the bedroom.*

m. *The friends are in the living room.*

n. *The grandparents are in the bedroom.*

o. *They are in the garden.*

p. *I am in a hurry.*

ANSWER KEY

1. g; 2. m; 3. n; 4. p; 5. l; 6. i; 7. c; 8. a; 9. e; 10. o; 11. h; 12. j; 13. k; 14. f; 15. b.

Lesson 5: Describing Things

Quinta Lezione: Descrivere le cose
QUEEN-tah leh-TSYOH-neh: deh-SCREE-veh-reh leh KOH-zeh

Bentornato! [BEHN-tohr-NAH-toh] *Welcome back!* In this lesson you'll learn how to:

☐ describe people and things

☐ use colors and other common adjectives in Italian

☐ use possessive words like *my, your, her, our,* and so on

☐ use more basic vocabulary to talk about people and the house

☐ put it all together in a brief conversation

As always, we'll start with some vocabulary.

Vocabulary Builder 1

▶ 5B Vocabulary Builder 1 (CD 1, Track 41)

The couch is new.	Il divano è nuovo.	eel dee-VAH-noh eh NWOH-voh
The house is old.	La casa è vecchia.	lah KAH-zah eh VEHK-kyah
The beds are small.	I letti sono piccoli.	ee LEH-tee SOH-noh PEEK-koh-lee
The bedrooms are beautiful.	Le camere da letto sono belle.	Leh KAH-meh-reh dah LEHT-toh SOH-noh BEHL-leh
The kitchen is big.	La cucina è grande.	lah koo-CHEE-nah eh GRAHN-deh
The bathroom is ugly.	Il bagno è brutto.	eel BAH-nyoh eh BROOT-toh
The rug is red.	Il tappeto è rosso.	eel TAHP-peh-toh eh ROHS-soh
The pillows are yellow.	I cuscini sono gialli.	ee koo-SHEE-nee SOH-noh JAHL-lee
The table is green.	Il tavolo è verde.	eel TAH-voh-loh eh VEHR-deh
The chairs are brown.	Le sedie sono marroni.	leh SEH-dyeh SOH-noh mahr-ROH-nee
The washing machine is white.	La lavatrice è bianca.	lah lah-vah-TREE-cheh eh BYAN-kah
The dishes are blue.	I piatti sono blu.	ee PYAT-tee SOH-noh bloo
The pans are black.	Le pentole sono nere.	leh PEHN-toh-leh SOH-noh NEH-reh

⏸

✎ Vocabulary Practice 1

Translate the following sentences into English. Read each sentence out loud.

1. **La casa è piccola.** _____

2. **Il bagno è brutto.** _____

3. **La lavatrice è bianca.** _____

4. **Il divano è nuovo.** _____

5. **I cuscini sono blu.** _____

6. **Le sedie sono marroni.** _____

7. **La cucina è grande.** _____

8. **Il tavolo è verde.** _____

ANSWER KEY

1. *The house is small.* 2. *The bathroom is ugly.* 3. *The washing machine is white.* 4. *The couch is new.*
5. *The pillows are blue.* 6. *The chairs are brown.* 7. *The kitchen is large.* 8. *The table is green.*

Grammar Builder 1

▶ 5C Grammar Builder 1 (CD 1, Track 42)

You just heard some common adjectives:

new/old	**nuovo/vecchio**
small/big	**piccolo/grande**
beautiful/ugly	**bello/brutto**

Did you notice how the ending of each adjective changed according to the
noun accompanying it? That's because Italian adjectives take the same gender
(masculine or feminine), and number (singular or plural) of the noun they refer
to. An adjective like *new* has four forms:

	MASCULINE	FEMININE
singular	**nuovo**	**nuova**
plural	**nuovi**	**nuove**

Therefore, we have:

il divano nuovo	i letti nuovi
the new couch	*the new beds*
(the masculine singular ending in -o)	(the masculine plural ending in -i)
la casa nuova	le camere nuove
the new house	*the new bedrooms*
(the feminine singular ending in -a)	(the feminine plural ending in -e)

Some adjectives, however, like **grande**, only have two endings: singular (-e) and plural (-i), with no distinction between masculine and feminine. This usually applies to adjectives that end in -e. Compare:

la cucina grande
the big kitchen

il bagno grande
the big bathroom

Cucina (f.) and **bagno** (m.) have a different gender, but the adjective form does not change.

Most colors work like other adjectives too. Some of them, like **rosso** (*red*), **giallo** (*yellow*), **bianco** (*white*), and **nero** (*black*), have four endings, while others, like **verde** (*green*) and **marrone** (*brown*), only have two. Some adjectives, like **blu** (*blue*), **arancione** (*orange*), and **rosa** (*pink*), are invariable—meaning they won't change according to the noun they are describing. Let's now move on to another family of adjectives: possessive adjectives.

Ⅱ

Vocabulary Builder 2

▶ 5D Vocabulary Builder 2 (CD 1, Track 43)

my house	la mia casa	lah MEE-ah KAH-zah
your apartment	il tuo appartamento	eel TOO-oh ahp-pahr-TAH-mehn-toh
his/her table	il suo tavolo	eel SOO-oh TAH-voh-loh
his/her kitchen	la sua cucina	lah SOO-ah koo-CHEE-nah
our bed	il nostro letto	eel NOHS-troh LEHT-toh
your (pl.) pillow	il vostro cuscino	eel VOHS-troh koo-SHEE-noh
their rug	il loro tappeto	eel LOH-roh TAHP-peh-toh
Your father is nice.	Tuo padre è simpatico.	TOO-oh PAH-dreh eh seem-PAH-tee-koh
Your mom is sweet.	La tua mamma è dolce.	lah TOOx-ah MAHM-mah eh DOHL-cheh
Your sister is intelligent.	Tua sorella è intelligente.	TOO-ah soh-REHL-lah eh een-tehl-lee-JEHN-teh

⏸

✎ Vocabulary Practice 2

Fill in the blanks following the model, and then read each new sentence aloud.

La mia mamma è dolce. (tua) → La tua mamma è dolce.

1. La mia casa è piccola. (tua) _____

2. Il mio tavolo è verde. (loro) _____

3. Il mio letto è grande. (suo) _____

4. Il loro tappeto è nuovo. (nostro) _____

5. **La sua cucina è bella. (vostra)** _____

6. **Mio padre è intelligente. (vostro)** _____

7. **Tua cugina è simpatica. (mia)** _____

8. **Vostra madre è dolce. (sua)** _____

ANSWER KEY

1. La tua casa è piccola. 2. Il loro tavolo è verde. 3. Il suo letto è grande. 4 Il nostro tappeto è nuovo.
5. La vostra cucina è bella. 6. Vostro padre è intelligente. 7. Mia cugina è simpatica. 8. Sua madre è dolce.

Grammar Builder 2

▶ 5E Grammar Builder 2 (CD 2, Track 1)

Let's take a short break and make a few comments on what you just heard. Each possessive adjective, like other adjectives, has four forms, according to gender and number. The only exception is the invariable form loro (*their*). Let's look at them all together:

	MASCULINE SINGULAR	FEMININE SINGULAR	MASCULINE PLURAL	FEMININE PLURAL
my	mio	mia	miei	mie
your (sg.)	tuo	tua	tuoi	tue
his, her	suo	sua	suoi	sue
our	nostro	nostra	nostri	nostre
your (pl.)	vostro	vostra	vostri	vostre
their	loro	loro	loro	loro

Italian possessives always agree with the object, and not with the object's owner. Therefore, *my house* is la mia casa (feminine singular), and *my apartment* is il mio appartamento (masculine singular), no matter whether the owner is male or female.

Italian possessives are always preceded by a definite article—il vostro cuscino (*your pillow*), il nostro letto (*our bed*)—unless they refer to family terms (like

padre, madre, fratello, sorella, figlio, nonna, zio, cugina, nipote, and so on) used
in the singular and not accompanied by other adjectives.

However, when using possessives to refer to the words mamma and papà (*mom*
and *dad*), you need to use the definite article, as mamma and papà are considered
terms of endearment.

Ⓘ

✎ Work Out 1

Let's practice what you've learned in a listening comprehension exercise. Listen
to the audio, and fill in each blank with the word that you hear.

▶ 5F Work Out 1 (CD 2, Track 2)

1. *My house is old.*

   La _____ casa è vecchia.

2. *Your pillows are green.*

   I tuoi _____ sono _____.

3. *His/Her table is big.*

   Il _____ tavolo è _____.

4. *His/Her chair is small.*

   La _____ sedia è _____.

5. *Our washing machines are white.*

   Le _____ lavatrici _____ bianche.

6. *Your (pl.) couch is red.*

   Il _____ divano è _____.

7. *Their beds are small.*

   I _____ letti sono _____.

8. *Their bedrooms are new.*

   Le loro _____ da letto sono _____.

9. *Your (sg.) dishes are yellow.*

   I _____ piatti sono _____.

10. *Her kitchen is beautiful.*

    La _____ cucina è _____.

ANSWER KEY

1. mia; 2. cuscini, verdi; 3. suo, grande; 4. sua, piccola; 5. nostre, sono; 6. vostro, rosso; 7. loro, piccoli; 8. camere, nuove; 9. tuoi, gialli; 10. sua, bella

Bring It All Together

Now let's bring it all together, and add a little bit more vocabulary and structure.

▶ 5G Bring It All Together (CD 2, Track 3)

My family is big.
La mia famiglia è numerosa.
lah MEE-ah fah-MEE-lyah eh noo-meh-ROH-sah

My father, Bob, is very nice.
Mio padre, Bob, è molto simpatico.
MEE-oh PAH-dreh, Bob, eh MOHL-toh seem-PAH-tee-koh

His car is red.
La sua automobile è rossa.
lah SOO-ah ah-oo-toh-MOH-bee-leh eh ROHS-sah

My mother, Laura, is a little stressed.
Mia madre, Laura, è un po' stressata.
MEE-ah MAH-dreh, LAH-oo-rah, eh oon poh strehs-SAH-tah

Her bike is green.
La sua bicicletta è verde.
lah SOO-ah bee-chee-CLEHT-tah eh VEHR-deh

My sister, Ann, is very intelligent.
Mia sorella, Ann, è molto intelligente.
MEE-ah soh-REHL-lah, Ann, eh MOHL-toh een-tehl-lee-JEHN-teh

Her bedroom is always clean.
La sua camera da letto è sempre pulita.
lah SOO-ah KAH-meh-rah dah LEHT-toh eh SEHM-preh poo-LEE-tah

My cousins are a little stressed, too.
Anche i miei cugini sono un po' stressati.
AHN-keh ee mee-EH-ee koo-JEE-nee SOH-noh oon poh strehs-SAH-tee

Their apartments are old.
I loro appartamenti sono vecchi.
ee LOH-roh ahp-pahr-TAH-mehn-tee SOH-noh VEHK-kee

My grandparents are happy.
I miei nonni sono felici.
ee mee-EH-ee NOHN-nee SOH-noh feh-LEE-chee

Their garden is very big.
Il loro giardino è molto grande.
eel LOH-roh jahr-DEE-noh eh MOHL-toh GRAHN-deh

My garden, on the other hand, is very small.

Il mio giardino, invece, è molto piccolo.

eel MEE-oh jahr-DEE-noh een-VEH-cheh eh MOHL-toh peek-KOH-loh

Take It Further

▶ 5H Take It Further (CD 2, Track 4)

Did you notice how the English *his* and *her* were both translated as **sua** because they referred to feminine objects?

la sua automobile
his car

la sua bicicletta
her bike

In case you want to avoid ambiguities, you can use a different structure and say **di lui** for *his,* and **di lei** for *her*. You also heard a few new words:

molto	*very*
un po'	*a little*
invece	*instead*
anche	*too, also*

Use **molto** and **un po'** to modify adjectives. **Invece** and **anche**, on the other hand, are used to express differences and similarities between people and things. Note the position of **anche**: in Italian, it's usually placed at the beginning of a sentence.

✎ Work Out 2

Let's practice what you've learned so far; we'll start with possessive adjectives.
Change the adjective to the appropriate form following the model. Remember to
read each sentence out loud.

Mia sorella è simpatica. → Le mie sorelle sono simpatiche.

1. **Mio fratello è intelligente. → I _____ fratelli sono intelligenti.**

2. **La loro casa è grande. → Le _____ case sono grandi.**

3. **Il tuo tavolo è marrone. → I _____ tavoli sono marroni.**

4. **La sua nipote è di Roma. → Le _____ nipoti sono di Roma.**

5. **Tuo zio è in camera da letto. → I _____ zii sono in camera da letto.**

6. **Il loro divano è vecchio. → I _____ divani sono vecchi.**

7. **Il suo bambino è in giardino. → I _____ bambini sono in giardino.**

8. **La nostra automobile è rossa. → Le _____ automobili sono rosse.**

ANSWER KEY
1. miei; 2. loro; 3. tuoi; 4. sue; 5. tuoi; 6. loro; 7. suoi; 8. nostre

▶ 5I Work Out 2 (CD 2, Track 5)

Now listen to the audio for some more audio-only practice with what you've
learned in this lesson.

⑪

✎ Drive It Home

Now we'll do some more practice with adjectives. This time, choose the correct ending of the adjective. Read each sentence out loud.

1. Le mie cugine sono intelligent- _____.

2. Il loro appartamento è grand- _____.

3. La camera da letto è piccol- _____.

4. Il tavolo in cucina è bianc- _____.

5. I cuscini sul divano sono bianch- _____.

6. Le studentesse sono simpatich- _____.

7. Le pentole sono ner- _____.

8. Mia sorella è dolc- _____.

ANSWER KEY
1. intelligenti; 2. grande; 3. piccola; 4. bianco; 5. bianchi; 6. simpatiche; 7. nere; 8. dolce

Parting Words

Molto bene! [MOHL-toh BEH-neh] *Very good!* You've finished your fifth lesson of Italian. You should know how to:

☐ describe people and things. (Still unsure? Go back to page 71.)

☐ use colors and other common adjectives in Italian. (Still unsure? Go back to page 72.)

☐ use possessive words like *my, your, her, our,* and so on. (Still unsure? Go back to page 75.)

☐ use more basic vocabulary to talk about people and the house. (Still unsure? Go back to page 74.)

☐ put it all together in a brief conversation. (Still unsure? Go back to page 77.)

Don't forget to practice and reinforce what you've learned by visiting **www.livinglanguage.com/ languagelab** for flashcards, games, and quizzes for Lesson Five!

Word Recall

Read the following paragraph aloud, and then translate it into English. Here are a few notes that will help you:

Tanti is a way of saying *many*. It's the plural form of tanto. The conjunction e (*and*) becomes ed before a vowel. Vive means *lives*, from vivere (*to live*). We'll cover verb conjugation later. Nell' is a contraction of in (*in*) and l' (*the*), so it simply means *in the*. Con means *with*.

Carla Betti è una studentessa. Carla ha tanti amici simpatici ed una famiglia molto grande. Lei ha tre sorelle e due fratelli. La famiglia di Carla vive a Milano. Carla vive in un appartamento piccolo. Nell'appartamento ci sono una camera da letto, una cucina, un bagno ed un piccolo soggiorno. La camera da letto di Carla è bella. Ci sono un letto grande, una scrivania marrone ed un divano blu. La cucina è grande. In cucina c'è un tavolo bianco con quattro sedie bianche. In cucina c'è una lavatrice. In soggiorno c'è un divano blu con tre cuscini gialli. In bagno ci sono una doccia ed un piccolo tappeto rosso.

_____

_____

_____

_____

_____

_____

_____

_____

_____

_____

_____

_____

_____

_____

_____

_____

ANSWER KEY

Carla Betti is a student. Carla has many nice friends and a very large family. She has three sisters and two brothers. Carla's family lives in Milano. Carla lives in a small apartment. In the apartment there is a bedroom, a kitchen, a bathroom and a small living room. Carla's bedroom is beautiful. There is a big bed, a brown desk, and a blue couch. The kitchen is large. In the kitchen there is a white table with four white chairs. In the kitchen there is a washing machine. In the living room there is a blue couch with three yellow cushions. In the bathroom there is a shower and a small red carpet.

Quiz 1

Let's see how you're doing. Here's a short quiz testing the material in Lessons One through Five. Answer all of the questions, and then score yourself to see if you could use a refresher. If you find that you need to go back and review, please do so before continuing on to Lesson Six.

Ready?

A. Match the following English words to the correct Italian translations:

1. mi chiamo
2. In cucina c'è il tavolo.
3. Ecco i miei amici.
4. C'è il fratello.
5. il tuo appartamento

a. *There's the brother.*
b. *your apartment*
c. *my name is*
d. *Here are my friends.*
e. *In the kitchen there is the table.*

B. Translate the following English expressions into Italian.

1. *How are you? (fml.)*

_____

2. *I'm from Boston.*

_____

3. *Pleased to meet you. (fml.)*

_____

4. *Where are you from? (fml.)*

_____

5. *You're welcome.*

_____

C. Fill in the table with the correct forms of essere (*to be*):

I am	1.
you are (sg., infml.)	2.
she/he is	3.
we are	4.
you are (pl.)	5.
they are	6.

D. Fill in the blanks with the appropriate Italian adjective in the correct form.

1. L'appartamento di Maria è _____. *(big)*

2. Mia sorella è _____. *(nice)*

3. I cuscini sono _____. *(yellow)*

4. Tua cugina è _____. *(intelligent)*

5. Le sedie sono _____. *(red)*

ANSWER KEY
A. 1. c; 2. e; 3. d; 4. a; 5. b
B: 1. Come sta? 2. (Io) sono di Boston. 3. Piacere di conoscerLa. 4. Lei di dov'è? 5. Prego.
C: 1. io sono; 2. tu sei; 3. lei/lui è; 4. noi siamo; 5. voi siete; 6. loro sono
D: 1. grande; 2. simpatica; 3. gialli; 4. intelligente; 5. rosse

How Did You Do?

Give yourself a point for every correct answer, then use the following key to determine whether or not you're ready to move on:

0-7 points: It's probably best to go back and study the lessons again to make sure you understood everything completely. Take your time; it's not a race! Make sure you spend time reviewing the vocabulary and reading through each Grammar Builder section carefully.

8-16 points: If the questions you missed were in sections A or B, you may want to review the vocabulary from previous lessons again; if you missed answers mostly in sections C or D, check the Grammar Builder sections to make sure you have your grammar basics down.

17-20 points: Feel free to move on to Lesson Six! You're doing a great job.

☐☐ points

Lesson 6: Around Town

Sesta Lezione: In giro per la città

Rieccoci! *Here we are again!* In this sixth lesson, all about **in giro per la città** (*around town*), you'll:

☐ learn important vocabulary for getting around town

☐ find out how to ask for and give directions

☐ learn how to express location and direction

☐ learn important prepositions and other useful vocabulary

☐ listen in on a brief conversation about asking for and getting directions

Let's start right away with some vocabulary. Remember to repeat the Italian a few times to practice pronunciation as you listen carefully to the native speakers.

Vocabulary Builder 1

Notice that from this point on, there won't be any more phonetics. But by now you've gotten enough vocabulary under your belt that you'll know how to pronounce words as they are spelled. Don't forget to listen to the audio for practice, and you'll do fine.

▶ 6B Vocabulary Builder 1 (CD 2, Track 7)

Is there a bank nearby?	C'è una banca qui vicino?
a post office	un ufficio postale
a supermarket	un supermercato
Where is the train station?	Dov'è la stazione?
the school	la scuola
the hospital	l'ospedale
There is a pharmacy in Dante Square.	C'è una farmacia in piazza Dante.
There is a church on Mazzini Street.	C'è una chiesa in via Mazzini.
There is a movie theater on Roma Avenue.	C'è un cinema in viale Roma.
The museum is next to the station.	Il museo è vicino alla stazione.
The restaurant is next to the school.	Il ristorante è vicino alla scuola.
The theater is next to the church.	Il teatro è vicino alla chiesa.

⏸

Take It Further

You'll learn a little more about the word vicino (near) shortly. For now, let's focus on the last three examples in Vocabulary Builder 1:

Il museo è vicino alla stazione.	The museum is next to the station.
Il ristorante è vicino alla scuola.	The restaurant is next to the school.
Il teatro è vicino alla chiesa.	The theater is next to the church.

The preposition *next to* is a fixed expression in Italian: vicino a. Vicino doesn't change, but a (*to*) forms a contraction with the definite article that follows it. In all three cases above, the word that follows a is feminine: la stazione, la scuola, la chiesa. When la follows a, the contraction alla (*to the*) is used: a + la stazione = alla stazione, and so on.

Don't worry too much about these contractions yet. There are lots of forms, also used with other common prepositions, such as nell' (in + l'), which you came across in the last lesson. For now you should just start to be on the lookout for them. And in fact, you probably know a few of them already. In the expression al fresco ("*in the fresh air*"), fresco is masculine, and a + il fresco = al fresco. If you like your pasta al dente, that means you like it to stick *to the tooth* a bit: a + il dente = al dente.

✎ Vocabulary Practice 1

Match the English expressions in the left column with the Italian in the right.

1. *Where is the train station?*	a. un supermercato
2. *There is a movie theater on Roma Avenue.*	b. un ufficio postale
3. *the school*	c. C'è un cinema in viale Roma.
4. *There is a pharmacy in Dante Square.*	d. C'è una banca qui vicino?
5. *Is there a bank nearby?*	e. C'è una farmacia in piazza Dante.
6. *a supermarket*	f. C'è una chiesa in via Mazzini.
7. *There is a church on Mazzini Street.*	g. l'ospedale
8. *The museum is next to the station.*	h. la scuola
9. *the hospital*	i. Dov' è la stazione?
10. *a post office*	j. Il museo è vicino alla stazione.

ANSWER KEY

1. i; 2. c; 3. h; 4. e; 5. d; 6. a; 7. f; 8. j; 9. g; 10. b

Grammar Builder 1
▶ 6C Grammar Builder 1 (CD 2, Track 8)

You just learned many names of common places you can find in giro per la città (*around town*):

(una) banca	bank
(un) ufficio postale	post office
(un) supermercato	supermarket
(una) stazione	train station
(una) scuola	school
(un) ospedale	hospital
(una) farmacia	pharmacy
(una) chiesa	church
(un) cinema	movie theater
(un) museo	museum
(un) ristorante	restaurant
(un) teatro	theater

To ask directions to these places, you need to know how to ask questions. One way to form questions in Italian is with a simple change in intonation. Compare:

C'è una banca qui vicino.
There is a bank nearby.

C'è una banca qui vicino?
Is there a bank nearby?

The word order doesn't change, but in the question version, you can hear the pitch rising at the end of the sentence. Another way to form questions in Italian is to begin a sentence with a question word (the intonation, however, is always important). You also heard the question word **dove?** (*where?*, shortened to **dov'** before **è**), as in:

Dov'è la stazione?
Where is the train station?

You'll learn more question words later on. For now, let's add some more vocabulary and learn how to give directions.

Vocabulary Builder 2
▶ 6D Vocabulary Builder 2 (CD 2, Track 9)

downtown	**in centro**
straight ahead	**sempre diritto**
on the left, to the left	**(a) sinistra**
on the right, to the right	**(a) destra**
through	**per**
then	**poi**
again	**ancora**
up to	**fino a**
intersection	**incrocio**
traffic light	**semaforo**
near	**vicino/vicina/vicini/vicine**
far	**lontano/lontana/lontani/lontane**

✎ Vocabulary Practice 2

Once again, match the English on the left with the Italian on the right.

1. *intersection*	a. **semaforo**
2. *on the right, to the right*	b. **vicino/vicina/vicini/vicine**
3. *then*	c. **a sinistra**
4. *downtown*	d. **fino a**
5. *on the left, to the left*	e. **ancora**
6. *near*	f. **in centro**
7. *straight ahead*	g. **incrocio**
8. *up to*	h. **lontano/lontana/lontani/lontane**
9. *again*	i. **sempre diritto**
10. *traffic light*	j. **a destra**
11. *far*	k. **poi**

ANSWER KEY

1. g; 2. j; 3. k; 4. f; 5. c; 6. b; 7. i; 8. d; 9. e; 10. a; 11. h.

Grammar Builder 2

▶ 6E Grammar Builder 2 (CD 2, Track 10)

When asking directions, don't forget to say:

scusi (*fml.*)	scusa (*infml.*)	*excuse me*

Let's now focus a moment on the word **vicino,** and its different meanings. You can use it as an adverb meaning *next to* or in the expression **qui vicino** (*nearby*). In both cases it is invariable.

Vicino is also an adjective meaning *near*. When used as an adjective, it will have four forms:

	MASCULINE	FEMININE
singular	vicino	vicina
plural	vicini	vicine

And it will agree with the noun it is referring to. Compare:

La scuola è vicino alla chiesa.
The school is next to the church.

La scuola è qui vicino.
The school is nearby.

La scuola è vicina.
The school is near/close.

Ⓘ

Take It Further

Let's take a closer look at those last three examples. Remember that **vicino a** (*next to*) and **qui vicino** (*nearby*) are fixed expressions, so the word **vicino** doesn't agree with anything. But when **vicino** is used on its own to directly describe a noun, it agrees with it.

La scuola è vicino alla chiesa.	*The school is next to the church.*	(Vicino a is a fixed expression, so vicino doesn't change.)
La scuola è qui vicino.	*The school is nearby.*	(Qui vicino is a fixed expression, so vicino doesn't change.)
La scuola è vicina.	*The school is near./ The school is close.*	(Vicino is describing the school, so it agrees by taking the feminine singular form, vicina.)

✎ Work Out 1

By now you're used to these listening comprehension exercises. Listen to the audio, and fill in each blank with the word you hear.

▶ 6F Work Out 1 (CD 2, Track 11)

1. *This is my hometown.*

   Questa è la mia _____ natale.

2. *The bank and the post office are downtown.*

   La _____ e l' _____ postale sono in centro.

3. *The church is downtown, too.*

   Anche la _____ è in _____.

4. *The train station is next to the school.*

   La _____ è _____ alla _____.

5. *The hospital is far.*

   L' _____ è _____.

6. *The pharmacy, on the other hand, is near.*

   La _____, invece, è _____.

7. *There's a movie theater on Mazzini Street.*

   _____ un _____ in via Mazzini.

8. *And there's a theater in Dante Square.*

   E c'è un _____ in _____ Dante.

⑪

ANSWER KEY
1. città; 2. banca, ufficio; 3. chiesa, centro; 4. stazione, vicino, scuola; 5. ospedale, lontano;
6. farmacia, vicina; 7. C'è, cinema; 8. teatro, piazza

⒢ Bring It All Together

Now let's bring it all together, and add a little bit more vocabulary and structure.

▶ 6G Bring It All Together (CD 2, Track 12)

Excuse me, where is the Museum of Modern Art?
Mi scusi, dov'è il museo di arte moderna?

It's on Manzoni Avenue, next to the Beccaria High School.
È in viale Manzoni, vicino al liceo Beccaria.

Is it far?
È lontano?

No, it's nearby. Straight ahead through Mazzini Street up to Dante Square. Then left on Verdi Street, and left again on Manzoni Avenue. The museum is on the right, after the second traffic light.
No, è qui vicino. Sempre diritto per via Mazzini fino a piazza Dante. Poi a sinistra in via Verdi e ancora a sinistra in viale Manzoni. Il museo è a destra, dopo il secondo semaforo.

One more question. Is there a good restaurant nearby?
Ancora una domanda: c'è un buon ristorante qui vicino?

Yes, there is an excellent restaurant on Garibaldi Street: the family restaurant "Buon appetito" ("Enjoy your meal").
Sì, c'è un ristorante eccellente in via Garibaldi: la trattoria "Buon appetito".

And where is Garibaldi Street?
E dov'è via Garibaldi?

*It's right here. The first street on the right after the intersection between Mazzini
Street and Cavour Avenue.*
**È proprio qui. La prima strada a destra dopo l'incrocio tra via Mazzini e corso
Cavour.**

Thank you very much! You're very kind.
Grazie mille! Lei è molto gentile.

No problem! Enjoy your walk and … enjoy your dinner!
Non c'è di che! Buona passeggiata e… buona cena!

Take It Further

6H Take It Further (CD 2, Track 13)

Did you notice the new adjectives used in the dialogue? Some of them belong to
the family of adjectives with two endings:

| gentile/gentili | *kind* |
| eccellente/eccellenti | *excellent* |

Others belong to the family of numeral adjectives, which always have four endings:

| primo/prima/primi/prime | *first* |
| secondo/seconda/secondi/seconde | *second* |

Finally, you heard the adjective **buono/buona/buoni/buone** (*good*) used in the
expression **un buon ristorante** (*a good restaurant*). Before a noun, the adjective
buono follows the same pattern as the indefinite article; thus **un buon ristorante**

and not **un buono ristorante**. The same happens in the expression **buon appetito** (*enjoy your meal*). You can use the appropriate form of **buono** followed by a noun when you want to wish someone well in their plans:

Buona passeggiata!	*Enjoy your walk! Have a good walk!*
Buona cena!	*Enjoy your dinner! Have a good dinner!*

(II)

✎ Work Out 2

Let's practice what we've learned so far. We'll start with the different forms of **vicino**.

Fill in the blanks with **vicino, vicina,** or **vicine**.

1. **La farmacia è qui** _____.

2. **La farmacia è** _____.

3. **La farmacia è** _____ **alla stazione.**

4. **Le scuole sono qui** _____.

5. **Le scuole sono** _____.

6. **Le scuole sono** _____ **alla banca.**

7. **La banca è qui** _____.

8. **La banca è** _____.

9. **La banca è** _____ **alla chiesa.**

ANSWER KEY

1. vicino; 2. vicina; 3. vicino; 4. vicino; 5. vicine; 6. vicino; 7. vicino; 8. vicina; 9. vicino.

Now let's practice some other adjective forms. Use the correct form of the adjective following the model:

La signora è gentile. Le signore sono gentili

1. **La scuola è vicina. Le scuole sono** _____.

2. **L'ospedale è lontano. Gli ospedali sono** _____.

3. **Il museo è interessante. I musei sono** _____.

4. **La madre è gentile. Le madri sono** _____.

5. **Il padre è simpatico. I padri sono** _____.

6. **Il semaforo è vicino. I semafori sono** _____.

7. **L'ufficio postale è vicino. Gli uffici postali sono** _____.

8. **La scuola è eccellente. Le scuole sono** _____.

9. **La banca è lontana. Le banche sono** _____.

10. **Il ristorante è eccellente. I ristoranti sono** _____.

ANSWER KEY

1. vicine; 2. lontani; 3. interessanti; 4. gentili; 5. simpatici; 6. vicini; 7. vicini; 8. eccellenti; 9. lontane; 10. eccellenti.

▶ 6I Work Out 2 (CD 2, Track 14)

Listen to the audio for additional audio-only practice with the material you've learned in this lesson.

⑪

✎ Drive It Home

Let's focus on expressions with vicino. Fill in the blanks with vicino, vicina, vicini, or vicine.

1. La stazione è _____ alla banca.

2. La chiesa è qui _____.

3. Il ristorante è _____ alla farmacia.

4. La scuola è _____.

5. L'ufficio postale è _____.

6. La banca è _____.

7. I supermercati sono _____ alla stazione.

8. Le scuole sono _____.

9. Gli ospedali sono _____.

10. Gli ospedali sono _____ alla scuola.

ANSWER KEY
1. vicino; 2. vicino; 3. vicino; 4. vicina; 5. vicino; 6. vicina; 7. vicino; 8. vicine; 9. vicini; 10. vicino

Parting Words

Eccellente! *Excellent!* You just finished Lesson Six, in which you were able to:

☐ learn important vocabulary for getting around town. (Still unsure? Go back to page 89.)

☐ find out how to ask for and give directions. (Still unsure? Go back to page 91.)

☐ learn how to express location and direction. (Still unsure? Go back to page 92.)

☐ learn important prepositions and other useful vocabulary. (Still unsure? Go back to page 93.)

☐ listen in on a brief conversation about asking for and getting directions. (Still unsure? Go back to page 96.)

Don't forget to practice and reinforce what you've learned by visiting **www.livinglanguage.com/languagelab** for flashcards, games, and quizzes for Lesson Six!

Take It Further

▶ 6J Take It Further (CD 2, Track 15)

We looked at **buono** earlier, so let's mention a few more common expressions that use this word:

buona fortuna	*good luck*
buon viaggio	*have a good trip*
buon riposo	*have a good rest*
buon compleanno	*happy birthday*
buon anniversario	*happy anniversary*
buone feste	*happy holidays*
buon Natale	*Merry Christmas*

⏸

Word Recall

Translate the following words, phrases, and sentences into Italian.

1. *I have* _____

2. *there are* _____

3. *there is* _____

4. *I am hungry.* _____

   _____

5. *I am cold.* _____

   _____

6. *You (sg., infml.) are in a hurry.* _____

   _____

7. *Here is a family.* _____

   _____

8. *Here are two families.* _____

   _____

9. *Here are my friends.* _____

   _____

10. *a bed* _____

11. *a closet* _____

12. *a rug* _____

13. *Here is a mirror.* _____

_____

14. *Here are four chairs.* _____

_____

15. *my house* _____

16. *your (sg., infml.) apartment* _____

17. *Marta's house* _____

18. *small (four forms)* _____

19. *large (two forms)* _____

20. *downtown* _____

21. *the supermarket* _____

22. *the station* _____

23. *the schools* _____

24. *Where is the station?* _____

_____

25. *Is there a restaurant nearby?* _____

_____

26. *the traffic light* _____

27. *on the left* _____

28. *on the right* _____

29. *straight ahead* _____

30. *an intersection* _____

ANSWER KEY

1. io ho; 2. ci sono; 3. c'è; 4. (Io) ho fame. 5. (Io) ho freddo. 6. (Tu) hai fretta. 7. Ecco una famiglia.
8. Ecco due famiglie. 9. Ecco i miei amici. 10. un letto; 11. un armadio; 12. un tappeto; 13. Ecco uno
specchio. 14. Ecco quattro sedie. 15. la mia casa; 16. il tuo appartamento; 17. la casa di Marta;
18. piccolo/piccola/piccoli/piccole; 19. grande/grandi; 20. in centro; 21. il supermercato;
22. la stazione; 23. le scuole; 24. Dov'è la stazione? 25. C'è un ristorante qui vicino? 26. il semaforo;
27. a sinistra; 28. a destra; 29. sempre diritto; 30. un incrocio.

Lesson 7: At the Restaurant

Settima Lezione: Al ristorante

Bentornati! *Welcome back!* In this seventh lesson, you'll:

☐ increase your vocabulary by learning essential words related to food and restaurants

☐ learn how to make polite requests with **posso?** (*can I?; may I?*) and **vorrei** (*I would like*)

☐ begin to use verbs in Italian

☐ continue to build your proficiency with more complex sentences

☐ put it all to work in a short conversation at an Italian restaurant

Let's start with some vocabulary.

Vocabulary Builder 1

7B Vocabulary Builder 1 (CD 2, Track 17)

the restaurant	**il ristorante**
the waiter	**il cameriere**
the waitress	**la cameriera**
the menu	**il menù**
the wine list	**la lista dei vini** (or **la carta dei vini**)
the appetizer	**l'antipasto**
the first (course)	**il primo (piatto)**
the main (course)	**il secondo (piatto)**
the side dish	**il contorno**
the dessert	**il dolce**
the fresh fruit	**la frutta fresca**
the check	**il conto**
the tip	**la mancia**
I'll have the grilled fish.	**Prendo il pesce alla griglia.**
I would like ravioli with meat sauce.	**Vorrei i ravioli al ragù.**
May I have the wine list?	**Posso avere la carta dei vini?**
Can I pay by credit card?	**Posso pagare con la carta di credito?**

Take It Further

Did you notice **alla** (**a** + **la**) in the expression **il pesce alla griglia** (*grilled fish*)? This is the same **alla** you came across earlier, in expressions such as **vicino alla scuola** (*near the school.*) You probably also notice **al** (**a** + **il**) in **i ravioli al ragù** (*ravioli with meat sauce*). And you were introduced to a contraction with a different preposition, **di** (*of*), as well. The *wine list* is **la carta dei vini**, and **dei** is a contraction of **di + i**, as in **i vini** (*the wines*). You'll get used to these contractions as you learn more Italian. They're very common!

✎ Vocabulary Practice 1

Match the English on the left with the Italian equivalent on the right.

1. *the side dish*	a. **Posso avere la carta dei vini?**
2. *the appetizer*	b. **il conto**
3. *the main (course)*	c. **il contorno**
4. *May I have the wine list?*	d. **il primo (piatto)**
5. *the first (course)*	e. **Posso pagare con la carta di credito?**
6. *the waiter*	f. **l'antipasto**
7. *the check*	g. **la mancia**
8. *the tip*	h. **il cameriere**
9. *I would like ravioli with meat sauce*	i. **il secondo (piatto)**
10. *Can I pay by credit card?*	j. **Vorrei i ravioli al ragù**

ANSWER KEY
1. c.; 2. f; 3. i; 4. a; 5. d; 6. h; 7. b; 8. g; 9. j; 10. e.

Grammar Builder 1

▶ 7C Grammar Builder 1 (CD 2, Track 18)

In Lesson Six you learned how to ask directions. Now let's learn how to make a polite request. A very simple and common way is to say **posso** (*can I, may I*), followed by the infinitive of a verb, just like you heard in the examples:

Posso pagare con la carta di credito?
May I pay by credit card?

Posso avere la carta dei vini?
May I have the wine list?

Another polite way to ask for something is by using the conditional form of the verb **volere** (*to want*): **vorrei** (*I would like*). You won't get as far as the conditional in this course, but if you keep in mind just the first person form (**io vorrei**), you'll make yourself understood and you'll sound very polite, which is always appreciated.

Now let's learn more about the present tense of regular verbs.

Take It Further

You just learned that you can use **posso** (*I can; I may*) with the infinitive form of a verb in Italian. Just to make sure you're clear on what that means, an infinitive is a basic, unconjugated verb. In English, an infinitive is the *to* form: *to speak, to swim, to laugh, to cry …*

We'll talk more about verbs in Italian in a moment, but here's the big picture. In Italian, the infinitive ends in **-are, -ere,** or **-ire**, and each type of infinitive has a special set of endings that are used in the verb's conjugation. **Pagare** (*to pay*) is, for example, an **-are** verb. It also happens to be regular, meaning that it follows the predictable pattern of endings when you conjugate it. You've also seen **avere** (*to have*) in Lesson Three and **essere** (*to be*) in Lesson Four, which both end in **-ere**, but which are also irregular. Still, it's worth reminding yourself of the forms, because some of the endings you already know will come in handy later in this lesson!

	AVERE *(TO HAVE)*	ESSERE *(TO BE)*
I	io ho	io sono
you (sg., infml.)	tu hai	tu sei
you (sg., fml.)	Lei ha	Lei è
he	lui ha	lui è
she	lei ha	lei è
we	noi abbiamo	noi siamo
you (pl.)	voi avete	voi siete
they	loro hanno	loro sono
you (pl., fml.)	Loro hanno	Loro sono

Vocabulary Builder 2

▶ 7D Vocabulary Builder 2 (CD 2, Track 19)

to order	ordinare
I order	io ordino
you order (sg., infml.)	tu ordini
you order (sg., fml.)	Lei ordina
he/she orders	lui/lei ordina
to take (or, to have, as in an order)	prendere
I take, I'll have	io prendo
you take, you'll have (sg., infml.)	tu prendi
you take, you'll have (sg., fml.)	Lei prende
he takes/she takes, he'll have/she'll have	lui/lei prende

⏸

✏ Vocabulary Practice 2

Let's practice the vocabulary you've learned. Match the English in the left column with the Italian equivalent in the right.

1. *He takes the dessert.*

2. *He orders the main course.*

3. *She orders the fruit.*

4. *I take the side dish.*

5. *You (infml.) order the first course.*

6. *You (infml.) take the ravioli with meat sauce.*

7. *You (fml.) take the first course.*

8. *I order the antipasto.*

a. **Lei (fml.) prende il primo.**

b. **Tu ordini il primo.**

c. **Lui prende il dolce.**

e. **Lui ordina il secondo.**

f. **Io ordino l'antipasto.**

g. **Lei ordina la frutta.**

h. **Tu prendi i ravioli al ragù.**

i. **Io prendo il contorno.**

ANSWER KEY

1. c; 2. e; 3. g; 4. i; 5. b; 6. h; 7. a; 8. f.

Grammar Builder 2

Let's take a closer look at verbs in Italian. You learned earlier that verbs are conjugated, meaning they take different forms depending on the subject, according to their infinitive ending, either -are, -ere, or -ire. The conjugations aren't drastically different, and in fact many of the endings are identical. To conjugate a verb, first take off its infinitive ending (-are, -ere, or -ire), and replace it with the right subject ending.

Let's start by just looking at the singular forms for io (*I*), tu (*you, infml.*), and lui/lei (*he/she*). First, let's start with -are verbs such as pagare (*to pay*) and ordinare (*to order*).

SUBJECT	ENDING	EXAMPLES
io (*I*)	-o	pago (*I pay*); ordino (*I order*)

*Notice the gh in paghi. That's to keep the hard g sound. Pagi would be pronounced PAH-jee, while paghi is pronounced PAH-gee, preserving the hard g of the verb stem.

SUBJECT	ENDING	EXAMPLES
tu *(you)*	-i	paghi* *(you pay);* ordini *(you order)*
lui/lei *(he/she)*	-a	paga *(he/she pays);* ordina *(he/she orders)*

*Notice the gh in paghi. That's to keep the hard g sound. Pagi would be pronounced PAH-jee, while paghi is pronounced PAH-gee, preserving the hard g of the verb stem.

Now, let's look at **-ere** verbs such as **prendere** *(to take)* and **chiedere** *(to ask for)*.

SUBJECT	ENDING	EXAMPLES
io *(I)*	-o	prendo *(I take);* chiedo *(I ask for)*
tu *(you)*	-i	prendi *(you take);* chiedi *(you ask for)*
lui/lei *(he/she)*	-e	prende *(he/she takes);* chiede *(he/she asks for)*

We'll leave -ire verbs for another lesson, but for now you can rest assured that the singular endings (io, tu, lui/lei) are the same as for -ere verbs. So really, you already know them! And in fact, you also already know another verb form. The Lei *(you, fml.)* form is identical to the lui/lei *(he/she)* form, no matter what the infinitive ending is:

Lei paga, Lei ordina, Lei prende, Lei chiede
you pay, you order, you take, you ask for

▶ 7E Grammar Builder 2 (CD 2, Track 20)

Let's go back over the verbs one more time. Listen to your audio for an audio-only version of this grammar note. That will help you digest the material more easily!

⏸

Lesson 7: At the Restaurant   111

✎ Work Out 1

Ready for some listening comprehension practice? Listen to your audio, and fill in the blanks with each word you heard.

▶ 7F Work Out 1 (CD 2, Track 21)

1. *We are at an Italian restaurant.*

   _____ in un _____ italiano.

2. *I order ravioli with meat sauce.*

   Io _____ i ravioli _____ ragù.

3. *You order grilled fish and mixed salad.*

   Tu _____ il pesce alla _____ e l'insalata mista.

4. *Maria orders mixed appetizers.*

   Maria _____ l'antipasto _____.

5. *You ask for dessert and coffee.*

   Tu _____ il dolce e il _____.

6. *Maria asks for the bill.*

   Maria _____ il _____.

7. *I pay the check by credit card.*

   Io _____ il conto con la _____ di credito.

⧀

ANSWER KEY

1. Siamo, ristorante; 2. ordino, al; 3. ordini, griglia; 4. ordina, misto; 5. chiedi, caffè; 6. chiede, conto; 7. pago, carta

Bring It All Together

Now let's bring it all together, and add a little bit more vocabulary and structure.

▶ 7G Bring It All Together (CD 2, Track 22)

Well, Giulia, what are you having?
Allora Giulia, che cosa prendi?

I would like the bruschette of the house.
Vorrei le bruschette della casa.

And what are you having as a first course?
E cosa prendi per primo?

I'll have the ravioli; they're very good.
Prendo i ravioli; sono molto buoni.

I, on the other hand, would like the penne with tomato and basil sauce. It's delicious.
Io invece vorrei le penne al pomodoro e basilico: sono squisite.

Are you having a main course, too?
Prendi anche il secondo?

Yes, the meat is excellent. I'll have a beefsteak with a side of salad.
Sì, la carne è eccellente. Prendo una bistecca con contorno di insalata.

Good idea! I'd like the pork roast with a side of potatoes instead.
Buona idea! Io invece vorrei il maiale al forno con contorno di patate.

Shall I order wine, too?
Ordino anche il vino?

Yes, sure. Half a liter of the house red. And a bottle of mineral water, still.
Sì, certo: mezzo litro di (vino) rosso della casa. E una bottiglia di acqua minerale naturale.

All right, I'll call the waiter right away.
Bene, chiamo subito il cameriere.

Take It Further

▶ 7H Take It Further (CD 2, Track 23)

You probably noticed some new vocabulary.

pomodoro e basilico	*tomato and basil*
la bistecca	*the beefsteak*
il maiale al forno	*the pork roast*
le patate	*the potatoes*
l'acqua minerale	*mineral water*
squisito/squisita/squisiti/squisite	*delicious*
naturale/naturali	*natural, non-carbonated, still*

You also heard a new question word: **che cosa?** (*what?*), as in **che cosa prendi?** (*what are you having?*), which can also be shortened into **che** or **cosa** (**che prendi?/cosa prendi?**).

A very useful expression to keep in mind when reading an Italian menu is **della casa** (*[of the] house*), which means a dish is prepared according to a special recipe created by the chef of that restaurant. You can also have **vino della casa** (*wine of the house, house wine*), which usually means a decent quality wine sold by the pitcher.

At the Restaurant

At Work

Review Dialogues

Around Town

Everyday Life

Socializing

✎ Work Out 2

Let's practice the verbs we have seen so far. Fill in the blank with the correct form of the infinitive that you see in parentheses.

1. Tu _____ il pesce della casa. (ordinare)

   You order the house fish.

2. Io _____ il cameriere. (chiamare)

   I call the waiter.

3. Lui _____ il conto. (chiedere)

   He asks for the check.

4. Lei _____ con la carta di credito. (pagare)

   She pays with a credit card.

5. Loro _____ la bistecca. (ordinare)

   They order steak.

6. Noi _____ il dolce ed il caffè. (prendere)

   We have (take) dessert and coffee.

7. Voi _____ il primo. (ordinare)

   You order the first course.

8. Noi _____ con la carta di credito. (pagare)

   We pay with a credit card.

   ANSWER KEY
   1. ordini; 2. chiamo; 3. chiede; 4. paga; 5. ordinano; 6. prendiamo; 7. ordinate; 8. paghiamo.

7I Work Out 2 (CD 2, Track 24)

Now listen to your audio for additional audio-only practice with the material you've learned in this lesson.

✎ Drive It Home

Let's practice the verb endings we have seen so far. We will focus on the present tense singular forms. Fill in the blanks with the appropriate present tense for the following infinitives.

1. avere

   io _____

   tu _____

   lui/lei _____

2. essere

   io _____

   tu _____

   lui/lei _____

3. ordinare

   io _____

   tu _____

   lui/lei _____

4. **pagare**

io _____

tu _____

lui/lei _____

5. **chiamare**

io _____

tu _____

lui/lei _____

6. **chiedere**

io _____

tu _____

lui/lei _____

7. **prendere**

io _____

tu _____

lui/lei _____

ANSWER KEY

1. ho, hai, ha; 2 sono, sei, è; 3. ordino, ordini, ordina; 4. pago, paghi, paga; 5. chiamo, chiami, chiama;
6. chiedo, chiedi, chiede; 7. prendo, prendi, prende.

Parting Words

Molto bene! *Very good!* You just finished Lesson Seven, in which you were able to:

- [ ] increase your vocabulary by learning essential words related to food and restaurants. (Still unsure? Go back to page 106.)

- [ ] learn how to make polite requests with **posso?** (*can I?; may I?*) and **vorrei** (*I would like*). (Still unsure? Go back to page 107.)

- [ ] begin to use verbs in Italian. (Still unsure? Go back to page 109.)

- [ ] continue to build your proficiency with more complex sentences. (Still unsure? Go back to page 110.)

- [ ] put it all to work in a short conversation at an Italian restaurant. (Still unsure? Go back to page 113.)

Don't forget to practice and reinforce what you've learned by visiting **www.livinglanguage.com/ languagelab** for flashcards, games, and quizzes for Lesson Seven!

Word Recall

Let's practice the key vocabulary you've learned over the past lesson. Translate the following sentences into Italian. You can omit the pronouns in Italian.

1. *We are in the kitchen.* _____

   _____

2. *In the bedroom there is the double bed.* _____

   _____

3. *Paola's flowers are in the garden.* _____

   _____

4. *My mom is nice.* _____

   _____

5. *Luigi's car is red.* _____

   _____

6. *Where is the pharmacy?* _____

   _____

7. *Is there a post office nearby?* _____

   _____

8. *May I have the wine list?* _____

   _____

9. *Can we pay by credit card?* _____

_____

10. *I would like the mineral water.* _____

_____

11. *I order the grilled fish.* _____

_____

12. *We pay by credit card.* _____

_____

13. *The bathroom is new.* _____

_____

14. *Carla's couch is old.* _____

_____

15. *The school is next to the station.* _____

_____

16. *I'll have ("take") the ravioli with meat sauce.* _____

_____

ANSWER KEY

1. Siamo in cucina. 2. Nella camera c'è il letto matrimoniale. 3. I fiori di Paola sono in giardino.
4. Mia mamma è simpatica. 5. L'automobile/la macchina di Luigi è rossa. 6. Dov'è la farmacia?
7. C'è un ufficio postale qui vicino? 8. Posso avere la carta dei vini? 9. Possiamo pagare con la carta
di credito? 10. Vorrei l'acqua minerale. 11. Ordino il pesce alla griglia. 12. Paghiamo con la carta di
credito. 13. Il bagno è nuovo. 14. Il divano di Carla è vecchio. 15. La scuola è vicino alla stazione.
16. Prendo i ravioli al ragù.

Lesson 8: Everyday Life

Ottava Lezione: La vita quotidiana

Ciao! *Hi!* Welcome to Lesson Eight, where you'll learn more vocabulary and continue to build on your foundation of *Essential Italian*. This lesson focuses on:

☐ essential vocabulary you'll need to talk about everyday life

☐ the plural forms of verbs

☐ the very important irregular verb **fare** (*to do, to make*)

☐ weather expressions

☐ a conversation about daily routines and everyday life

As always, we'll start with some vocabulary.

Vocabulary Builder 1

▶ 8B Vocabulary Builder 1 (CD 2, Track 26)

to work	lavorare
We work in the morning.	Noi lavoriamo la mattina.
You (pl.) work in the afternoon.	Voi lavorate il pomeriggio.
They work in the evening.	Loro lavorano la sera.
to live	vivere
We live in town.	Noi viviamo in città.
You (pl.) live in the suburbs.	Voi vivete in periferia.
They live in the countryside.	Loro vivono in campagna.
to leave	partire
We leave by train.	Noi partiamo in treno.
You (pl.) leave by bus.	Voi partite in autobus.
They leave by car.	Loro partono in automobile.

⑈

✎ Vocabulary Practice 1

Translate the following sentences. Here are a few expressions with in that will
come in handy for this exercise: in treno *(by train)*, in macchina *(by car)*, in città
(in town), in campagna *(in the country)*. Don't forget that the time expressions
you just learned that use *in* in English don't use in in Italian!

1. *You (pl.) leave by train.* _____

2. *We live in the country.* _____

3. *They live in town.* _____

4. *You (pl.) live in the country.* _____

5. *They leave by car.* _____

6. *We work in the evening.* _____

7. *They work in the morning.* _____

ANSWER KEY
1. Voi partite in treno. 2. Noi viviamo in campagna. 3. Loro vivono in città. 4. Voi vivete in campagna. 5. Loro partono in macchina. 6. Noi lavoriamo la sera. 7. Loro lavorano la mattina.

Take It Further

Let's quickly review the singular forms of **-are** and **-ere** verbs, and also go over the singular forms of **-ire** verbs. Remember that **-ere** and **-ire** verbs take the same endings in the singular. First, here are the singular endings for all three types of verbs.

	-ARE	-ERE	-IRE
io	-o	-o	-o
tu	-i	-i	-i
lui/lei/Lei	-a	-e	-e

And now let's look at a few examples.

	ORDINARE *(TO ORDER)*	PRENDERE *(TO TAKE)*	PARTIRE *(TO LEAVE)*
io	ordino	prendo	parto
tu	ordini	prendi	parti
lui/lei/Lei	ordina	prende	parte

Grammar Builder 1

Now let's look at the plural forms of -are, -ere, and -ire verbs, also known as the first, second, and third conjugations, respectively. We'll start with the -are, or first conjugation, verbs **lavorare** (*to work*) and **ordinare** (*to order*).

SUBJECT	ENDING	EXAMPLES
noi (*we*)	-iamo	lavoriamo (*we work*); ordiniamo (*we order*)
voi (*you, pl.*)	-ate	lavorate (*you work*); ordinate (*you order*)
loro (*they*)	-ano	lavorano (*they work*); ordinano (*they order*)

Now let's move on to the -ere, or second conjugation, verbs **vivere** (*to live*) and **vedere** (*to see*).

SUBJECT	ENDING	EXAMPLES
noi (*we*)	-iamo	viviamo (*we live*); vediamo (*we see*)
voi (*you, pl.*)	-ete	vivete (*you live*); vedete (*you see*)
loro (*they*)	-ono	vivono (*they live*); vedono (*they see*)

And finally, here are two -ire, or third conjugation, verbs, **partire** (*to leave*) and **dormire** (*to sleep*).

SUBJECT	ENDING	EXAMPLES
noi (*we*)	-iamo	partiamo (*we leave*); dormiamo (*we sleep*)
voi (*you, pl.*)	-ite	partite (*you leave*); dormite (*you sleep*)
loro (*they*)	-ono	partono (*they leave*); dormono (*they sleep*)

As you can see, all of the **noi** (*we*) forms share the same ending: -iamo. The **voi** (*you, pl.*) forms all end in -te, preceded by the same vowel as the vowel of the infinitive ending: -ate for -are verbs, -ete for -ere verbs, and -ite for -ire verbs. The **loro** (*they*) forms end in -ano for -are verbs, and -ono for both -ere and -ire verbs.

▶ 8C Grammar Builder 1 (CD 2, Track 27)

Now listen to your audio for an audio-only version of this grammar note. This will give you more practice with verbs, and the more practice you have, the more easily you'll remember how to use them.

Ⓘ

Take It Further

Let's take a moment to review all three types of regular verbs that you've learned so far in Italian. First, here are the endings for each group:

INFINITIVE	-ARE	-ERE	-IRE
io	-o	-o	-o
tu	-i	-i	-i
lui/lei/Lei	-a	-e	-e
noi	-iamo	-iamo	-iamo
voi	-ate	-ete	-ite
loro/Loro	-ano	-ono	-ono

Notice that the endings for io (*I*), tu (*you, sg., infml.*), and noi (*we*) are all identical. For the lui/lei/Lei (*he/she/you fml.*) and loro/Loro (*they/you pl. fml.*) forms, the endings are the same for both -ere and -ire verbs. The voi forms all take different endings, but remember that the vowel before the -te ending is identical to the vowel of the infinitive.

Now let's look at the full conjugation of three verbs that you're familiar with by now: lavorare (*to work*), prendere (*to take*), and partire (*to leave*).

INFINITIVE	LAVORARE	PRENDERE	PARTIRE
io	lavoro	prendo	parto

INFINITIVE	LAVORARE	PRENDERE	PARTIRE
tu	lavori	prendi	parti
lui/lei/Lei	lavora	prende	parte
noi	lavoriamo	prendiamo	partiamo
voi	lavorate	prendete	partite
loro	lavorano	prendono	partono

With this information, you can use any regular Italian verb in the present tense!

Vocabulary Builder 2

8D Vocabulary Builder 2 (CD 2, Track 28)

to make, to do	fare
I do the shopping at the mall.	Io faccio la spesa al centro commerciale.
You exercise outdoors.	Tu fai ginnastica all'aperto.
You have breakfast (sg., fml.) at the café.	Lei fa colazione al bar.
He/She takes a walk.	Lui/Lei fa un giro a piedi.
We pay attention.	Noi facciamo attenzione.
You (pl.) make a good impression.	Voi fate bella figura.
They make friends.	Loro fanno amicizia.
What's the weather like?	Che tempo fa?
Today, it's nice (weather).	Oggi fa bello.
Today, it's bad (weather).	Oggi fa brutto.
It's hot.	Fa caldo.
It's cold.	Fa freddo.

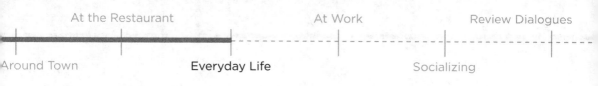
✎ Vocabulary Practice 2

Match the Italian in the left column with the English equivalent in the right.

1. *You have breakfast (sg., fml.) at the café.*

2. *We pay attention.*

3. *It's cold.*

4. *What's the weather like?*

5. *It's hot.*

6. *They make friends.*

7. *You exercise outdoors.*

8. *He/She takes a walk.*

9. *I do the shopping at the mall.*

10. *You (pl.) make a good impression.*

a. **Faccio la spesa al centro commerciale.**

b. **Che tempo fa?**

c. **Fai ginnastica all'aperto.**

d. **Fate bella figura.**

e. **Fanno amicizia.**

f. **Lei fa colazione al bar.**

g. **Fa caldo.**

h. **Facciamo attenzione.**

i. **Fa freddo.**

j. **Fa un giro a piedi.**

ANSWER KEY

1. f; 2. h; 3. i; 4. b; 5. g; 6. e; 7. c; 8. j; 9. a; 10. d.

Grammar Builder 2

▶ 8E Grammar Builder 2 (CD 2, Track 29)

Let's take a short break and focus on the verb **fare** (*to do, to make*). This verb is irregular; it's not conjugated like the regular **-are** verbs. Let's look at how it's conjugated again:

io faccio	noi facciamo
tu fai	voi fate
lui/lei/Lei fa	loro fanno

You may have noticed in the vocabulary building section that this verb has several different meanings. In fact, the verb **fare** translates into English as *to do* and *to* make—consider for instance **fare la spesa** (*to do the shopping,* usually referring to grocery shopping)—but **fare** is also used in a number of other expressions:

fare ginnastica	to exercise
fare colazione	to have breakfast
fare un giro a piedi	to go for a walk
fare attenzione	to pay attention
fare bella figura	to make a good impression
fare amicizia	to make friends

The third person singular of the verb **fare** is also used to make comments about the weather:

Fa bello.	It's nice (weather.)
Fa brutto.	It's bad (weather.)
Fa caldo.	It's hot (weather.)
Fa freddo.	It's cold (weather.)

Finally, if you want to ask what the weather is like, simply say **che tempo fa?**

✎ Work Out 1

Now listen to the audio and fill in each blank with the verb form you hear.

▶ 8F Work Out 1 (CD 2, Track 30)

1. *Today, it's nice.*

   Oggi _____ bello.

2. *We live in town.*

   Noi _____ in città.

3. *We take a walk.*

   _____ un giro a piedi.

4. *Today, it's bad.*

   Oggi _____ brutto.

5. *You (pl.) live in the suburbs.*

   Voi _____ in periferia.

6. *You (pl.) do the shopping at the mall.*

   _____ la spesa al centro commerciale.

7. *Today, it's hot.*

   Oggi _____ caldo.

8. *They live in the countryside.*

   Loro _____ in campagna.

9. *They exercise outdoors.*

   _____ ginnastica all'aperto.

(II)

ANSWER KEY

1. fa; 2. viviamo; 3. Facciamo; 4. fa; 5. vivete; 6. Fate; 7. fa; 8. vivono; 9. Fanno

◖ Bring It All Together

▶ 8G Bring It All Together (CD 2, Track 31)

Now let's bring it all together, and add a little bit more vocabulary and structure.

Mario and I live in Milan.
Io e Mario viviamo a Milano.

We work in a boutique on Montenapoleone Street.
Lavoriamo in una boutique in via Montenapoleone.

We always make a good impression on our customers.
Facciamo sempre bella figura con i nostri clienti.

You and Valeria live in New York City.
Tu e Valeria vivete a New York.

You (pl.) read the Corriere della Sera every day.
Leggete il Corriere della Sera tutti i giorni.

Lucio and Nicolina live and work in Rome.
Lucio e Nicolina vivono e lavorano a Roma.

In the morning they often have breakfast at a café.
Spesso la mattina fanno colazione al bar.

In the afternoon Lucio usually does the shopping and Nicolina exercises.
Di solito il pomeriggio Lucio fa la spesa e Nicolina fa ginnastica.

In the evening they often take a walk downtown.
Spesso la sera fanno un giro a piedi in centro.

Sometimes they make friends with the foreign tourists.
A volte fanno amicizia con i turisti stranieri.

Ⓘ

Take It Further

▶ 8H Take It Further (CD 2, Track 32)

As usual, in the passage you just heard there were some new words like **clienti** (*customers*), **turisti** (*tourists*), and the **voi** form of the regular -ere verb **leggere** (*to read*): **leggete.** You probably noticed there were some frequency adverbs and expressions, too:

sempre	*always*
tutti i giorni	*every day*
spesso	*often*
di solito	*usually*
a volte	*sometimes*

Try to memorize at least some of them and you'll be able to express your thoughts more accurately.

Ⓘ

✎ Work Out 2

Conjugate each verb in the parentheses.

1. **Tutti i giorni io** _____ **una passeggiata in centro. (fare)**

   Everyday I take a walk downtown.

2. Spesso Carla e Marco _____ in macchina. (partire)

Carla and Marco often leave by car.

3. Lui _____ sempre in treno. (viaggiare)

He always travels by train.

4. Loro a volte _____ la sera. (lavorare)

They sometimes work at night.

5. Loro _____ colazione al bar tutte le mattine. (fare)

They have breakfast at the café every morning.

6. Noi spesso _____ la spesa la sera. (fare)

We often go shopping in the evening.

7. Di solito tu _____ il treno. (prendere)

Usually you take the train.

8. Loro _____ vicino alla stazione. (vivere)

They live close to the station.

9. Carla _____ in centro. (lavora)

Carla works downtown.

10. A New York noi spesso _____ al ristorante. (mangiare)

In New York we often eat at the restaurant.

11. La mattina lei _____ l'autobus. (prendere)

In the morning she takes the bus.

12. La sera io _____ il treno. (prendere)

In the evening I take the train.

ANSWER KEY

1. faccio; 2. partono; 3. viaggia; 4. lavorano; 5. fanno; 6. facciamo; 7. prendi; 8. vivono; 9. lavora;
10. mangiamo; 11. prende; 12. prendo

▶ 8I Work Out 2 (CD 2, Track 33)

Now listen to your audio for additional audio-only practice with the material
you've learned in this lesson.

⫿

✎ Drive It Home

Let's practice the verb endings we have seen so far. In Lesson Seven we practiced
the present tense singular forms. Now we'll move to the plural forms. But first,
we'll practice all the forms of the verbs **avere**, **essere**, **fare**, because these forms
appear a lot in combinations with other verb tenses. Fill in the blanks with the
appropriate present tense for the following infinitives.

1. avere

io _____

tu _____

lui/lei _____

noi _____

voi _____

loro _____

2. essere

io _____

tu _____

lui/lei _____

noi _____

voi _____

loro _____

3. fare

io _____

tu _____

lui/lei _____

noi _____

voi _____

loro _____

ANSWER KEY
1. ho, hai, ha, abbiamo, avete, hanno; 2. sono, sei, è, siamo, siete, sono; 3. faccio, fai, fa, facciamo, fate, fanno

Now let's just look at the plural forms. Fill in the blank with the appropriate form of the verb.

1. pagare

noi _____

voi _____

loro _____

2. **chiamare**

noi _____

voi _____

loro _____

3. **prendere**

noi _____

voi _____

loro _____

4. **lavorare**

noi _____

voi _____

loro _____

5. **vivere**

noi _____

voi _____

loro _____

6. **partire**

noi _____

voi _____

loro _____

ANSWER KEY

1. paghiamo, pagate, pagano; 2. chiamiamo, chiamate, chiamano; 3. prendiamo, prendete, prendono; 4. lavoriamo, lavorate, lavorano; 5. viviamo, vivete, vivono; 6. partiamo, partite, partono

Parting Words

Benissimo! *Wonderful!* You've finished your eighth lesson, which means that you should be familiar with the following:

☐ essential vocabulary you'll need to talk about everyday life. (Still unsure? Go back to page 122.)

☐ the plural forms of verbs. (Still unsure? Go back to page 124.)

☐ the very important irregular verb **fare** (*to do*, *to make*). (Still unsure? Go back to page 126.)

☐ weather expressions. (Still unsure? Go back to page 127.)

☐ a conversation about daily routines and everyday life. (Still unsure? Go back to page 130.)

Don't forget to practice and reinforce what you've learned by visiting **www.livinglanguage.com/ languagelab** for flashcards, games, and quizzes for Lesson Eight!

Word Recall

Translate the following sentences into Italian.

1. *We live in the countryside.* _____

   _____

2. *We travel by train.* _____

   _____

3. *Their apartment is large.* _____

   _____

4. *My house is small.* _____

   _____

5. *In the living room there is a brown couch.* (Note: **in** + **il** = **nel**) _____

   _____

6. *Is there a post office nearby?* _____

   _____

7. *The library is next to the school.* _____

   _____

8. *I'll order the main course with the side dish.* _____

   _____

9. *He'll have the appetizer and the first course.* _____

_____

10. *The first course is delicious.* _____

_____

11. *I would like the check.* _____

_____

12. *What's the weather like?* _____

_____

13. *It's hot.* _____

_____

14. *It's cold.* _____

_____

15. *She always shops downtown.* _____

_____

16. *He sometimes has breakfast at the café.* _____

_____

17. *We often take a walk.* _____

_____

18. *I exercise in the garden.* _____

_____

19. *We live and work in town.* _____

_____

20. *We often make friends with tourists.* _____

_____

ANSWER KEY

1. Viviamo in campagna. 2. Viaggiamo in treno. 3. Il loro appartamento è grande. 4. La mia casa è piccola. 5. Nel soggiorno c'è un divano marrone. 6. C'è un ufficio postale qui vicino? 7. La biblioteca è vicino alla scuola. 8. Ordino il secondo con il contorno. 9. Lui prende l'antipasto e il primo. 10. Il primo è squisito. 11. Vorrei il conto. 12. Che tempo fa? 13. Fa caldo. 14. Fa freddo. 15. Lei fa sempre la spesa in centro. 16. Lui a volte fa colazione al bar. 17. Spesso facciamo un giro a piedi. 18. Faccio ginnastica in giardino. 19. Viviamo e lavoriamo in città. 20. Spesso facciamo amicizia con i turisti.

Lesson 9: At Work

Nona Lezione: Al lavoro

Bentornati! *Welcome back!* In this second-to-last lesson of *Essential Italian*, you'll focus on:

☐ the days of the week

☐ telling time

☐ the names of common professions

☐ your job or profession

☐ a conversation about work and the work week, including the useful verb **andare** (*to go*)

As always, let's begin with some vocabulary.

Vocabulary Builder 1

▶ 9B Vocabulary Builder 1 (CD 2, Track 35)

to work from Monday to Friday	**lavorare dal lunedì al venerdì**
I work on Mondays and Thursdays.	**Io lavoro il lunedì e il giovedì.**
You work on Tuesdays, Wednesdays, and Fridays.	**Tu lavori il martedì, il mercoledì e il venerdì.**
He/She doesn't work on Saturdays and Sundays.	**Lui/Lei non lavora il sabato e la domenica.**
What's the time?	**Che ora è? Che ore sono?**
It's noon.	**È mezzogiorno.**
It's midnight.	**È mezzanotte.**
It's 1:00 am.	**È l'una di notte.**
It's 11:15 am.	**Sono le undici e un quarto di mattina.**

Ⅱ

✎ Vocabulary Practice 1

Translate the following sentences into Italian.

1. *They work Monday to Friday.* _____

   _____

2. *You (pl.) work Tuesday to Saturday.* _____

   _____

3. *I don't work on Sundays.* _____

   _____

4. *What time is it?* _____

_____

5. *It's noon.* _____

_____

6. *It's eleven am.* _____

_____

ANSWER KEY

1. Loro lavorano dal lunedì al venerdì. 2. Voi lavorate dal martedì al sabato. 3. Io non lavoro la domenica. 4. Che ora è?/Che ore sono? 5. È mezzogiorno. 6. Sono le undici di mattina.

Grammar Builder 1

▶ 9C Grammar Builder 1 (CD 2, Track 36)

In the example sentences, you heard the days of the week in Italian, which, by the way, are not capitalized.

lunedì, martedì, mercoledì	*Monday, Tuesday, Wednesday*
giovedì, venerdì	*Thursday, Friday*
sabato, domenica	*Saturday, Sunday*

The Italian week begins with lunedì (*Monday*) and ends with domenica (*Sunday*). To say *on Mondays* or *on Tuesdays*, you need to say the day of the week in the singular accompanied by the definite article:

il lunedì
on Mondays

il martedì
on Tuesdays

Finally, you heard how to ask and tell the time. Let's quickly review that. To ask the time, say **Che ora è?** or **Che ore sono?**, using either the singular or the plural form. In this answer you'll use the singular form only in the expressions:

È mezzogiorno.	*It's noon.*
È mezzanotte.	*It's midnight.*
È l'una.	*It's one o'clock.*

In every other case you'll say **sono le ...** (*lit., they are the ...*) followed by the number indicating the hour of the day:

Sono le due.	*It's two (o'clock).*
Sono le tre.	*It's three (o'clock).*
Sono le quattro.	*It's four (o'clock).*

Also keep in mind that instead of *pm* and *am*, in Italian you'll say:

di mattina	*in the morning, from 4 to 11 am*
di pomeriggio	*in the afternoon, from 1 to 5 pm*
di sera	*in the evening, from 6 to 11 pm*
di notte	*in the night, from midnight to 3 am*

Finally, **un quarto** means *a quarter*, and **mezza** (when used with **ora**) or **mezzo** (when used with a specific time) mean *a half (hour)*.

| Il viaggio è durato due ore e mezza. | *The trip lasted two and a half hours.* |
| Ci vediamo alle sette e mezzo. | *Let's meet at 7:30.* |

It's important to know that in Italy, like in many other European countries, in official time schedules the day is divided into 24 hours. Therefore, if you hear someone say: **Prendiamo l'aereo alle 21:00 (ventuno)**, that means they are taking the 9:00 pm flight.

In Lesson Three, you studied the numbers from one to twelve, here is a list of the numbers from thirteen to twenty:

tredici	thirteen
quattordici	fourteen
quindici	fifteen
sedici	sixteen
diciassette	seventeen
diciotto	eighteen
diciannove	nineteen
venti	twenty

From twenty on you'll just combine **venti** with **uno, due,** etc. to form **ventuno, ventidue, ventitré, ventiquattro,** and so on.

⏸

Vocabulary Builder 2
▶ 9D Vocabulary Builder 2 (CD 2, Track 37)

the teacher (male or female)	l'insegnante
the artist (male or female)	l'artista
the vendor (male)	il commerciante
the vendor (female)	la commerciante
the clerk (male)	l'impiegato
the clerk (female)	l'impiegata
the worker (male)	l'operaio
the worker (female)	l'operaia
the businessman	l'imprenditore
the businesswoman	l'imprenditrice

I am a professor. (male)	**Sono un professore.**
I am a professor. (female)	**Sono una professoressa.**
You are a doctor. (male)	**Sei un dottore.**
You are a doctor. (female)	**Sei una dottoressa.**
He is a medical doctor.	**Lui fa il medico.**
She is a medical doctor.	**Lei fa il medico.**
I am a lawyer.	**Faccio l'avvocato.**
You are an engineer. (male or female)	**Fai l'ingegnere.**
He is an architect.	**Lui fa l'architetto.**
She is an architect.	**Lei fa l'architetto.**

✎ Vocabulary Practice 2

1. *He is a businessman.*

2. *I am a professor. (female)*

3. *She is a businesswoman.*

4. *He is a vendor.*

5. *He is a professor.*

6. *She is a worker.*

7. *She is an engineer.*

8. *He is a clerk.*

9. *She is a vendor.*

10. *She is a clerk.*

11. *You are a doctor. (male)*

12. *You are a doctor. (female)*

a. **Tu sei un dottore.**

b. **Lei fa l'impiegata.**

c. **Lui è un imprenditore.**

d. **Lui è un professore.**

e. **Lui fa l'impiegato.**

f. **Lei fa l'imprenditrice.**

g. **Tu sei una dottoressa.**

h. **Lei fa l'operaia.**

i. **Lei è una commerciante.**

j. **Lei fa l'ingegnere.**

k. **Lui è un commerciante.**

l. **Io sono una professoressa.**

ANSWER KEY
1. c; 2. l; 3. f; 4. k; 5. d; 6. h; 7. j; 8. e; 9. i; 10. b; 11. a; 12. g

Grammar Builder 2

▶ 9E Grammar Builder 2 (CD 3, Track 1)

Okay, let's pause for a moment and make some comments. You just heard several new words related to jobs and professions. Did you pay attention to the gender? Some of them, like insegnante (*teacher*), artista (*artist*), or commerciante (*vendor*), can be used for both masculine and feminine, but don't ever forget to use the correct article.

In most cases, you'll have one form for the masculine and one for the feminine:

impiegato/impiegata	*male/female clerk*
operaio/operaia	*male/female worker*
imprenditore/imprenditrice	*businessman/businesswoman*
professore/professoressa	*male/female professor*
dottore/dottoressa	*male/female doctor*

However, for some professions (like medico, avvocato, ingegnere, and architetto), which used to be traditionally considered 'masculine professions', you'll use the masculine form even if you are talking about a woman:

Maria fa l'architetto.
Maria is an architect.

By the way, did you notice that the English '*I am* + profession' can be translated into Italian with the verb essere followed by the indefinite article (sono un medico), or with the verb fare followed by the definite article (faccio il medico)? The meaning is exactly the same, so you can choose, and use, the form you like better.

(II)

✎ Work Out 1

Let's practice listening comprehension. Turn on your audio, and fill in each blank with the word that you hear.

▶ 9F Work Out 1 (CD 3, Track 2)

1. *My name is Mike.*

   _____ Mike.

2. *I am an architect.*

   _____ architetto.

3. *I work from Monday to Friday.*

   _____ dal lunedì al _____ .

4. *Sometimes I work on Saturdays.*

   A volte lavoro _____ .

5. *I don't usually work on Sundays.*

   Di solito non lavoro la _____ .

6. *My wife is a (medical) doctor.*

   _____ moglie _____ il medico.

7. *She works at 7:30 am.*

   Lavora alle _____ e _____ di _____ .

8. *Our children don't go to work.*

   I _____ figli non vanno a _____ .

9. *They don't work because they are students.*

   Non _____ perché sono _____ .

Bring It All Together
▶ 9G Bring It All Together (CD 3, Track3)

Now let's bring it all together, and add a little bit more vocabulary and structure.

Good morning Laura, where are you going?
Buon giorno Laura, dove vai?

I'm going to work.
Vado al lavoro.

At 10:30 am!? You are really lucky.
Alle dieci e mezzo di mattina!? Sei proprio fortunata.

Actually, I usually work from 8:15 am to 5:00 pm. But on Tuesdays I have shorter working hours, from 10:45 am to 3:00 pm. And you? What time are you going to work today?
Veramente di solito lavoro dalle otto e un quarto di mattina alle cinque di pomeriggio. Però il martedì faccio orario ridotto: dalle undici meno un quarto alle tre. E tu? A che ora vai al lavoro oggi?

Well, this week I am not working. I am on vacation.
Beh, questa settimana non lavoro. Sono in ferie.

And what are you doing still here? Aren't you going out of town?
E che ci fai ancora qui? Non vai fuori città?

Unfortunately my wife is working until Thursday. She is a lawyer and is always very busy.
Purtroppo mia moglie lavora fino a giovedì. Lei fa l'avvocato ed è sempre molto impegnata.

Then you are leaving on Friday …
Allora partite venerdì …

Actually we are leaving on Thursday evening. We'll take the plane at 9:00 pm and go to Paris for the weekend.
Veramente partiamo giovedì sera. Prendiamo l'aereo alle 21:00 e andiamo a Parigi per il fine settimana.

Lucky you (good for you): Paris is such a romantic city!
Beati voi: Parigi è una città così romantica!

Take It Further
▶ 9H Take It Further (CD 3, Track 4)

You just heard a new verb: the irregular verb andare (*to go*). This verb has an irregular conjugation:

io vado	noi andiamo
tu vai	voi andate
lui/lei va	loro vanno

Basically, the endings are regular, but the stem is not. In fact, you have vad- for the first person singular (io vado), and- for the first and second person plural (noi andiamo, voi andate), and va- for the other forms (tu vai, lui/lei va, loro vanno).

You also heard some new expressions:

l'orario ridotto	the shorter working hours
in ferie	on vacation
fuori città	out of town

You also heard the expression dalle ... alle ... (*from ... to ...*):

Di solito lavoro dalle otto e un quarto di mattina alle cinque di pomeriggio.
I usually work from 8:15 am to 5:00 pm.

This is a useful expression when talking about time periods.

Did you pay attention to the many examples of negative forms in the dialogue you just listened to, as well as in the rest of the lesson? It's very easy to make an Italian sentence negative: just put non (*not*) before the verb:

Questa settimana non lavoro.
I am not working this week.

The same happens if you want to make a negative question:

Non vai fuori città?
Aren't you going out of town?

✎ Work Out 2

Fill in the blanks with the appropriate time, following the model below:

Sono l'una e un quarto della mattina *[1:15 am]*

1. _____ *[2:30 pm]*

2. _____ *[4:15 pm]*

3. _____ *[6:30 am]*

4. _____ *[12 pm]*

5. _____ *[12:20 pm]*

6. _____ *[8:10 am]*

7. _____ *[9:30 pm]*

8. _____ *[12:10 am]*

9. _____ *[5:30 pm]*

10. _____ *[9:45 am]*

11. _____ *[11:45 am]*

12. _____ *[1 am]*

ANSWER KEY

1. Sono le due e mezzo del pomeriggio. 2. Sono le quattro e un quarto del pomeriggio. 3. Sono le sei e mezzo della mattina. 4. È mezzogiorno. 5. È mezzogiorno e venti. 6. Sono le otto e dieci della mattina. 7. Sono le nove e mezzo di sera. 8. È mezzanotte e dieci. 9. Sono le cinque e mezzo del pomeriggio. 10. Sono le dieci meno un quarto della mattina. 11. È mezzogiorno meno un quarto. 12. È l'una di notte.

Now fill in the blanks with the appropriate form (masculine/feminine, singular/plural) of the profession corresponding to the English in parentheses.

1. Mario fa _____ . (architect)

2. Carla è una _____ . (professor)

3. Lei fa _____ . (engineer)

4. La mamma di Carla fa _____ . (lawyer)

5. Giulia e Maria sono _____ . (clerks)

6. La zia di Giulia fa _____ . (teacher)

7. La zio è un _____ . (artist)

8. Il cugino fa _____ . (businessman)

9. Il nipote fa _____ . (worker)

10. Lucia e Carla sono _____ . (professors, female)

11. Loro sono _____ . (vendors)

12. Noi siamo _____ . (teachers)

ANSWER KEY
1. l'architetto; 2. professoressa; 3. l'ingegnere; 4. l'avvocato; 5. impiegate; 6. l'insegnante; 7. artista;
8. l'imprenditore; 9. l'operaio; 10. professoresse; 11. commercianti; 12. insegnanti.

▶ 9I Work Out 2 (CD 3, Track 5)

Now listen to your audio for some additional practice with the material covered
in this lesson.

⑾

✎ Drive It Home

Let's practice andare. Fill in the blanks with the forms of andare that correspond to each subject given in parentheses.

1. _____ a scuola. (io)

2. _____ al lavoro (lui/lei)

3. _____ alla stazione (noi)

4. _____ al bar (loro)

5. _____ alla farmacia (tu)

6. _____ al ristorante (voi)

ANSWER KEY
1. vado; 2. va; 3. andiamo; 4. vanno; 5. vai; 6. andate.

Parting Words

Perfetto! *Great!* You just finished Lesson Nine, so by now you should be familiar with:

☐ talking about the days of the week (Still unsure? Go back to page 141.)

☐ telling time (Still unsure? Go back to page 142.)

☐ the names of common professions (Still unsure? Go back to page 144.)

☐ talking about your job or profession (Still unsure? Go back to page 146.)

☐ a conversation about work and the work week, including the useful verb andare (*to go*) (Still unsure? Go back to page 148.)

Don't forget to practice and reinforce what you've learned by visiting **www.livinglanguage.com/languagelab** for flashcards, games, and quizzes for Lesson Nine!

Take It Further

▶ 9J Take It Further (CD 3, Track 6)

In Italy, it's very common to address someone by his or her professional or academic title (often followed by someone's last name): **Buona sera, architetto!**, **Buon giorno, avvocato Boccagna!, ArrivederLa, dottoressa Valoroso!** The most frequently used titles are **dottore** and **dottoressa**: in fact, they can be used for anyone who has earned a university degree.

Word Recall

Let's practice some of the vocabulary from previous lessons. Translate the following paragraph into English.

Buongiorno, sono Carla Mattei. Sono di Milano e faccio l'avvocato. Vivo in centro in un appartamento molto grande vicino alla mia famiglia. Lavoro dal lunedì al venerdì, dalle nove della mattina alle sei di sera. Di solito vado al lavoro in macchina. A volte la sera sono impegnata (*busy*) con il lavoro. Spesso vado al ristorante vicino all'ufficio e ordino un secondo con contorno di verdure, e a volte il dolce. Dopo pranzo faccio un giro a piedi in centro e prendo un caffè al bar. Lunedì, mercoledì e giovedì faccio ginnastica dalle sette alle otto di sera. Spesso per il fine settimana vado fuori città.

_____

_____

_____

_____

_____

_____

_____

_____

_____

_____

_____

_____

_____

_____

_____

_____

_____

_____

_____

_____

Hello I am Carla Mattei. I am from Milano and I am a lawyer. I live downtown in a very large apartment close to my family. I work Monday to Friday from 9 am to 6 pm. I usually drive to work. Sometimes in the evening I am busy with work. I often go to the restaurant close to the office and I order a main course with a side of vegetables, and sometimes dessert. After lunch I take a walk downtown and I have coffee at a café. Monday, Wednesday and Thursday I exercise from 7 pm to 8 pm. Often on weekends I go out of the city.

Lesson 10: Socializing

Decima Lezione: La vita sociale

Benvenuti alla decima e ultima lezione! *Welcome to the tenth and final lesson!* In this lesson you'll learn about:

☐ expressing likes and dislikes

☐ pronouns such as *to me, to you, to her,* and so on

☐ talking about common hobbies and pastimes

☐ using a common type of **-ire** verb

☐ having a conversation about hobbies, interests, and preferences

As always, let's begin with some new vocabulary.

Vocabulary Builder 1

10B Vocabulary Builder 1 (CD 3, Track 8)

I like the movies.	**Mi piace il cinema.**
I don't like love stories.	**Non mi piacciono le storie d'amore.**
You (sg., infml.) like theater.	**Ti piace il teatro.**
You (sg., fml.) don't like classical music concerts.	**Non Le piacciono i concerti di musica classica.**
He likes pop music.	**Gli piace la musica pop.**
She likes British bands.	**Le piacciono i gruppi inglesi.**
We like traveling.	**Ci piace viaggiare.**
We don't like expensive hotels.	**Non ci piacciono gli alberghi costosi.**
You (pl.) like dancing.	**Vi piace ballare.**
You (pl.) like Latin American dancing.	**Vi piacciono i balli latinoamericani.**
They like reading.	**Gli piace leggere.**
They like contemporary novels.	**Gli piacciono i romanzi contemporanei.**

Take It Further

Did you notice that in Italian, the definite article (il, la, i, gli, le, and so on) is used to express a generic or general noun, while it's omitted in English? So, in English, you like *expensive hotels* in general, but in Italian, **ti piacciono gli alberghi costosi**. Take another look at these examples, and compare the English (with an article) to the Italian (without one.) Note that gli can mean *(to) him* or *(to) them*.

Non mi piacciono le storie d'amore.
I don't like love stories.

Non Le piacciono i concerti di musica classica.
You (sg., fml.) don't like classical music concerts.

Gli piace la musica pop.
He likes pop music. / They like pop music.

Le piacciono i gruppi inglesi.
She likes British bands.

Non ci piacciono gli alberghi costosi.
We don't like expensive hotels.

Vi piacciono i balli latinoamericani.
You (pl.) like Latin American dancing.

Keep in mind that if you like *doing* something, you'll just use the infinitive, without any article. And the most natural translation in these cases is with an *-ing* form of the verb in English.

Ci piace viaggiare.
We like traveling.

Vi piace ballare.
You (pl.) like dancing.

Gli piace leggere.
He likes reading. / They like reading.

✎ Vocabulary Practice 1

Let's practice the vocabulary we have learned above. Translate the following phrases into Italian, using the definite article with the generic/general nouns that you might like (or not!)

1. *we like* _____

2. *you (sg., infml.) like* _____

3. *they like* _____

4. *(the) expensive hotels* _____

5. *(the) classical music* _____

6. *(the) contemporary novels* _____

7. *(the) theater* _____

8. *reading/to read* _____

9. *traveling/to travel* _____

10. *dancing/to dance* _____

ANSWER KEY
1. ci piace; 2. ti piace; 3. gli piace; 4. gli alberghi costosi; 5. la musica classica; 6. i romanzi contemporanei; 7. il teatro; 8. leggere; 9. viaggiare; 10. ballare

Grammar Builder 1

▶ 10C Grammar Builder 1 (CD 3, Track 9)

Before we learn how to use **piacere**, let's quickly review the forms of the indirect object pronouns:

mi (*to me*)	**ci** (*to us*)
ti (*to you, informal*)	**vi** (*to you, plural*)
Le (*to you, formal*) **gli** (*to him*) **le** (*to her*)	**gli** (*to them*)

Note that **gli** can translate as both *to him* and *to them*. Indirect object pronouns are always placed before the verb.

The structure of the verb **piacere** (*to like*) is similar to the English *to be pleasing to*. Whoever or whatever is being liked is the subject of the sentence, and the person who is doing the liking is the indirect object. When the indirect object is expressed by a noun, it is always preceded by the preposition **a**:

A Maria piace il libro.
(*"The book is pleasing to Maria."*)/Maria likes the book.*

If you are using indirect object pronouns, like in the example you just heard, the preposition is not needed:

Le piace il libro.
(*"The book is pleasing to her."*)/She likes the book.*

Piacere always agrees with the subject—the object of affection—so you have:

Ci piace la musica. (Piace is singular because **la musica** is singular.)
We like music.

But:

Ci piacciono i concerti. (Piacciono is plural because **i concerti** is plural.)
We like concerts.

When **piacere** is followed by an infinitive, it is always in the third person singular:

Ti piace leggere.
You like reading.

To express dislikes, just add **non** (*not*) before the indirect pronoun:

Non ci piacciono gli alberghi costosi.
We don't like expensive hotels.

When using a noun or proper name, place **non** right before the verb:

A Maria non piace il cinema.
Maria doesn't like movies.

Finally, the subject in this construction is always preceded by the definite article:

Le piace il teatro.
She likes [the] theater.

Ci piacciono i romanzi contemporanei.
We like [the] contemporary novels.

However, when the subject is a verb in the infinitive, the article isn't necessary:

Vi piace ballare.
You (pl.) like dancing.

Vocabulary Builder 2

10D Vocabulary Builder 2 (CD 3, Track 10)

to prefer	preferire
I prefer to run.	(Io) preferisco correre.
to swim	nuotare
to play tennis	giocare a tennis
to ride a bike	andare in bicicletta
to watch sports on TV	guardare lo sport in televisione
basketball	la pallacanestro, il basket
soccer	il calcio
to understand	capire
I don't understand American football.	(Io) non capisco il football americano.
to finish, to end	finire
The game ends at midnight.	La partita finisce a mezzanotte.

Vocabulary Practice 2

Let's practice the vocabulary you learned above. Translate the following words and phrases into Italian.

1. *to understand* _____

2. *to play tennis* _____

3. *to finish* _____

4. *to prefer* _____

5. *soccer* _____

6. *to ride a bicycle* _____

7. *to watch sports on TV* _____

8. *basketball* _____

ANSWER KEY
1. capire; 2. giocare a tennis; 3. finire; 4. preferire; 5. il calcio; 6. andare in bicicletta; 7. guardare lo
sport alla televisione; 8. la pallacanestro/il basket

Grammar Builder 2
▶ 10E Grammar Builder 2 (CD 3, Track 11)

Okay, let's pause for a moment. You just heard the conjugation of **preferire** (*to prefer*).
Preferire is not exactly irregular, but its conjugation is somewhat different from the
-ire verbs you studied in Lessons 7 and 8, like **partire**. The endings are the same as
for **partire**, but the stem is modified in all forms except in the first and second person
plural, by adding -isc- before the regular endings. Let's review all the forms.

io preferisco	noi preferiamo
tu preferisci	voi preferite
lui/lei preferisce	loro preferiscono

Preferire is usually followed either by a noun:

Preferisco il calcio.
I prefer soccer.

Or by a verb in the infinitive:

Preferisci correre.
You prefer to run.

Three more verbs that are conjugated like **preferire** are **capire** (*to understand*), **finire** (*to end, to finish*), and **pulire** (*to clean*).

Take It Further

Let's do a side-by-side comparison of an -ire verb that does not take the -isc- infix, **partire** (*to leave*), and one that does, **capire** (*to understand*). Remember that the endings are identical, and that -isc- appears in all forms except the **noi** and **voi** forms. Also remember that **sc-** is pronounced like the *sh* in *shoe* before **i** and **e**, but otherwise like the *sk* in *skip*.

	PARTIRE (**NO -ISC-**)	CAPIRE (-ISC-)
io	parto	capisco
tu	parti	capisci
lui/lei/Lei	parte	capisce
noi	partiamo	capiamo
voi	partite	capite
loro	partono	capiscono

✎ Work Out 1

Let's do some listening comprehension practice. Fill in each blank with the word you hear on your audio.

▶ 10F Work Out 1 (CD 3, Track 12)

1. *I like sports.*

   Mi _____ **sport.**

2. *I prefer soccer.*

   _____ il calcio.

3. *But I like tennis and basketball, too.*

   Ma _____ anche il tennis e la pallacanestro.

4. *I don't understand American football.*

   _____ il football americano.

5. *You, on the other hand, prefer to watch sports on TV.*

   Tu, invece, _____ guardare lo sport _____ televisione.

6. *But you don't like soccer games.*

   Ma _____ piacciono le _____ di calcio.

7. *You like theater.*

   Ti _____ il _____.

8. *And you like concerts of classical music.*

   E ti _____ i concerti di _____.

9. *I, on the other hand, prefer pop music.*

   Io, _____, _____ la musica pop.

10. *I like British bands.*

    Mi piacciono i _____.

Ⅱ

ANSWER KEY
1. piace, lo; 2. Preferisco; 3. mi, piacciono; 4. Non, capisco; 5. preferisci, alla; 6. non, ti, partite;
7. piace, teatro; 8. piacciono, musica, classica; 9. invece, preferisco; 10. gruppi, inglesi

At the Restaurant

At Work

Review Dialogues

Around Town

Everyday Life

Socializing

🎧 Bring It All Together

Now let's bring it all together, and add a little bit more vocabulary and structure.

My family and I have many interests.
Io e i miei familiari abbiamo molti interessi.

My son Michael loves winter sports.
Mio figlio Michael ama gli sport invernali.

He likes skiing a lot.
Gli piace molto sciare.

He prefers cross-country skiing, but he likes Alpine skiing, too.
Preferisce lo sci di fondo, ma gli piace anche lo sci alpino.

Snow is his passion.
La neve è la sua passione.

My daughter Jane doesn't like snow, she prefers the sea.
A mia figlia Jane non piace la neve, preferisce il mare.

She likes swimming and sailing.
Le piace nuotare e andare in barca a vela.

My husband and I, on the other hand, are not athletic people.
Io e mio marito, invece, non siamo persone sportive.

We prefer to watch sports on TV.
Preferiamo guardare lo sport alla televisione.

We like movies a lot.
Ci piace molto il cinema.

I prefer comedies and my husband prefers action movies.
Io preferisco le commedie e mio marito preferisce i film d'azione.

But we share (lit., have in common) a passion for Roberto Benigni's movies.
Però abbiamo in comune la passione per i film di Roberto Benigni.

(II)

Take It Further

(▶) 10H Take It Further (CD 3, Track 14)

You just heard some new words and expressions:

interessi	*interests*
la passione per	*a passion for*
avere in comune	*to share*
sci di fondo	*cross-country skiing*
sci alpino	*Alpine skiing*
andare in barca a vela	*to sail*

Amare (*to love*) is used similarly to **preferire**: it can be followed either by a noun:

Mio figlio ama gli sport invernali.
My son loves winter sports.

Or by a verb in the infinitive:

Mia figlia ama nuotare.
My daughter loves swimming.

Finally, remember you can formulate your likes (and dislikes) in a more nuanced way by adding adverbs like **molto** (*a lot*), **un poco** (*a little*), **abbastanza** (*fairly*), or **così così** (*so-so*) right after **piacere**:

Mi piace molto …
I like … a lot.

Mi piace un poco …
I like … a little.

Mi piace abbastanza …
I like … pretty well.

Mi piace così così …
I like … well enough/so-so.

�(II)

✎ Work Out 2

Let's practice the use of **piacere** with different indirect objects. Select the appropriate form following the model:

Mi piace ballare. (tu) <u>Ti</u> piace ballare.

1. **Mi piace correre. (lei) _____ piace correre.**

2. **Mi piace il cinema. (loro) _____ piace il cinema.**

3. **Ti piace il museo. (noi) _____ piace il museo.**

4. **Ti piace la musica. (lui) _____ piace la musica.**

5. Mi piace il dolce. (voi) _____ piace il dolce.

ANSWER KEY
1. le; 2. gli; 3. ci; 4. gli; 5. vi

Now let's continue practicing with piacere. This time fill in the appropriate form of the verb piacere.

1. A Marta _____ nuotare.

2. A Carla _____ gli sport invernali.

3. A Giulia _____ lo sci di fondo.

4. Mi _____ i concerti.

5. Le _____ andare in bicicletta.

6. A Mario _____ leggere.

7. Gli _____ i romanzi contemporanei.

8. Ti _____ guardare gli sport alla televisione.

ANSWER KEY
1. piace; 2. piacciono; 3. piace; 4. piacciono; 5. piace; 6. piace; 7. piacciono; 8. piace

▶ 10I Work Out 2 (CD 3, Track 15)

Now listen to your audio for some additional audio-only practice.

⏸

✎ Drive It Home

Let's practice -ire verbs with -isc. Fill in the blanks with the forms of **preferire** that correspond to each subject given in parentheses.

1. _____ la bistecca. (io)

2. _____ la musica classica. (lui/lei)

3. _____ lo sci di fondo. (noi)

4. _____ ballare. (loro)

5. _____ nuotare. (tu)

6. _____ sciare. (voi)

ANSWER KEY
1. **Preferisco**; 2. **Preferisce**; 3. **Preferiamo**; 4. **Preferiscono**; 5. **Preferisci**; 6. **Preferite**

Parting Words

Molto bene! *Wonderful!* You finished the last lesson. In this lesson, you studied

☐ expressing likes and dislikes (Still unsure? Go back to page 158.)

☐ pronouns such as *to me, to you, to her*, and so on (Still unsure? Go back to page 161.)

☐ talking about common hobbies and pastimes (Still unsure? Go back to page 163.)

☐ using a common type of **-ire** verb (Still unsure? Go back to page 164.)

☐ having a conversation about hobbies, interests, and preferences (Still unsure? Go back to page 167.)

Don't forget to practice and reinforce what you've learned by visiting **www.livinglanguage.com/languagelab** for flashcards, games, and quizzes for Lesson Ten!

Word Recall

Let's practice the vocabulary we have learned so far. Translate the following sentences into Italian.

1. *I prefer classical music.* _____

_____

2. *Carla likes to ride a bicycle.* _____

_____

3. *He likes to read.* _____

_____

4. *My daughter loves to sail.* _____

_____

5. *I don't understand soccer.* _____

_____

6. *They like to travel.* _____

_____

7. *She likes Italian restaurants.* _____

_____

8. *My family likes winter sports.* _____

_____

9. *My grandmother likes the theater.* _____

_____

10. *My brother likes watching sports on tv.* _____

_____

11. *My sister prefers reading.* _____

_____

12. *What time is it?* _____

_____

13. *It's noon.* _____

_____

14. *Where is the hospital?* _____

_____

15. *May I have the wine list?* _____

_____

16. *My house is small.* _____

_____

17. *The station is near.* _____

_____

18. *They are always hungry.* _____

_____

19. *We take a walk downtown.* _____

_____

20. *In my hometown there are three theaters.* _____

_____

21. *The bank is on the right.* _____

_____

22. *The pharmacy is on the left.* _____

_____

ANSWER KEY

1. Preferisco la musica classica. 2. A Carla piace andare in bicicletta. 3. Gli piace leggere. 4. Mia figlia ama andare in barca a vela. 5. Non capisco il calcio. 6. Gli piace viaggiare. 7. Le piacciono i ristoranti italiani. 8. Alla mia famiglia piacciono gli sport invernali. 9. A mia nonna piace il teatro. 10. A mio fratello piace guardare lo sport alla televisione. 11. Mia sorella preferisce leggere. 12. Che ora è/che ore sono. 13. È mezzogiorno. 14. Dov'è l'ospedale? 15. Posso avere la carta dei vini? 16. La mia casa è piccola. 17. La stazione è vicina. 18. (Loro) hanno sempre fame. 19. (Noi) facciamo un giro in centro. 20. Nella mia città natale ci sono tre teatri. 21. La banca è a destra. 22. La farmacia è a sinistra.

Quiz 2

Now it's time for another review! Here is a final quiz testing what you learned in Lessons 6-10. Once you've worked through it, score yourself to see how well you've done. If you find that you need to go back and review, do so before continuing on to the final section with review dialogues and comprehension questions.

A. Match the following English words to the correct Italian translations:

1. a destra   a. *the check*

2. fa caldo   b. *noon*

3. la carta dei vini   c. *on the right*

4. mezzogiorno   d. *the wine list*

5. il conto   e. *it's hot*

B. Translate the following expressions into Italian

1. *I'll have the first course, the side dish and the dessert.* _____

2. *Marco works from Monday to Friday.* _____

_____

3. *The museum is next to the station.* _____

_____

4. *There is a restaurant near the museum.* _____

_____

5. *In the morning I often have breakfast at the café.* _____

_____

C. Fill in the table with the correct forms of **avere** (*to have*):

I have	1.
you have (sg.)	2.
she/he has	3.
we have	4.
you have (pl.)	5.
they have	6.

D. Fill in the blank with the appropriate form of the verb provided

1. **Mio fratello** _____ **un libro. (leggere)**

2. **Tu** _____ **a Roma. (vivere)**

3. **Carla e Marta** _____ **in centro. (lavorare)**

4. **Lei** _____ **il dolce. (ordinare)**

5. **Noi** _____ **in treno. (viaggiare)**

How Did You Do?

Give yourself a point for every correct answer, then use the following key to determine whether or not you're ready to move on:

0-7 points: Go back and study the lessons again to make sure you understood everything completely. Take your time; it's not a race! Make sure you spend time reviewing the vocabulary and reading through each Grammar Builder section carefully.

8-16 points: If the questions you missed were in sections A or B, you may want to review the vocabulary from previous lessons again; if you missed answers mostly in sections C or D, check the Grammar Builder sections to make sure you have your grammar basics down.

17-20 points: You're doing a wonderful job! You're ready to move on to the Review Dialogues!

☐☐ points

ANSWER KEY

A 1. c; 2. e; 3. d; 4. b; 5. a

B. 1. Io prendo il primo, il contorno e il dolce. 2. Marco lavora dal lunedì al venerdì. 3. Il museo è vicino alla stazione. 3. C' è un ristorante vicino al museo. 5. Spesso la mattina faccio colazione al bar.

C. 1. io ho; 2. tu hai; 3. lui/lei ha; 4. noi abbiamo; 5. voi avete; 6. loro hanno

D. 1. legge; 2. vivi; 3. lavorano; 4. ordina; 5. viaggiamo

Review Dialogues
Welcome!

Here's your chance to practice everything you've mastered in the ten lessons of *Living Language Essential Italian* with these five everyday dialogues. Each dialogue is followed by comprehension questions.

Have fun!

To practice your pronunciation, don't forget to listen to the audio! As always, look for ▶ and ⏸. You'll hear the dialogue in Italian first, then in Italian and English. Next, for practice, you'll do some role play by taking part in the conversation yourself!

🗨 Dialogue 1
INTRODUCTIONS

First, try to read (and listen to!) the whole dialogue in Italian. Then read and listen to the Italian and English together. How much did you understand? Next, take part in the role play exercise on the audio and answer the comprehension questions here in the book.

Note that there will be words and phrases in these dialogues that you haven't seen yet. This is because we want to give you the experience of a real Italian conversation, where you'll come upon words that you may not have heard before. You can often guess at their meaning from context in these situations. Of course, you'll see the English translations for each line here, but see how well you can do without looking at them first.

▶ 12A Dialogue 1 Italian Only (CD 3, Track 17); 12B Dialogue 1 Italian and English (CD 3, Track 18); 12C Dialogue 1 Role Play Exercise (CD 3, Track 19)

Maria:	**Ciao, mi chiamo Maria e tu?**
	Hi, my name's Maria, and you?
Steven:	**Mi chiamo Steven. Molto piacere!**
	My name's Steven. Nice to meet you!
Maria:	**Piacere mio.**
	Nice to meet you, too.
Steven:	**Come stai, Maria?**
	How are you, Maria?
Maria:	**Molto bene, grazie. E tu come stai?**
	Very well, thank you. And how are you?
Steven:	**Così così.**
	So-so.
Maria:	**Io sono italiana. Sono di Milano e tu?**
	I'm Italian. I'm from Milan, and you?
Steven:	**Io sono di New York, ma ho una madre italiana. Lei è di Venezia.**
	I'm from New York, but I have an Italian mother. She's from Venice.
Maria:	**Hai un fratello o una sorella?**
	Do you have a brother or a sister?
Steven:	**Ho una sorella: Margaux. Lei è una dottoressa.**
	I have a sister: Margaux. She's a doctor.
Maria:	**Hai una famiglia piccola!**
	You have a small family!
Steven:	**E tu hai una sorella o un fratello?**
	And do you have a sister or a brother?
Maria:	**Io ho una sorella, Elena e un fratello, Marco. Marco è un poliziotto e Elena è una studentessa.**
	I have a sister, Elena, and a brother, Marco. Marco is a police officer and Elena is a student.
Steven:	**Anche io sono uno studente. E tu?**
	I'm a student too. And you?

Maria:	Io sono una professoressa e ho una figlia piccola: Martina.
	I'm a professor and I have a little girl: Martina.
Steven:	Hai anche un nipote o una nipote?
	Do you also have a nephew or a niece?
Maria:	Ho un nipote, Giorgio, il figlio di Marco. E tu?
	I have a nephew, Giorgio. He's Marco's son. And you?
Steven:	No, ma ho una nonna, uno zio, un cugino e una cugina.
	No, but I have a grandmother, an uncle, a male and a female cousin.
Maria:	Arrivederci Steven.
	Good-bye, Steven.
Steven:	Ciao ciao, Maria. Buona serata!
	Bye-bye, Maria. Have a good evening!
Maria:	Grazie mille. A presto.
	Thank you very much. See you later.

✎ Dialogue 1 Practice

Now let's check your comprehension of the dialogue and review what you learned in Lessons 1-10. Ready?

1. Maria è italiana o americana? _____

_____

2. Di dov'è? _____

_____

3. Steven ha una madre italiana o un padre italiano? _____

_____

4. Sua madre è di Roma o di Venezia? _____

_____

5. **Come si chiama la sorella di Steven?** _____

_____

6. **Margaux è una professoressa o una dottoressa?** _____

_____

7. **Maria ha un fratello?** _____

_____

8. **Cosa fa?** _____

_____

9. **Come si chiama la figlia di Maria?** _____

_____

10. **Il nipote di Maria è il figlio di suo fratello o il figlio di sua sorella?** _____

_____

ANSWER KEY
1. Maria è italiana. 2. È di Milano. 3. Steven ha una madre italiana. 4. Sua madre è di Venezia. 5. La sorella di Steven si chiama Margaux. 6. È una dottoressa. 7. Sì, ha un fratello. 8. Fa il poliziotto. (Or: È un poliziotto.) 9. Si chiama Martina. 10. Il nipote di Maria è il figlio di suo fratello.

🔊 Dialogue 2
A BUSY FAMILY

As with Dialogue 1, first read and listen to the whole dialogue in Italian. Then read and listen to the Italian and English together. How much did you understand? Next, do the role play in the audio as well as the comprehension exercises here in the book.

▶ 13A Dialogue 2 Italian Only (CD 3, Track 20); 13B Dialogue 2 Italian and English (CD 3, Track 21); 13C Dialogue 2 Role Play Exercise (CD 3, Track 22)

Greta: **Sei solo in casa oggi? Dov'è Marco?**
         Are you alone at home today? Where is Marco?

Peter: **È in camera sua con Marina e Franco, due amici di scuola.**
         He is in his room with Marina and Franco, two friends from school.

Greta: **E Marisa dov'è? È in giardino?**
         And where's Marisa? Is she in the garden?

Peter: **No, è in camera da letto. Ha sonno e ha bisogno di fare un pisolino.**
         No, she is in the bedroom. She is sleepy and needs a nap.

Greta: **Anche io ho sonno …**
         I am sleepy, too …

Peter: **Hai voglia di un caffè?**
         Do you feel like having a coffee?

Greta: **Sì, grazie. Ho proprio bisogno di un caffè.**
         Yes, please. I really need a coffee.

Peter: **Ecco le tazze e il caffè. Ma dov'è lo zucchero?**
         Here are the cups and coffee. But where's the sugar?

Greta: **Forse è in cucina.**
         Maybe it's in the kitchen.

Peter: **Hai ragione. Ecco lo zucchero.**
         You're right. Here is the sugar.

Greta: **I libri in soggiorno sono di Marco vero?**
         The books in the living room belong to Marco (are Marco's), right?

Peter: **Veramente sono di Marina, l'amica di Marco.**
         Actually, they belong to Marina, Marco's friend.

Greta: **La madre di Marina si chiama Teresa vero?**
         The name of Marina's mother is Teresa, right?

Peter: **Sì, hai ragione, si chiama proprio Teresa.**
         Yes, you're right: her name is actually Teresa.

Greta: **Lei è amica di mio cugino Paolo.**
         She is friends with my cousin Paolo.

Peter:	**Hai voglia di un altro caffè?**
	Do you feel like having one more coffee?
Greta:	**Grazie mille, ma ho fretta. Ho bisogno di essere a casa per le sette e sono già in ritardo.**
	Thanks a lot, but I am in a hurry. I have to be home by seven and I am already late.
Peter:	**Ma tu sei sempre in ritardo!**
	Well, you are always late!
Greta:	**Non sono d'accordo. Purtroppo quando io sono puntuale tutti gli altri sono in ritardo!!!**
	I don't agree! Unfortunately, when I'm on time, everyone else is late!!!

(II)

✎ Dialogue 2 Practice

Answer each of the following comprehension questions.

1. **Peter è a casa da solo o con Marco ed i suoi amici?** _____

_____

2. **Marisa è in giardino o in camera da letto?** _____

_____

3. **I libri in soggiorno sono di Marco o di Marina?** _____

_____

4. **Come si chiama la madre di Marina?** _____

_____

5. **Cosa offre Marco a Greta?** _____

_____

6. **Dov'è lo zucchero?** _____

_____

7. **Teresa è amica del cugino o della cugina di Greta?** _____

_____

8. **Come si chiama il cugino di Greta?** _____

_____

9. **A che ora ha bisogno di essere a casa Greta?** _____

_____

10. **Greta è in anticipo o in ritardo?** _____

_____

ANSWER KEY
1. **Peter è a casa con Marco e i suoi amici.** 2. **Marisa è in camera da letto.** 3. **I libri sono di Marina.**
4. **La madre di Marina si chiama Teresa.** 5. **Le offre un caffè.** 6. **Lo zucchero è in cucina.** 7. **Teresa è amica del cugino di Greta.** 8. **Il cugino di Greta si chiama Paolo.** 9. **Greta ha bisogno di essere a casa alle sette.** 10. **È in ritardo.**

‹‹ Dialogue 3
A VISIT WITH A FRIEND

Remember, feel free to use your dictionary or the glossary to look up any words you don't know.

▶ 14A Dialogue 3 Italian Only (CD 3, Track 23); 14B Dialogue 3 Italian and English (CD 3, Track 24); 14C Dialogue 3 Role Play Exercise (CD 3, Track 25)

Marco: **Il tuo nuovo soggiorno è proprio bello: un divano rosso, un tavolo grande e quattro sedie verdi!**
Your new living room is really nice: a red couch, a big table and four green chairs!

Gina:	Veramente soltanto il divano è nuovo, le sedie e il tavolo sono vecchi.
	Actually, only the couch is new, the chairs and table are old.
Marco:	Vecchi?
	Old?
Gina:	Sì, sono di mia nonna Maria. Lei ha un nuovo appartamento, ma è un po' piccolo per tutti i suoi mobili.
	Yes, they belong to my grandmother Maria. She has a new apartment, but it's a little small for all her furniture.
Marco:	Tua nonna è molto simpatica! Mia nonna, invece, è un po' stressata.
	Your grandma is very nice! My grandmother, on the other hand, is a little stressed.
Gina:	Anche io sono un po' stressata!
	I am a little stressed, too!
Marco:	Forse hai bisogno di una piccola pausa. Hai voglia di fare una passeggiata in centro?
	Maybe you need a little break. Do you feel like taking a walk downtown?
Gina:	È una buona idea. C'è una bella mostra al museo di arte moderna.
	Good idea. There's a beautiful exhibition at the Museum of Modern Art.
Marco:	Ma dov'è il museo? In viale Roma?
	But where's the museum? (is it) On Roma Avenue?
Gina:	No, in viale Roma c'è la biblioteca. Il museo è in piazza Verdi, vicino all'ufficio postale.
	No, on Roma Avenue there's the library. The museum is in Verdi Square, by the post office.
Marco:	È un po' lontano per una passeggiata. C'è un autobus per piazza Verdi?
	It's a little far for a walk. Is there a bus to Verdi Square?

Gina:	No, ma c'è un autobus per via Giulio Cesare.
	No, but there's a bus to Giulio Cesare Street.
Marco:	E poi?
	And then?
Gina:	Beh, via Giulio Cesare è molto vicina a piazza Verdi. È una passeggiata piacevole.
	Well, Giulio Cesare Street is very close to Verdi Square. It's a pleasant walk.
Marco:	È vero! Sempre diritto e poi a destra per via Mazzini.
	That's right! Straight ahead and then left through Mazzini Street.
Gina:	A proposito, in via Mazzini c'è una eccellente caffetteria. Anche il loro gelato è molto buono.
	By the way, on Mazzini Street there's an excellent coffee shop. Their ice cream is very good, too.
Marco:	Molto bene. Ecco il nostro programma antistress per il pomeriggio: prima un buon gelato e poi il museo.
	Very well. Here is our anti-stress afternoon program: first a good ice cream and then the museum.

✎ Dialogue 3 Practice

1. Nel soggiorno di Gina ci sono un divano rosso, un tavolo piccolo e quattro sedie marroni? _____

   _____

2. I mobili di Gina sono nuovi o vecchi? _____

   _____

3. Di chi sono il tavolo e le sedie? _____

   _____

4. **La nonna di Marco è simpatica?** _____

_____

5. **Gina ha voglia di fare una passeggiata in centro?** _____

_____

6. **Dov'è la mostra di arte moderna?** _____

_____

7. **Il museo di arte moderna è in via Roma?** _____

_____

8. **C'è un autobus per piazza Verdi?** _____

_____

9. **Dov'è via Giulio Cesare?** _____

_____

10. **Come vanno Gina e Marco al museo?** _____

_____

ANSWER KEY

1. No, ci sono un divano rosso, un tavolo grande e quattro sedie verdi. 2. Il divano è nuovo, ma
il tavolo e le sedie sono vecchi. 3. Sono della nonna di Gina, Maria. 4. No, la nonna di Marco è
stressata. 5. Si, ha voglia di fare una passeggiata in centro. 6. Al museo di arte moderna. 7. No, è in
piazza Verdi. 8. No, non c'è un autobus per piazza Verdi, ma c'è un autobus per via Giulio Cesare.
9. Via Giulio Cesare è vicina a piazza Verdi. 10. Gina e Marco vanno in autobus e poi a piedi.

◖ Dialogue 4
DINING OUT

▶ 15A Dialogue 4 Italian Only (Track 26, CD3); 15B Dialogue 4 Italian and English
(Track 27, CD3); 15C Dialogue 4 Role Play Exercise (Track 28, CD3)

Jeff: **Allora Vera, sei pronta per ordinare?**
Well, Vera, are you ready to order?

Vera: **Veramente sono un po' indecisa. Tu cosa prendi?**
Actually I'm a bit undecided. What are you having?

Jeff: **Prendo l'antipasto della casa e le fettuccine al pomodoro.**
*I'll have the appetizer of the house and the fettuccine with tomato
sauce.*

Vera: **Prendi anche il secondo?**
Are you having a main course, as well?

Jeff: **Forse prendo il pesce alla griglia: è delizioso!**
Maybe I'll have the grilled fish: it's delicious.

Vera: **Buona idea! Prendo anch'io il pesce alla griglia.**
Good idea! I'll have the grilled fish, too.

Jeff: **E per primo?**
And as a first course?

Vera: **No, io non prendo il primo. Ordino solo una bella insalata verde
per contorno.**
*No, I am not having a first course. I'll just have a nice green salad as
a side dish.*

Jeff: **Ordiniamo anche del vino bianco?**
Shall we order some white wine, too?

Vera: **Sì certo, ma solo un po'. Questa sera lavoro fino a tardi perché
domani io e Mike partiamo per la Toscana.**
*Yes, sure, but just a little bit. This evening, I am working late
because tomorrow, Mike and I are leaving for Tuscany.*

Jeff: **Fate una vacanza?**
Are you going on vacation?

Vera: **Sì, ma solo per pochi giorni.**
Yes, but just for a few days.

Jeff: **Che bello! Io e Suzy invece lavoriamo domani e sabato. Però domenica, se fa bello, facciamo una gita a Rimini.**
How nice! Suzy and I, on the other hand, are working tomorrow and Saturday. But on Sunday, if it's nice, we'll take a trip to Rimini.

Vera: **Ho molti parenti a Rimini. I miei cugini vivono in centro e la sorella di mia madre vive al porto, vicino al famoso ristorante "Il capitano".**
I have many relatives in Rimini. My cousins live downtown, and my mother's sister lives at the harbor, next to the famous restaurant "Il capitano."

Jeff: **A proposito, è ora di ordinare la nostra cena.**
By the way, it's time to order our dinner.

Vera: **Hai ragione. Ecco la cameriera!**
You're right. Here comes the waitress!

⏸

✎ Dialogue 4 Practice

1. **Vera è pronta ad ordinare?** _____

_____

2. **Cosa ordina Jeff?** _____

_____

3. **Vera prende il primo?** _____

_____

4. **Vera e Jeff ordinano il vino rosso o bianco?** _____

_____

5. **Cosa fa Vera stasera?** _____

_____

6. **Cosa fanno Vera e Mike?** _____

_____

7. **Cosa fanno Jeff e Suzy questo fine settimana?** _____

_____

8. **Dove vivono i parenti di Vera?** _____

_____

ANSWER KEY
1. No, Vera è indecisa. 2. Jeff ordina l'antipasto della casa, le fettuccine al pomodoro e di secondo il pesce alla griglia. 3. No, Vera prende il secondo e una insalata. 4. Ordinano il vino bianco. 5. Stasera Vera lavora. 6. Vera e Mike fanno una vacanza in Toscana. 7. Jeff e Suzy lavorano venerdì e sabato. Se fa bello domenica vanno a Rimini. 8. I cugini vivono in centro e la zia vive al porto.

Dialogue 5
A NIGHT AT THE THEATER

▶ 16A Dialogue 5 Italian Only (Track 29, CD3); 16B Dialogue 5 Italian and English (Track 30, CD3); 16C Dialogue 5 Role Play Exercise (Track 31, CD3)

Avvocato Santi: **Buona sera professoressa Marini!**
                   Good evening, professor Marini!
Dottoressa Marini: **Buona sera avvocato Santi, anche Lei a teatro!**
                   Good evening, counselor Santi, you're at the theater too!

Avvocato Santi: Sì, il teatro è la mia passione. Di solito vado a teatro il giovedì sera, ma questa settimana ho un appuntamento di lavoro fuori città e quindi sono qui di martedì.

Yes, theater is my passion. I usually go to the theater on Thursdays, but this week I will be out of town for a meeting, and so I am here on a Tuesday.

Dottoressa Marini: Capisco. Io invece preferisco il martedì perché il mercoledì faccio orario ridotto: dalle due alle sei di pomeriggio.

I see. I prefer Tuesdays, instead, since on Wednesdays, I have a shorter working shift: from two to six pm.

Avvocato Santi: Le piace lo spettacolo di questa sera?

How do you like tonight's show?

Dottoressa Marini: Francamente non mi piace molto. Amo Shakespeare, ma preferisco le versioni tradizionali, non mi piacciono le ambientazioni moderne.

Frankly, I don't like it very much. I love Shakespeare, but I prefer traditional versions, I don't like modern settings.

Avvocato Santi: Sì, sono d'accordo, però gli attori sono molto bravi. Romeo e Mercuzio mi piacciono molto.

Yes, I agree, however, the actors are very talented. I really like Romeo and Mercutio.

Dottoressa Marini: Le piace anche Giulietta?

Do you like Juliet, too?

Avvocato Santi: No, lei non mi piace. Parla troppo veloce.

No, I don't like her. She speaks too fast.

Dottoressa Marini: Beh, l'intervallo finisce tra cinque minuti. Forse abbiamo tempo di prendere qualcosa da bere.

Well, the intermission is up in five minutes. Maybe we have time for a drink.

Avvocato Santi: Buona idea! A proposito, a che ora finisce la seconda parte dello spettacolo?

Good idea! By the way, when does the second act finish?

Dottoressa Marini:	Intorno a mezzanotte.
	Around midnight.
Avvocato Santi:	Ma adesso sono le dieci meno un quarto!
	But it's (only) a quarter to ten right now!
Dottoressa Marini:	Adesso forse anche Lei capisce perché io preferisco le
	messinscene tradizionali!
	Maybe now you too understand why I prefer traditional
	stagings!

⏸

✎ Dialogue 5 Practice

1. All'avvocato Santi piace il teatro? _____

   _____

2. Di solito l'avvocato Santi va al teatro di martedì o di giovedì? _____

   _____

3. Che giorno preferisce la dottoressa Marini? _____

   _____

4. Alla dottoressa Marini piace lo spettacolo di stasera? _____

   _____

5. La dottoressa Marini preferisce le versioni tradizionali, o le ambientazioni

   moderne di Shakespeare? _____

   _____

6. All'avvocato Santi piacciono Romeo, Mercuzio e Giulietta? _____

   _____

7. Che ore sono quando parlano l'avvocato Santi e la Dottoressa Marini? _____

_____

8. A che ora finisce lo spettacolo? _____

_____

ANSWER KEY

1. Sì, il teatro è la sua passione. 2. Di solito va il giovedì. 3. La dottoressa Marini preferisce il martedì. 4. No, non le piace lo spettacolo di stasera. 5. Preferisce le versioni tradizionali. 6. Gli piacciono Romeo e Mercuzio, ma non gli piace Giulietta. 7. Sono le dieci meno un quarto. 8. Lo spettacolo finisce a mezzanotte.

You've come to the end of *Living Language Essential Italian*! Congratulations! We hope you've enjoyed your experience. If you purchased the *Complete Italian* package, you can now continue on to *Intermediate Italian*. And of course, feel free to go back and review any or all of *Essential Italian* at any time if you need to.

For more information on other Living Language Italian courses and supplementary materials, visit **www.livinglanguage.com.**

Pronunciation Guide

Italian pronunciation

Many Italian sounds are like English sounds, though the differences are enough that you need to familiarize yourself with them in order to make yourself understood properly in the Italian language. Some key things to remember:

1. Each vowel is pronounced clearly and crisply.

2. A single consonant is pronounced with the following vowel.

3. Some vowels bear an accent mark, sometimes used to show the accentuated syllable (la città, *the city*), and sometimes merely to distinguish words (e, *and*; è, *is*). An acute accent, on the other hand, gives a more closed pronunciation (perché, *why*).

4. When the accent is on the letter e, it gives it a more open pronunciation (caffè, *coffee*).

5. The apostrophe is used to mark elision, the omission of a vowel. For example, when the word dove (*where*) is combined with è (*is*), the e in dove is dropped: Dov'è? (*Where is?*).

The rest is a matter of listening and repeating, which you should do with each word in this section as you start to learn how the Italian language sounds.

VOWELS

Now that you've looked at the difference between Italian and English on a broad scale, let's get down to the specifics by looking at individual sounds, starting with Italian vowels.

LETTER	PRONUNCIATION	EXAMPLES
a	*ah* in *father*	a, amico, la, lago, pane, parlare
e	*e* in *bent*	era, essere, pera, padre, carne, treno, tre, estate, se
i	*i* in *police, machine, marine*	misura, sì, amica, oggi, piccolo, figlio
o	*o* in *no*	no, poi, ora, sono, corpo, con, otto, come, forma, voce
u	*oo* in *noon*	uno, una, tu, ultimo

There are also several diphthongs in Italian, vowel-and-vowel combinations which create a new sound.

LETTER	PRONUNCIATION	EXAMPLES
ai	*i* in *ripe*	guai
au	*ow* in *now*	auto
ei	*ay* in *say*	sei
eu	*ay* in *say* + *oo* in *noon*	neutro
ia	*ya* in *yarn*	italiano
ie	*ye* in *yet*	miele
io	*yo* in *yodel*	campione
iu	*you*	fiume
oi	*oy* in *boy*	poi

LETTER	PRONUNCIATION	EXAMPLES
ua	*wa* in *wand*	quando
ue	*we* in *wet*	questo
uo	*wa* in *war*	suono
ui	*wee* in *sweet*	guido

1. CONSONANTS

Next, let's take a look at Italian consonants. The consonants **b**, **d**, **f**, **k**, **l**, **m**, **n**, **p**, **q**, **t**, and **v** are all pronounced as they are in English. The rest differ slightly, as you'll see below.

LETTER	PRONUNCIATION	EXAMPLES
c	before **e** or **i**, *ch* in *church*	cena, cibo
c	before **a**, **o**, and **u**, *k* in *bake*	caffè, conto, cupola
g	before **e** or **i**, *j* in *joy*	gente, gita
g	before **a**, **o**, or **u**, *g* in *gold*	gala, gondola, gusto
h	silent	hotel
r	trilled	rumore
s	generally, *s* in *set*	pasta
s	between two vowels, or before **b**, **d**, **g**, **l**, **m**, **n**, **r**, or **v**, *z* in *zero*	sbaglio
z	generally, *ts* in *pits*	zucchero, grazie
z	sometimes, *ds* in *toads*	zingaro, zanzara

2. SPECIAL ITALIAN SOUNDS

There are several sound combinations in Italian that appear quite often as exceptions to the above rules, so study them carefully.

CLUSTER	PRONUNCIATION	EXAMPLES
ch	before **e** or **i**, *c* in *can*	amiche, chilo

CLUSTER	PRONUNCIATION	EXAMPLES
gh	*g* in *get*	spaghetti, ghiotto
	gh in *ghost*	funghi
gl	before a vowel + consonant, *gl* in *globe*	globo, negligente
gli	*lli* in *scallion*	gli
glia	*lli* in *scallion* + *ah*	famiglia
glie	*lli* in *scallion* + *eh*	moglie
glio	*lli* in *scallion* + *oh*	aglio
gn	*ny* in *canyon*	Bologna
sc	before e or i, *sh* in *fish*	pesce, sci
sc	before a, o, or u, *sc* in *scout*	scala, disco
sch	before e or i, *sk* in *sky*	pesche, fischi

Grammar Summary

1. ARTICLES

a. Definite

	MASCULINE	FEMININE
Singular	il (in front of a consonant) l' (in front of a vowel) lo (in front of s + consonant, z-, ps-, or gn-)	la (in front of a consonant) l' (in front of a vowel)
Plural	i (in front of consonants) gli (in front of s + consonant, z-, ps-, gn-, or vowels)	le (in front of consonants or vowels)

b. Indefinite

	MASCULINE	FEMININE
Singular	un (in front of a consonant or vowel) uno (in front of s + consonant, z-, ps-, gn-)	una (in front of a consonant) un' (in front of a vowel)

2. PLURALS OF NOUNS AND ADJECTIVES

GENDER	SINGULAR ENDING	PLURAL ENDING
Masculine	-o	-i
Masculine/Feminine	-e	-i
Feminine	-a	-e

Some exceptions:

a. A few nouns ending in -o are feminine.

b. Some masculine nouns ending in -o have two plurals, with different meanings for each.

c. Masculine nouns ending in -a form their plural in –i.

SPECIAL CASES

1. Nouns ending in -ca or -ga insert h in the plural in order to keep the "k" and "g" sound in the plural.

2. Nouns ending in -cia or -gia (with unaccented i) form their plural in -ce or -ge if the c or g is double or is preceded by another consonant. Nouns ending in -cia or -gia form their plural in -cie or -gie if c or g is preceded by a vowel or if the i is accented.

3. Nouns ending in -io (without an accent on the i) have a single i in the plural. If the i is accented, the plural has ii.

4. Nouns ending in -co or -go form their plural in -chi or -ghi if the accent falls on the syllable before the last. If the accent falls on the third-to-last syllable, the plural is in -ci or -gi.

5. Nouns in the singular with the accent on the last vowel do not change in the plural.

6. There is no special plural form for:

- Nouns with a written accent on the last vowel.

- Nouns ending in i in the singular, and almost all the nouns in ie.

- Nouns ending in a consonant.

3. THE PARTITIVE

a. di + a form of the definite article il, lo, la, l', i, le, gli
b. qualche (only with singular nouns)
c. alcuni, alcune (only in the plural)
d. un po' di

4. COMPARISON

Equality	(così) … come	as … as
Equality	tanto … quanto	as much/as many as
Superiority	più … di or che	More … than
Inferiority	meno … di or che	less/fewer … than

5. RELATIVE SUPERLATIVE

a. The relative superlative (expressed in English using *the most/the least/the . . . -est of/in*) is formed by placing the appropriate definite article before più or meno followed by the adjective. *Of/in* is translated with di, whether by itself or combined with the definite article.

b. If a clause follows the superlative, the verb is often in the subjunctive form.

c. With the superlative of adverbs, the definite article is often omitted, unless *possibile* is added to the adverb.

6. ABSOLUTE SUPERLATIVE

a. The absolute superlative is formed by dropping the last vowel of the adjective and adding -issimo, -issima, -issimi, -issime.

b. By putting the words molto, troppo, or assai in front of the adjectives.

c. By using a second adjective of almost the same meaning, or by repeating the adjective.

d. By using stra-, arci-, sopra-, super-, extra-.

7. IRREGULAR COMPARATIVES AND SUPERLATIVES

ADJECTIVE	COMPARATIVE	SUPERLATIVE
good: buono(a)	*better:* più buono(a) migliore	*the best:* il più buono buonissimo(a) ottimo(a) il/la migliore
bad: cattivo(a)	*worse:* peggiore più cattivo(a) peggio	*the worst:* il/la più cattivo(a) cattivissimo(a) pessimo(a) il/la peggiore
big/great: grande	*bigger/greater:* maggiore più grande	*the biggest/greatest:* il/la più grande grandissimo(a) massimo(a) il/la maggiore
small/little: piccolo(a)	*smaller/lesser:* minore più piccolo(a)	*the smallest:* il/la più piccolo(a) piccolissimo(a) minimo(a) il/la minore

ADVERB	COMPARATIVE	SUPERLATIVE
well: bene	*better:* meglio (il migliore)	*the best:* il meglio
badly: male	*worse:* peggio (il peggiore)	*the worst:* il peggio

8. DIMINUTIVES AND AUGMENTATIVES

a. The endings -ino, -ina, -ello, -ella, -etto, -etta, -uccio, -uccia imply smallness.

b. The endings -one, -ona, -otta imply largeness or hyperbole.

c. The endings -uccia, -uccio indicate endearment.

d. The endings -accio, -accia, -astro, -astra, -azzo, -azza indicate depreciation.

9. DEMONSTRATIVES

questo, -a, -i, -e	*this, these*
quello, -a, -i, -e	*that, those*

There are also the masculine forms quel, quell', quei, quegli. Here is how they are used:

a. If the article il is used before the noun, use quel.

b. If the article l' is used before the noun, then use quell'.

c. If i is used before the noun, use quei.

d. If gli is used before the noun, use quegli.

Note that the same rules apply to bel, bell', bei, begli, from bello, -a, -i, -e (*beautiful*).

10. POSSESSIVE ADJECTIVES

	MASCULINE SINGULAR	MASCULINE PLURAL	FEMININE SINGULAR	FEMININE PLURAL
my	il mio	i miei	la mia	le mie
your	il tuo	i tuoi	la tua	le tue
his, her, its	il suo	i suoi	la sua	le sue
your (fml.)	il Suo	i Suoi	la Sua	le Sue
our	il nostro	i nostri	la nostra	le nostre
your	il vostro	i vostri	la vostra	le vostre
their	il loro	i loro	la loro	le loro
your (fml. pl.)	il Loro	i Loro	la Loro	le Loro

11. INDEFINITE ADJECTIVES AND PRONOUNS

some	qualche *(sg.)*, alcuni *(pl.)*
any	qualunque, qualsiasi *(no pl.)*
each, every	ogni *(no pl.)*, ciascun, ciascuno, ciascuna *(no pl.)*
other, more	altro, altra, altri, altre
no, no one, none of	nessuno, nessun, nessuna *(no pl.)*

12. INDEFINITE PRONOUNS

some	alcuni
someone, somebody	qualcuno
anybody, anyone	chiunque
each one, each person	ognuno
everybody, everyone	tutti *(pl.)*
each, each one	ciascuno
everything	tutto
the other, the others, else (in interrogative or negative sentences), anything else (in interrogative or negative sentences)	l'altro, l'altra, gli altri, le altre, altro
another one	un altro
nothing	niente, nulla
nobody, no one	nessuno *(no pl.)*

13. RELATIVE PRONOUNS

chi	*who*
che	*who, whom, that, which*
cui	*whom, which*

a cui	to whom, to which
di cui	of whom, of which
in cui	in which

a. **che**: For masculine, feminine, singular, plural; for persons, animals, things. Not used if there is a preposition.

b. **cui**: Masculine, feminine, singular, plural; for persons, animals, things; used instead of **che** when there is a preposition.

c. **il quale, la quale, i quali, le quali**: For persons, animals, things, with the same English meanings as **che**; can be used with or without prepositions. When used with prepositions, the contracted forms are used, e.g., **alla quale, dei quali**, etc.

14. PRONOUNS

	SUBJECT	DIRECT OBJECT	INDIRECT OBJECT	WITH PREPOSITION	REFLEXIVE
1st sg.	io	mi	mi	me	mi
2nd sg.	tu	ti	ti	te	ti
3rd m. sg.	lui	lo	gli	lui	si
3rd f. sg.	lei	la	le	lei	si
2nd sg. fml.	Lei	La	Le	Lei	Si
1st pl.	noi	ci	ci	noi	ci
2nd pl.	voi	vi	vi	voi	vi
3rd pl.	loro	li/le	gli/loro	loro	si
2nd pl. fml.	Loro	Li/Le	Gli/Loro	Loro	Si

15. DOUBLE OBJECT PRONOUNS

INDIRECT OBJECT	+ LO	+ LA	+ LI	+ LE	+ NE
mi	me lo	me la	me li	me le	me ne
ti	te lo	te la	te li	te le	te ne
gli/le/ Le	glielo	gliela	glieli	gliele	gliene
ci	ce lo	ce la	ce li	ce le	ce ne
vi	ve lo	ve la	ve li	ve le	ve ne
gli	glielo/ Glielo	gliela/ Gliela	glieli/Glieli	gliele/ Gliele	gliene/ Gliene
loro/ loro	lo ... loro/Loro	la ... loro/Loro	li ... loro/Loro	le ... loro/Loro	ne ... loro/Loro

16. ADVERBS

a. Many adverbs end in -mente.

b. Adjectives ending in -le or -re drop the final e before adding -mente if the l or r is preceded by a vowel.

c. Adverbs may have a comparative and superlative form.

17. PREPOSITIONS

di	of
a	at, to
da	from
in	in
con	with
su	above
per	through, by means of, on
tra, fra	between, among

Prepositions + Definite Articles

	DI	A	SUL	CON
il	del	al	sul	col
lo	dello	allo	sullo	-
la	della	alla	sulla	-
l'	dell'	all'	sull'	-
i	dei	ai	sui	coi
gli	degli	agli	sugli	-
le	delle	alle	sulle	-

18. NEGATION

a. **Non** (*not*) comes before the verb.

b. Note that **non** can be combined with negative pronouns in the same sentence (double negative).

c. If the negative pronoun begins the sentence, **non** is not used.

19. QUESTION WORDS

Perché?	*Why?*
Come?	*How?*
Quando?	*When?*
Dove?	*Where?*
Quanto/quanta?	*How much?*
Quanti/quante?	*How many?*

20. THE SUBJUNCTIVE

The subjunctive mood expresses doubt, uncertainty, hope, fear, desire, supposition, possibility, probability, or granting. It is mostly found in clauses dependent upon another verb.

The subjunctive is used:

a. after verbs expressing hope, wish, desire, command, doubt.

b. after verbs expressing an opinion (penso, credo).

c. after expressions made with a form of essere and an adjective or an adverb (è necessario, è facile, è possibile), or some impersonal expressions like bisogna, importa, etc.

d. after conjunctions such as sebbene, quantunque, per quanto, benché, affinché, prima che (subjunctive to express a possibility; indicative to express a fact).

21. "IF" CLAUSES

An "*if*" clause can express:

a. REALITY. In this case, the indicative present and future is used.

b. POSSIBILITY. The imperfect subjunctive and the conditional present are used to express possibility in the present. The past perfect subjunctive and the past conditional are used to express a possibility in the past.

c. IMPOSSIBILITY or COUNTERFACTUALITY. Use the same construction as in (b); the only difference is that we know that the condition cannot be fulfilled.

amare
to love, to like

io	noi
tu	voi
lui/lei/ Lei	loro/Loro

Present		Imperative	
amo	amiamo		Amiamo!
ami	amate	Ama!	Amate!
ama	amano	Ami!	Amino!

Past		Imperfect	
ho amato	abbiamo amato	amavo	amavamo
hai amato	avete amato	amavi	amavate
ha amato	hanno amato	amava	amavano

Future		Conditional	
amerò	ameremo	amerei	ameremmo
amerai	amerete	ameresti	amereste
amerà	ameranno	amerebbe	amerebbero

Future Perfect		Past Conditional	
avrò amato	avremo amato	avrei amato	avremmo amato
avrai amato	avrete amato	avresti amato	avreste amato
avrà amato	avranno amato	avrebbe amato	avrebbero amato

Past Perfect		Subjunctive	
avevo amato	avevamo amato	ami	amiamo
avevi amato	avevate amato	ami	amiate
aveva amato	avevano amato	ami	amino

temere
to fear

io	noi
tu	voi
lui/lei/Lei	loro/Loro

Present		Imperative	
temo	temiamo		Temiamo!
temi	temete	Temi!	Temete!
teme	temono	Tema!	Temano!

Past		Imperfect	
ho temuto	abbiamo temuto	temevo	temevamo
hai temuto	avete temuto	temevi	temevate
ha temuto	hanno temuto	temeva	temevano

Future		Conditional	
temerò	temeremo	temerei	temeremmo
temerai	temerete	temeresti	temereste
temerà	temeranno	temerebbe	temerebbero

Future Perfect		Past Conditional	
avrò temuto	avremo temuto	avrei temuto	avremmo temuto
avrai temuto	avrete temuto	avresti temuto	avreste temuto
avrà temuto	avranno temuto	avrebbe temuto	avrebbero temuto

Past Perfect		Subjunctive	
avevo temuto	avevamo temuto	tema	temiamo
avevi temuto	avevate temuto	tema	temiate
aveva temuto	avevano temuto	tema	temano

sentire
to hear

io	noi
tu	voi
lui/lei/ Lei	loro/Loro

Present		Imperative	
sento	sentiamo		Sentiamo!
senti	sentite	Senti!	Sentite!
sente	sentono	Senta!	Sentano!

Past		Imperfect	
ho sentito	abbiamo sentito	sentivo	sentivamo
hai sentito	avete sentito	sentivi	sentivate
ha sentito	hanno sentito	sentiva	sentivano

Future		Conditional	
sentirò	sentiremo	sentirei	sentiremmo
sentirai	sentirete	sentiresti	sentireste
sentirà	sentiranno	sentirebbe	sentirebbero

Future Perfect		Past Conditional	
avrò sentito	avremo sentito	avrei sentito	avremmo sentito
avrai sentito	avrete sentito	avresti sentito	avreste sentito
avrà sentito	avranno sentito	avrebbe sentito	avrebbero sentito

Past Perfect		Subjunctive	
avevo sentito	avevamo sentito	senta	sentiamo
avevi sentito	avevate sentito	senta	sentiate
aveva sentito	avevano sentito	senta	sentano

capire
to understand

io	noi
tu	voi
lui/lei/ Lei	loro/Loro

Present		Imperative	
capisco	capiamo		Capiamo!
capisci	capite	Capisci!	Capite!
capisce	capiscono	Capisca!	Capiscano!

Past		Imperfect	
ho capito	abbiamo capito	capivo	capivamo
hai capito	avete capito	capivi	capivate
ha capito	hanno capito	capiva	capivano

Future		Conditional	
capirò	capiremo	capirei	capiremmo
capirai	capirete	capiresti	capireste
capirà	capiranno	capirebbe	capirebbero

Future Perfect		Past Conditional	
avrò capito	avremo capito	avrei capito	avremmo capito
avrai capito	avrete capito	avresti capito	avreste capito
avrà capito	avranno capito	avrebbe capito	avrebbero capito

Past Perfect		Subjunctive	
avevo capito	avevamo capito	capisca	capiamo
avevi capito	avevate capito	capisca	capiate
aveva capito	avevano capito	capisca	capiscano

essere
to be

io	noi
tu	voi
lui/lei/ Lei	loro/Loro

Present		Imperative	
sono	siamo		Siamo!
sei	siete	Sii!	Siate!
è	sono	Sia!	Siano!

Past		Imperfect	
sono stato/a	siamo stati/e	ero	eravamo
sei stato/a	siete stati/e	eri	eravate
è stato/a	sono stati/e	era	erano

Future		Conditional	
sarò	saremo	sarei	saremmo
sarai	sarete	saresti	sareste
sarà	saranno	sarebbe	sarebbero

Future Perfect		Past Conditional	
sarò stato/a	saremo stati/e	sarei stato/a	saremmo stati/e
sarai stato/a	sarete stati/e	saresti stato/a	sareste stati/e
sarà stato/a	saranno stati/e	sarebbe stato/a	sarebbero stati/e

Past Perfect		Subjunctive	
ero stato/a	eravamo stati/e	sia	siamo
eri stato/a	eravate stati/e	sia	siate
era stato/a	erano stati/e	sia	siano

avere
to have

io	noi
tu	voi
lui/lei/ Lei	loro/Loro

Present		Imperative	
ho	abbiamo		Abbiamo!
hai	avete	Abbi!	Abbiate!
ha	hanno	Abbia!	Abbiano!

Past		Imperfect	
ho avuto	abbiamo avuto	avevo	avevamo
hai avuto	avete avuto	avevi	avevate
ha avuto	hanno avuto	aveva	avevano

Future		Conditional	
avrò	avremo	avrei	avremmo
avrai	avrete	avresti	avreste
avrà	avranno	avrebbe	avrebbero

Future Perfect		Past Conditional	
avrò avuto	avremo avuto	avrei avuto	avremmo avuto
avrai avuto	avrete avuto	avresti avuto	avreste avuto
avrà avuto	avranno avuto	avrebbe avuto	avrebbero avuto

Past Perfect		Subjunctive	
avevo avuto	avevamo avuto	abbia	abbiamo
avevi avuto	avevate avuto	abbia	abbiate
aveva avuto	avevano avuto	abbia	abbiano

andare
to go

io	noi
tu	voi
lui/lei/ Lei	loro/Loro

Present		Imperative	
vado	andiamo		Andiamo!
vai	andate	Va!/Va'!/Vai!	Andate!
va	vanno	Vada!	Vadano!

Past		Imperfect	
sono andato/a	siamo andati/e	andavo	andavamo
sei andato/a	siete andati/e	andavi	andavate
è andato/a	sono andati/e	andava	andavano

Future		Conditional	
andrò	andremo	andrei	andremmo
andrai	andrete	andresti	andreste
andrà	andranno	andrebbe	andrebbero

Future Perfect		Past Conditional	
sarò andato/a	saremo andati/e	sarei andato/a	saremmo andati/e
sarai andato/a	sarete andati/e	saresti andato/a	sareste andati/e
sarà andato/a	saranno andati/e	sarebbe andato/a	sarebbero andati/e

Past Perfect		Subjunctive	
ero andato/a	eravamo andati/e	vada	andiamo
eri andato/a	eravate andati/e	vada	andiate
era andato/a	erano andati/e	vada	vadano

bere
to drink

io	noi
tu	voi
lui/lei/ Lei	loro/Loro

Present		Imperative	
bevo	beviamo		Beviamo!
bevi	bevete	Bevi!	Bevete!
beve	bevono	Beva!	Bevano!

Past		Imperfect	
ho bevuto	abbiamo bevuto	bevevo	bevevamo
hai bevuto	avete bevuto	bevevi	bevevate
ha bevuto	hanno bevuto	beveva	bevevano

Future		Conditional	
berrò	berremo	berrei	berremmo
berrai	berrete	berresti	berreste
berrà	berranno	berrebbe	berrebbero

Future Perfect		Past Conditional	
avrò bevuto	avremo bevuto	avrei bevuto	avremmo bevuto
avrai bevuto	avrete bevuto	avresti bevuto	avreste bevuto
avrà bevuto	avranno bevuto	avrebbe bevuto	avrebbero bevuto

Past Perfect		Subjunctive	
avevo bevuto	avevamo bevuto	beva	beviamo
avevi bevuto	avevate bevuto	beva	beviate
aveva bevuto	avevano bevuto	beva	bevano

dare
to give

io	noi
tu	voi
lui/lei/ Lei	loro/Loro

Present		Imperative	
do	diamo		Diamo!
dai	date	Dai!/Dà!/Da'!	Date!
dà	danno	Dia!	Diano!

Past		Imperfect	
ho dato	abbiamo dato	davo	davamo
hai dato	avete dato	davi	davate
ha dato	hanno dato	dava	davano

Future		Conditional	
darò	daremo	darei	daremmo
darai	darete	daresti	dareste
darà	daranno	darebbe	darebbero

Future Perfect		Past Conditional	
avrò dato	avremo dato	avrei dato	avremmo dato
avrai dato	avrete dato	avresti dato	avreste dato
avrà dato	avranno dato	avrebbe dato	avrebbero dato

Past Perfect		Subjunctive	
avevo dato	avevamo dato	dia	diamo
avevi dato	avevate dato	dia	diate
aveva dato	avevano dato	dia	diano

dire
to say

io	noi
tu	voi
lui/lei/ Lei	loro/Loro

Present		Imperative		
dico	diciamo			Diciamo!
dici	dite	Di'!/Dì!	Dite!	
dice	dicono	Dica!	Dicano!	

Past		Imperfect	
ho detto	abbiamo detto	dicevo	dicevamo
hai detto	avete detto	dicevi	dicevate
ha detto	hanno detto	diceva	dicevano

Future		Conditional	
dirò	diremo	direi	diremmo
dirai	direte	diresti	direste
dirà	diranno	direbbe	direbbero

Future Perfect		Past Conditional	
avrò detto	avremo detto	avrei detto	avremmo detto
avrai detto	avrete detto	avresti detto	avreste detto
avrà detto	avranno detto	avrebbe detto	avrebbero detto

Past Perfect		Subjunctive	
avevo detto	avevamo detto	dica	diciamo
avevi detto	avevate detto	dica	diciate
aveva detto	avevano detto	dica	dicano

dovere
to owe, to be obliged, to have to

io	noi
tu	voi
lui/lei/ Lei	loro/Loro

Present

		Imperative	
devo (debbo)	dobbiamo		Dobbiamo!
devi	dovete	Devi!	Dovete!
deve	devono (debbono)	Debba!	Debbano!

Past

		Imperfect	
ho dovuto	abbiamo dovuto	dovevo	dovevamo
hai dovuto	avete dovuto	dovevi	dovevate
ha dovuto	hanno dovuto	doveva	dovevano

Future

		Conditional	
dovrò	dovremo	dovrei	dovremmo
dovrai	dovrete	dovresti	dovreste
dovrà	dovranno	dovrebbe	dovrebbero

Future Perfect

		Past Conditional	
avrò dovuto	avremo dovuto	avrei dovuto	avremmo dovuto
avrai dovuto	avrete dovuto	avresti dovuto	avreste dovuto
avrà dovuto	avranno dovuto	avrebbe dovuto	avrebbero dovuto

Past Perfect

		Subjunctive	
avevo dovuto	avevamo dovuto	debba	dobbiamo
avevi dovuto	avevate dovuto	debba	dobbiate
aveva dovuto	avevano dovuto	debba	debbano

Essential Italian

fare
to do

io	noi
tu	voi
lui/lei/ Lei	loro/Loro

Present		Imperative	
faccio	facciamo		Facciamo!
fai	fate	Fa!/Fai!/Fa'!	Fate!
fa	fanno	Faccia!	Facciano!

Past		Imperfect	
ho fatto	abbiamo fatto	facevo	facevamo
hai fatto	avete fatto	facevi	facevate
ha fatto	hanno fatto	faceva	facevano

Future		Conditional	
farò	faremo	farei	faremmo
farai	farete	faresti	fareste
farà	faranno	farebbe	farebbero

Future Perfect		Past Conditional	
avrò fatto	avremo fatto	avrei fatto	avremmo fatto
avrai fatto	avrete fatto	avresti fatto	avreste fatto
avrà fatto	avranno fatto	avrebbe fatto	avrebbero fatto

Past Perfect		Subjunctive	
avevo fatto	avevamo fatto	faccia	facciamo
avevi fatto	avevate fatto	faccia	facciate
aveva fatto	avevano fatto	faccia	facciano

potere
to be able, can

io	noi
tu	voi
lui/lei/ Lei	loro/Loro

Present		Imperative	
posso	possiamo		Possiamo!
puoi	potete	Puoi!	Possiate!
può	possono	Possa!	Possano!

Past		Imperfect	
ho potuto	abbiamo potuto	potevo	potevamo
hai potuto	avete potuto	potevi	potevate
ha potuto	hanno potuto	poteva	potevano

Future		Conditional	
potrò	potremo	potrei	potremmo
potrai	potrete	potresti	potreste
potrà	potranno	potrebbe	potrebbero

Future Perfect		Past Conditional	
avrò potuto	avremo potuto	avrei potuto	avremmo potuto
avrai potuto	avrete potuto	avresti potuto	avreste potuto
avrà potuto	avranno potuto	avrebbe potuto	avrebbero potuto

Past Perfect		Subjunctive	
avevo potuto	avevamo potuto	possa	possiamo
avevi potuto	avevate potuto	possa	possiate
aveva potuto	avevano potuto	possa	possano

rimanere
to stay

io	noi
tu	voi
lui/lei/ Lei	loro/Loro

Present		Imperative	
rimango	rimaniamo		Rimaniamo!
rimani	rimanete	Rimani!	Rimanete!
rimane	rimangono	Rimanga!	Rimangano!

Past		Imperfect	
sono rimasto/a	siamo rimasti/e	rimanevo	rimanevamo
sei rimasto/a	siete rimasti/e	rimanevi	rimanevate
è rimasto/a	sono rimasti/e	rimaneva	rimanevano

Future		Conditional	
rimarrò	rimarremo	rimarrei	rimarremmo
rimarrai	rimarrete	rimarresti	rimarreste
rimarrà	rimarranno	rimarrebbe	rimarrebbero

Future Perfect		Past Conditional	
sarò rimasto/a	saremo rimasti/e	sarei rimasto/a	saremmo rimasti/e
sarai rimasto/a	sarete rimasti/e	saresti rimasto/a	sareste rimasti/e
sarà rimasto/a	saranno rimasti/e	sarebbe rimasto/a	sarebbero rimasti/e

Past Perfect		Subjunctive	
ero rimasto/a	eravamo rimasti/e	rimanga	rimaniamo
eri rimasto/a	eravate rimasti/e	rimanga	rimaniate
era rimasto/a	erano rimasti/e	rimanga	rimangano

sapere
to know

io	noi
tu	voi
lui/lei/ Lei	loro/Loro

Present		Imperative	
so	sappiamo		Sappiamo!
sai	sapete	Sappi!	Sappiate!
sa	sanno	Sappia!	Sappiano!

Past		Imperfect	
ho saputo	abbiamo saputo	sapevo	sapevamo
hai saputo	avete saputo	sapevi	sapevate
ha saputo	hanno saputo	sapeva	sapevano

Future		Conditional	
saprò	sapremo	saprei	sapremmo
saprai	saprete	sapresti	sapreste
saprà	sapranno	saprebbe	saprebbero

Future Perfect		Past Conditional	
avrò saputo	avremo saputo	avrei saputo	avremmo saputo
avrai saputo	avrete saputo	avresti saputo	avreste saputo
avrà saputo	avranno saputo	avrebbe saputo	avrebbero saputo

Past Perfect		Subjunctive	
avevo saputo	avevamo saputo	sappia	sappiamo
avevi saputo	avevate saputo	sappia	sappiate
aveva saputo	avevano saputo	sappia	sappiano

Essential Italian

scegliere
to choose

io	noi
tu	voi
lui/lei/ Lei	loro/Loro

Present		Imperative	
scelgo	scegliamo		Scegliamo!
scegli	scegliete	Scegli!	Scegliete!
sceglie	scelgono	Scelga!	Scelgano!

Past		Imperfect	
ho scelto	abbiamo scelto	sceglievo	sceglievamo
hai scelto	avete scelto	sceglievi	sceglievate
ha scelto	hanno scelto	sceglieva	sceglievano

Future		Conditional	
sceglierò	sceglieremo	sceglierei	sceglieremmo
sceglierai	sceglierete	sceglieresti	scegliereste
sceglierà	sceglieranno	sceglierebbe	sceglierebbero

Future Perfect		Past Conditional	
avrò scelto	avremo scelto	avrei scelto	avremmo scelto
avrai scelto	avrete scelto	avresti scelto	avreste scelto
avrà scelto	avranno scelto	avrebbe scelto	avrebbero scelto

Past Perfect		Subjunctive	
avevo scelto	avevamo scelto	scelga	scegliamo
avevi scelto	avevate scelto	scelga	scegliate
aveva scelto	avevano scelto	scelga	scelgano

uscire
to go out

io	noi
tu	voi
lui/lei/ Lei	loro/Loro

Present		Imperative	
esco	usciamo		Usciamo!
esci	uscite	Esci!	Uscite!
esce	escono	Esca!	Escano!

Past		Imperfect	
sono uscito/a	siamo usciti/e	uscivo	uscivamo
sei uscito/a	siete usciti/e	uscivi	uscivate
è uscito/a	sono usciti/e	usciva	uscivano

Future		Conditional	
uscirò	usciremo	uscirei	usciremmo
uscirai	uscirete	usciresti	uscireste
uscirà	usciranno	uscirebbe	uscirebbero

Future Perfect		Past Conditional	
sarò uscito/a	saremo usciti/e	sarei uscito/a	saremmo usciti/e
sarai uscito/a	sarete usciti/e	saresti uscito/a	sareste usciti/e
sarà uscito/a	saranno usciti/e	sarebbe uscito/a	sarebbero usciti/e

Past Perfect		Subjunctive	
ero uscito/a	eravamo usciti/e	esca	usciamo
eri uscito/a	eravate usciti/e	esca	usciate
era uscito/a	erano usciti/e	esca	escano

vedere
to see

io	noi
tu	voi
lui/lei/ Lei	loro/Loro

Present

vedo	vediamo
vedi	vedete
vede	vedono

Imperative

	Vediamo!
Vedi!/Ve'!	Vedete!
Veda!	Vedano!

Past

ho visto	abbiamo visto
hai visto	avete visto
ha visto	hanno visto

Imperfect

vedevo	vedevamo
vedevi	vedevate
vedeva	vedevano

Future

vedrò	vedremo
vedrai	vedrete
vedrà	vedranno

Conditional

vedrei	vedremmo
vedresti	vedreste
vedrebbe	vedrebbero

Future Perfect

avrò visto	avremo visto
avrai visto	avrete visto
avrà visto	avranno visto

Past Conditional

avrei visto	avremmo visto
avresti visto	avreste visto
avrebbe visto	avrebbero visto

Past Perfect

avevo visto	avevamo visto
avevi visto	avevate visto
aveva visto	avevano visto

Subjunctive

veda	vediamo
veda	vediate
veda	vedano

venire
to come

io	noi
tu	voi
lui/lei/ Lei	loro/Loro

Present		Imperative	
vengo	veniamo		Veniamo!
vieni	venite	Vieni!	Venite!
viene	vengono	Venga!	Vengano!

Past		Imperfect	
sono venuto/a	siamo venuti/e	venivo	venivamo
sei venuto/a	siete venuti/e	venivi	venivate
è venuto/a	sono venuti/e	veniva	venivano

Future		Conditional	
verrò	verremo	verrei	verremmo
verrai	verrete	verresti	verreste
verrà	verranno	verrebbe	verrebbero

Future Perfect		Past Conditional	
sarò venuto/a	saremo venuti/e	sarei venuto/a	saremmo venuti/e
sarai venuto/a	sarete venuti/e	saresti venuto/a	sareste venuti/e
sarà venuto/a	saranno venuti/e	sarebbe venuto/a	sarebbero venuti/e

Past Perfect		Subjunctive	
ero venuto/a	eravamo venuti/e	venga	veniamo
eri venuto/a	eravate venuti/e	venga	veniate
era venuto/a	erano venuti/e	venga	vengano

volere
to want

io	noi
tu	voi
lui/lei/ Lei	loro/Loro

Present		Imperative	
voglio	vogliamo		vogliamo!
vuoi	volete	vogli!	vogliate!
vuole	vogliono	voglia!	vogliano!

Past		Imperfect	
ho voluto	abbiamo voluto	volevo	volevamo
hai voluto	avete voluto	volevi	volevate
ha voluto	hanno voluto	voleva	volevano

Future		Conditional	
vorrò	vorremo	vorrei	vorremmo
vorrai	vorrete	vorresti	vorreste
vorrà	vorranno	vorrebbe	vorrebbero

Future Perfect		Past Conditional	
avrò voluto	avremo voluto	avrei voluto	avremmo voluto
avrai voluto	avrete voluto	avresti voluto	avreste voluto
avrà voluto	avranno voluto	avrebbe voluto	avrebbero voluto

Past Perfect		Subjunctive	
avevo voluto	avevamo voluto	voglia	vogliamo
avevi voluto	avevate voluto	voglia	vogliate
aveva voluto	avevano voluto	voglia	vogliano

Glossary

Note that the following abbreviations will be used in this glossary: (m.) = masculine, (f.) = feminine, (inv.) = invariable, (sg.) = singular, (pl.) = plural, (fml.) = formal/polite, (infml.) = informal/familiar. If a word has two grammatical genders, (m./f.) or (f./m.) is used.

Italian-English

A

a *to, at, in, by*
  a + definite article *in the style of*
  A dopo. *See you later.*
  a tempo pieno *full-time*
  A presto. *See you soon.*
  a proposito *by the way*
  a proposito di ... *speaking of ...*
  a volte *sometimes*
abbastanza *fairly, enough*
abbigliamento (m.) *clothing*
  negozio (m.) di abbigliamento *clothing store*
abbondante *abundant, plentiful*
  cena (f.) abbondante *large dinner*
abbracciarsi *to hug*
abitabile *habitable*
  cucina (f.) abitabile *eat-in kitchen*
abitare *to live*
abito (m.) *suit (men's), dress (women's)*
  abito da uomo *men's suit*
accessorio (m.) *accessory*
accettare *to accept*
accettazione (f.) *reception desk*
accomodante *accommodating*
accompagnare *to accompany*
accordo (m.) *agreement*
  essere d'accordo *to agree*
  d'accordo *agreed, O.K.*
acqua (f.) *water*
  acqua minerale *mineral water*
  acqua minerale naturale *still mineral water*
  acqua minerale frizzante *sparkling mineral water*
adatto *appropriate*
addormentarsi *to fall asleep*

adesso *now*
adolescente (m./f.) *teenager*
adorabile *adorable*
adulto/a (m./f.) *adult*
aereo (m.) *airplane*
  in aereo *by plane*
aerobico *aerobic*
  fare ginnastica aerobica *to do aerobics*
aeroporto (m.) *airport*
affari (m. pl.) *business*
  uomo (m.) d'affari *businessman*
  donna (f.) d'affari *businesswoman*
affatto *completely*
  non ... affatto *not ... at all*
affermare *to claim*
affettare *to slice*
affettato (m.) *sliced cold meat*
  affettati misti *mixed cold cuts*
affinché *in order that, so that*
affittare *to rent*
affollato *crowded*
affrettato *fast, rushed*
affumicato *smoked*
agenzia (f.) *agency*
aggettivo (m.) *adjective*
aggiungere *to add*
agitarsi *to get nervous*
agosto (m.) *August*
aiutare *to help*
  aiutare a ... *to help ... ing*
aiutarsi *to help each other*
aiuto (m.) *help*
albergo (m.) *hotel*
albero (m.) *tree*
albicocca (f.) *apricot*
albicocco (m.) *apricot tree*
alcuni/e *a few, some*
alimentari (m. pl.) *groceries*

negozio (m.) di alimentari *grocery store*
alla brace *grilled/barbecued*
  carne alla brace *grilled/barbecued meat*
allegare *to attach*
  allegare un file *to attach a file*
  allegare un documento *to attach a document*
allegato (m.) *attachment*
allenatore/trice (m./f.) *coach*
alloggio (m.) *accommodation, apartment*
allora *then, well then, so*
alluce (m.) *big toe*
almeno *at least*
alpino *alpine*
  sci (m.) alpino *alpine skiing*
alternare *to alternate*
alto *tall*
altro *other*
  un altro/un'altra *another*
  tutti gli altri *everyone else*
alzarsi *to get up*
amaramente *bitterly*
amare *to love*
  Ti amo. *I love you.*
amaro *sour, bitter*
ambientazione (f.) *settings*
americano *American*
  futbol (m.) americano *American football*
amicizia (f.) *friendship*
  fare amicizia *to make friends*
amico (m.)/amici (m. pl.) *friend*
ammalato *ill, sick*
amore (m.) *love*
  storie (f. pl.) d'amore *love stories*
ampio *spacious, wide*
ananas (m. sg./pl.) *pineapple*
anche *also, too*
ancora *again, still, yet*
andare *to go*
  andare a … *to go … ing*
  andare a trovare *to go visit*
  andare in barca a vela *to sail*
  andare in bicicletta *to ride a bike*
  Andiamoci. *Let's go there.*
  Come va? *How's it going?*
  Va meglio. *It's better.*
  Va' avanti. *Go ahead.*
  Vacci. *Go there.*
anello (m.) *ring*

animale (m.) *animal*
anniversario (m.) *anniversary*
  Buon anniversario. *Happy anniversary.*
anno (m.) *year*
  anno scorso *last year*
  Ho … anni. *I am … years old.*
  Quanti anni hai? *How old are you?* (infml.)
  tutti gli anni *every year*
annoiarsi *to get bored*
anticipo (m.) *advance*
  essere in anticipo *to be early*
antico *ancient*
antipasto (m.) *appetizer*
antipatico *unfriendly*
antistress (m. sg./pl.) *anti-stress*
anzi *on the contrary*
aperitivo (m.) *aperitif*
aperto *open*
  all'aperto *outdoors*
apparecchiare *to set (a table)*
appartamento (m.) *apartment*
appena *just*
appetito (m.) *appetite*
  Buon appetito. *Enjoy your meal.*
apprendere *to learn*
appuntamento (m.) *appointment*
aprile (m.) *April*
aprire *to open*
  aprire un documento *to open a document*
  aprire un file *to open a file*
arabo *Arab*
aragosta (f.) *lobster*
arancia (f.) *orange (fruit)*
arancione (inv.) *orange (color)*
archeologico (m.)/archeologici (m.
  pl.) *archeological*
architetto (m.) *architect*
aria (f.) *air*
  aria condizionata *air conditioning*
armadietto (m.) *medicine cabinet*
armadio (m.) *closet, wardrobe*
aroma (m.) *aroma*
arrivare *to arrive*
  Arrivederci. *Good-bye* (infml.)
  ArrivederLa. *Good-bye* (sg. fml.)
arrosto *roast*
arte (f.) *art*
  arte moderna *modern art*

articolo (m.) *article*
artista (m./f.) *artist*
asciugamano (m.) *towel*
ascoltare *to listen to*
aspettare *to wait for*
asse (f.) *board*
  asse da stiro *ironing board*
assistente (m./f.) *assistant*
assolutamente *absolutely*
assorbire *to absorb*
astronauta (m./f.) *astronaut*
atleta (m./f.) *athlete*
attaccare *to attach*
attento *attentive, careful*
  Sta' attento! *Pay attention!/Be careful!/Watch*
    out!
attenzione (f.) *attention*
  fare attenzione *to pay attention*
attico (m.)/attici (m. pl.) *penthouse*
attività (f.)/attività (f. pl.) *activity*
attore (m.) *actor*
attorno *around*
  attorno a … *around …*
attrice (f.) *actress*
attuale *current*
autobus (m.) *bus*
automobile (f.) *car*
autore/trice (m./f.) *author*
autunno (m.) *fall*
  in/d'autunno *in the fall*
avanti *forward, before, ahead*
  Va' avanti. *Go ahead.*
avere *to have*
  avere bisogno di … *to need …*
  avere caldo *to be hot*
  avere freddo *to be cold*
  avere in comune *to share*
  avere fretta *to be in a hurry*
  avere la febbre *to have a fever*
  avere male a … *to have a pain in …*
  avere paura (di) *to be afraid (of)*
  avere ragione *to be right*
  avere sete *to be thirsty*
  avere sonno *to be sleepy*
  avere tempo *to have time*
  avere torto *to be wrong*
  avere un dolore a … *to have a pain in …*
  avere voglia di … *to feel like …*

  Ho … anni. *I am … years old.*
  Quanti anni hai? *How old are you?* (infml.)
avocado (m. sg./pl.) *avocado*
avvocato (m.) *lawyer*
azione (f.) *action*
  film (m. pl.) d'azione *action movies*

B

baciarsi *to kiss*
bagno (m.) *bathroom*
  costume (m.) da bagno *bathing trunks,*
    bathing suit
  fare il bagno *to take a bath*
  vasca (f.) (da bagno) *bath tub*
bagnoschiuma (m.) *bath gel*
ballare *to dance*
ballo (m.) *dance*
bambino/a (m./f.) *baby, child (from 0 to 10 years*
  old)
banana (f.) *banana*
banca (f.) *bank*
banchiere/a (m./f.) *banker*
bar (m.) *café*
barba (f.) *beard*
  crema (f.) da barba *shaving cream*
  farsi la barba *to shave*
barca (f.) *boat*
  andare in barca a vela *to sail*
barocco (m.) *baroque*
barzelletta (f.) *joke*
baseball (m.) *baseball*
basilico (m.) *basil*
basket (m.) *basketball*
basso *short, low*
bastare *to be enough*
  Basta così! *That's enough!*
beato *lucky*
  Beati voi. *Lucky you.* (pl.)
  Beato te! *Lucky you!* (sg. infml.)
Beh … *Well …*
beige (inv.) *beige*
bello *beautiful*
  bellissimo *very beautiful*
  Che bello! *How nice!/How beautiful!*
  Che bel piatto! *What a beautiful dish!*
  Fa bello. *It's beautiful. (weather)*
  fare bella figura *to make a good impression*
benché *although*

benda (f.) *bandage*
bene *well*
  (Sto) bene, grazie. *Fine, thanks.*
  Benissimo! *Wonderful!/Very well!*
  Molto bene, grazie. *Very well, thanks.*
  Va bene. *All right.*
Bentornato. *Welcome back.*
benvenuto *welcome*
bere *to drink*
  qualcosa da bere *something to drink*
bevanda (f.) *drink*
bianco *white*
  vino (m.) bianco *white wine*
bibita (f.) *soft drink, soda*
biblioteca (f.) *library*
bicchiere (m.) *glass*
bichini (m.) *bikini*
bici (f. sg./pl.) *bike*
bicicletta (f.) *bicycle*
  andare in bicicletta *to ride a bike*
biglietto (m.) *ticket*
biliardo (m.) *pool, billiards*
biologia (f.) *biology*
birra (f.) *beer*
bisogno (m.) *need*
  avere bisogno di … *to need …*
  essere nel bisogno *to need*
bistecca (f.) *beefsteak*
blu (inv.) *blue*
blue jeans (m. pl.) *jeans*
bocca (f.) *mouth*
  In bocca al lupo! *Break a leg! (lit. In the mouth of the wolf!)*
bocciare *to reject*
  essere bocciato *to fail (an exam)*
bollire *to boil*
bollitore (m.) *tea kettle*
borotalco (m.) *powder (talcum)*
borsa (f.) *bag, purse*
bosco (m.) *wood*
botte (f.) *cask*
bottiglia (f.) *bottle*
boutique (f.) *boutique*
braccialetto (m.) *bracelet*
braccio (m.) *arm*
  braccia (f. pl.) *arms*
braciola (f.) *chop*
  braciola di maiale *pork chop*

bravo *skillful, talented, nice*
broccolo (m.) *broccoli*
bruschetta (f.) *bruschetta*
brutto *ugly*
  Fa brutto. *It's bad. (weather)*
bucato (m.) *laundry*
  detersivo (m.) per il bucato *laundry detergent*
  fare il bucato *to do the laundry*
bugia (f.) *lie*
buono/buon (before masculine nouns except when they begin with the letter s followed by a consonant, or with the letter z) *good*
  Buon anniversario. *Happy anniversary.*
  Buon appetito. *Enjoy your meal.*
  Buon compleanno. *Happy birthday.*
  Buon giorno. *Good morning.*
  Buon Natale. *Merry Christmas.*
  Buon pomeriggio. *Good afternoon. (from 1 p.m. to 6 p.m.)*
  Buon riposo. *Have a good rest.*
  Buon viaggio. *Have a good trip.*
  Buona cena. *Enjoy your dinner./Have a good dinner.*
  Buona fortuna. *Good luck.*
  Buona giornata. *Have a good day.*
  Buona notte. *Good night.*
  Buona passeggiata. *Enjoy your walk./Have a good walk.*
  Buona sera. *Good evening.*
  Buona serata. *Have a good evening.*
  Buone feste. *Happy holidays.*
burro (m.) *butter*
business (m. sg./pl.) *business*

C

C'è … *There is …*
  C'è il sole. *It's sunny.*
  C'è nebbia. *It's foggy.*
  C'è un temporale. *It's stormy.*
  C'è vento. *It's windy.*
cachemire (m.) *cashmere*
  di cachemire *made out of cashmere*
cadere *to fall*
caffè (m. sg./pl.) *coffee, coffee shop*
caffetteria (f.) *coffee shop*
caffettiera (f.) *coffee maker (stovetop)*
calcio (m.) *soccer*
caldo (m.) *heat*

avere caldo *to be hot*
Fa caldo. *It's hot.*
calpestare *to tread on*
calze (f. pl.) *socks*
cambiare *to change*
  cambiare canale *to flip channels*
camera (f.) *room, bedroom, cabinet*
  camera da letto *bedroom*
  camera doppia *double room
    (two twin-size beds)*
  camera matrimoniale *double room
    (one queen-size bed)*
  camera singola *single room (one twin bed)*
cameriera (f.) *waitress*
cameriere (m.) *waiter*
camicetta (f.) *blouse*
camicia (f.) *shirt*
camminare *to walk*
  camminare in montagna *to go hiking*
campagna (f.) *countryside, country*
  in campagna *to the country*
campeggio (m.) *camping*
  fare il campeggio *to go camping*
campione/essa (m./f.) *champion*
campo (m.) *field*
canale (m.) *channel*
  cambiare canale *to flip channels*
cancellare *to delete*
candeggina (f.) *bleach*
canottiera (f.) *undershirt*
cantare *to sing*
canzone (f.) *song*
capacità (f. sg./pl.) *ability*
capelli (m. pl.) *hair*
capire *to understand*
capo/a (m./f.) *boss*
cappello (m.) *hat*
cappotto (m.) *coat (to the knees or longer)*
cappuccino (m.) *cappuccino*
carino *cute, pretty*
carne (f.) *meat*
  carne alla brace *grilled/barbecued meat*
caro *expensive*
carota (f.) *carrot*
carta (f.) *paper, card*
  carta di credito *credit card*
  carta igienica *toilet paper*
  giocare a carte *to play cards*

cartella (f.) *file*
cartina (f.) *map*
casa (f.) *house, home*
  a casa *at home*
  in giro per la casa *around the house*
casalinga (f.) *stay-at-home mom*
casalingo (m.) *stay-at-home dad*
caso (m.) *chance, case*
  in ogni caso *in any event*
  per caso *by any chance*
cassetto (m.) *drawer*
cattivo *naughty*
caviglia (f.) *ankle*
cavo (m.) *cable*
  cavo adsi *cable (dsl)*
cd rom (m.) *CD-ROM*
celebrare *to celebrate*
celibe (m.) *single (man)*
cellulare (m.) *cell phone*
cena (f.) *dinner*
Buona cena. *Enjoy your dinner./Have a good
  dinner.*
centimetro (m.) *centimeter*
cento *hundred*
centro (m.) *center*
  centro acquisti, centro
    commerciale *shopping mall*
  centro informazioni *information center*
  in centro *downtown, to/in the city*
cercare *to look for*
  cercare di … *to try to …*
cerimonia (f.) *ceremony*
cerotto (m.) *bandage*
certamente *certainly*
certo *some, a few*
certo/a (m./f.) *certain, certain ones*
cervello (m.) *brain*
cetriolo (m.) *cucumber*
chatroom (f.) *chatroom*
che *what* (question); *what, how* (exclamation);
  who, whom, which, that (relative pronoun); *that*
  (conjunction); *than* (comparative)
  Che bello! *How nice!/How beautiful!*
  Che cosa? *What?*
  Che ora è?/Che ore sono? *What time is it?*
  Che tempo fa? *What's the weather like?*
  meno … che *less … than*
  Non c'è di che. *Don't mention it.*

più ... che *more/-er ... than*
sia ... che *as/so ... as, both ... and*
chi *who* (question)*; he/she who, the one who,*
whoever (relative pronoun)
Di chi è ... ? *Whose ... is it ?*
Di chi sono ... ? *Whose ... are they?*
chiamare *to call, to telephone*
chiamarsi *to be named*
Mi chiamo ... *My name is ...*
Si chiama ... *His/Her name is ...*
chiaro (adjective) *clear*
chiaro (adverb), chiaramente *clearly*
chiedere *to ask, to ask for*
chiedere (un) consiglio *to ask for advice*
chiesa (f.) *church*
chilo (m.) *kilo*
chilometro *kilometer*
chimica (f.) *chemistry*
chimico (m. pl *chimici*) *chemical*
chitarra (f.) *guitar*
chiudere *to close*
chiudere un documento/file *to close a*
document/file
chiunque *anyone*
ci *us* (direct object pronoun)*; to us* (indirect object
pronoun)*; here, there; about/of/on it*
Andiamoci. *Let's go there.*
Arrivederci. *Good-bye* (infml.)
C'è ... *There is ...*
Ci penserò. *I'll think about it.*
Ci sono ... *There are ...*
Rieccoci! *Here we are again!*
Ciao. *Hi./Hello./Good-bye.*
Ciao ciao! *Bye-bye!*
ciascuno *each*
ciascuno/a (m./f.) *each one*
cibo (m.) *food*
ciclismo (m.) *biking*
cielo (m.) *sky*
ciglio (m.) *eyelash*
ciglia (f. pl.) *eyelashes*
Cina (f.) *China*
cinema (m. sg./pl.) *movie theater*
cinese (m.) *Chinese (language)*
parlare cinese *to speak Chinese*
cinquanta *fifty*
cinque *five*
tra cinque minuti *in five minutes*

cintura (f.) *belt*
ciotola (f.) *bowl*
cipolla (f.) *onion*
circa *about*
circo (m.) *circus*
città (f. sg./pl.) *city*
città natale *hometown*
fuori città *out of town*
in giro per la città *around town*
cittadina (f.) *town*
cittadinanza (f.) *citizenship*
civile *civil*
stato (m.) civile *marital status*
classe (f.) *classroom, class*
classico (m.)/classici (m. pl.) *classical*
musica (f.) classica *classical music*
cliente (m./f.) *customer*
clima (m.) *climate*
club (m. sg./pl.) *club*
colazione (f.) *breakfast*
fare colazione *to have breakfast*
collana (f.) *necklace*
collega (m./f.) *colleague*
collina (f.) *hill*
collo (m.) *neck*
colloquio (m.) *talk, conversation, interview*
colloquio di lavoro *job interview*
colonia (f.) *cologne*
coltello (m.) *knife*
coltivare *to grow*
comandare *to command*
come *how, as*
Com'è? *How is ... ?*
Come mi sta? *How do I look?*
Come sono? *How are ... ?*
Come sta? *How are you doing* (fml.)?
Come stai? *How are you doing* (infml.)?
Come va? *How's it going?*
così ... come *as/so ... as*
Ma come! *How's it possible!/How can this be!*
cominciare *to begin*
cominciare a ... *to begin to ...*
commedia (f.) *comedy*
commerciante (m./f.) *vendor*
commercio (m.) *business, commerce*
comodo *comfortable*
compagnia (f.) *company*
competenza (f.) *competence*

compiere *to complete*
compleanno (m.) *birthday*
  Buon compleanno. *Happy birthday.*
complimento (m.) *compliment*
  Complimenti! *Congratulations!*
comprare *to buy*
computer (m., pl.) *computer*
comune (m.) *common*
  avere in comune *to share*
comunità (f. sg./pl.) *community*
comunque *in any case*
con *with*
  con talento *talented*
concerto (m.) *concert*
condividere *to share*
condizionato *conditionin*
  aria (f.) condizionata *air conditioned*
condizione (f.) *condition, situation*
  a condizione che … *provided that …*
condominio (m.)/condomini (m. pl.) *apartment building*
confessare *to confess*
congiuntivo (m.) *subjunctive mood (grammar)*
  congiuntivo presente *present subjunctive*
conoscere *to know (a person), to meet (a person for the first time)*
conoscersi *to know each other*
consiglio (m.) *advice*
  chiedere (un) consiglio *to ask for advice*
contadino/a (m./f.) *farmer*
contare *to count*
contemporaneo *contemporary*
  romanzi (m. pl.) contemporanei *contemporary novels*
contento *happy*
  contento di … *happy to …*
continuare *to continue*
  orario (m.) continuato *open all day*
conto (m.) *check, bill*
contorno (m.) *side dish*
  di/per contorno *as a side dish*
controllare *to check*
convincere *to convince*
  convincere a … *to convince to …*
convinto *convinced*
coordinare *to coordinate*
coppia (f.) *couple*
corda (f.) *rope*

saltare la corda *to jump rope*
correre *to run*
corso (m.) *course*
cortile (m.) *back yard, courtyard*
corto *short*
cosa (f.) *thing*
  Che cosa? *What?*
  cose da fare *things to do*
  mille cose *tons of things, a thousand things*
  Tu cosa prendi? *What are you having?*
così *so*
  Basta così! *That's enough!*
  così … come *as/so … as*
  Così, così. *So so./Not bad.*
costa (f.) *coast, rib*
  di velluto a coste *made out of corduroy*
  velluto a coste *corduroy*
costare *to cost*
  Quanto costa? *How much does it cost?*
costo (m.) *cost*
  a tutti i costi *at all costs*
costoso *expensive*
costume (m.) *costume*
  costume da bagno *bathing trunks, bathing suit*
cotone (m.) *cotton*
cottura (f.) *cooking*
cravatta (f.) *tie*
credenza (f.) *cupboard*
credere *to believe*
  Non credo. *I don't think so.*
credito (m.) *credit*
  carta (f.) di credito *credit card*
crema (f.) *cream*
  crema da barba *shaving cream*
crescere *to grow, to raise*
croce (f.) *tail (of coin)*
  fare testa o croce *to flip a coin*
cucchiaio (m.) *spoon*
cucina (f.) *kitchen*
  cucina a gas *stove*
  cucina abitabile *eat-in kitchen*
  cucina elettrica *stove*
cucinare *to cook*
cugino/a (m./f.) *cousin*
cui *which, whom* (relative pronoun)
  il modo in cui … *the way in which …*
  la ragione/il motivo per cui … *the reason*

why ...
cultura (f.) *culture*
cuocere *to cook*
cuore (m.) *heart*
curare *to treat, to cure*
cuscino (m.) *pillow*

D

da *from, to, at, for, since*
  dal lunedì al venerdì *from Monday to Friday*
  dalle ... alle ... *from ... to ... (time periods)*
  dalle undici meno un quarto alle tre *from 10:45 a.m. to 3:00 p.m.*
dare *to give*
  dare una festa *to have a party*
data (f.) *date, day*
dati (m. pl.) *data*
  dati anagrafici *personal information*
davanti *in front*
  davanti a ... *in front of ...*
davvero *really*
debole *weak*
decidere *to decide*
  decidere di ... *to decide to ...*
decimo *tenth*
decollare *to take off*
delizioso *delicious*
denaro (m.) *money*
dente (m.) *tooth*
dentista (m./f.) *dentist*
deodorante (m.) *deodorant*
depresso *depressed*
descrivere *to describe*
deserto (m.) *desert*
desiderare *to want, to desire*
destra (f.)
  (a) destra *right, on the right, to the right*
determinare *to determine*
detersivo (m.) *detergent*
  detersivo per il bucato *laundry detergent*
  detersivo per i piatti *dishwashing detergent*
di *of, from, than*
  di + definite article *some, any*
  Di chi è ... ? *Whose ... is it?*
  Di chi sono ... ? *Whose ... are they?*
  Di dov'è? *Where are you from? (sg. fml.)/Where is he/she from?*
  Di dove sei? *Where are you from? (infml.)*

di legno *wooden*
di lei *her*
di lui *his*
di mattina *in the morning, from 4 to 11 a.m.*
di notte *at night, from midnight to 3 a.m*
di pomeriggio *in the afternoon, from 1 to 5 p.m.*
di sera *in the evening, from 6 to 11 p.m.*
di solito *usually*
È di ... *It belongs to ...*
È ora di ... *It's time to ...*
meno ... di *less ... than*
più ... di *more/-er ... than*
Sono di ... *I'm from ...*
dicembre (m.) *December*
diciannove *nineteen*
diciassette *seventeen*
diciotto *eighteen*
dieci *ten*
dietro *behind* (adv.)
differenza (f.) *difference*
difficile *difficult*
dimagrire *to lose weight*
dimenticare
  dimenticare di ... *to forget, to forget to ... (do something)*
diploma (m.) *diploma*
dire *to say, to tell*
  Non c'è di che. *Don't mention it.*
direttore (m.) *director*
diritto *straight*
  sempre diritto *straight ahead*
discorso (m.) *speech, talk*
discoteca (f.) *disco, club*
disoccupato/a (m./f.) *unemployed*
dispiacere *to displease, to upset*
  Mi dispiace. *I'm sorry.*
disponibile *available*
disponibilità (f.) *availability*
distruggere *to destroy*
dito (m.) *finger*
  dita (f. pl.) *fingers*
divano (m.) *sofa, couch*
diventare *to become*
diverso *different*
divertente *amusing, funny*
divertirsi *to have fun, to enjoy oneself*
divorziarsi *to get a divorce*

divorziarsi da ... *to divorce ... (someone)*
doccia (f.) *shower*
  fare la doccia *to take a shower*
docciaschiuma (m.) *bath gel*
documentario (m.) *documentary*
documento (m.) *document, file*
  allegare un documento *to attach a file*
  aprire un documento *to open a file*
  chiudere un documento *to close a file*
  inviare un documento *to send a file*
  salvare un documento *to save a file*
dodici *twelve*
dolce *sweet*
dolce (m.) *dessert*
dollaro (m.) *dollar*
  un milione di dollari *a million dollars*
dolore (m.) *pain*
  avere un dolore a ... *to have a pain in ...*
domanda (f.) *question*
  fare una domanda *to ask a question*
domani *tomorrow*
domenica (f.) *Sunday*
donna (f.) *woman*
  donna d'affari *businesswoman*
  donna poliziotto *police woman*
dopo *after*
  A dopo. *See you later.*
doppio *double*
  camera (f.) doppia *double room (two twin-size beds)*
dormire *to sleep*
  farsi una bella dormita *to take a nice long nap*
dottore/essa (m./f.) *doctor*
dove *where*
  Di dov'è? *Where are you from?* (sg. fml.)/*Where is he/she from?*
  Di dove sei? *Where are you from?* (infml.)
  Dov'è ... ? *Where is ... ?*
  Dove sono ... ? *Where are ... ?*
dovere *must, to have to*
dovuto *due*
  dovuto a ... *due to ...*
dramma (m.) *drama*
dubitare *to doubt*
due *two*
  due ore e mezzo *two and a half hours*
  duemila *two thousand*
  Sono le due. *It's two (o'clock).*

dunque *therefore*
durare *to last*
dvd (m.) *DVD player*

E

e/ed (before a vowel) *and*
  ... e Lei? *... and you?* (sg. fml.)
  ... e tu? *... and you?* (infml.)
eccellente *excellent*
eccetto *except*
eccezionale *exceptional*
ecco *here*
  Ecco ... *Here is ...*
economia (f.) *economics*
edificio (m.) *building*
elegante *elegant*
elegantemente *elegantly*
elementare *elementary*
  la prima elementare *the first grade at elementary school*
elettricista (m.) *electrician*
elettrico *electric*
  cucina (f.) elettrica *electric stove*
elettrocardiogramma (m.) *electrocardiogram*
elettronica (f.) *electronics*
  negozio (m.) di elettronica *electronics store*
eliminare *to delete*
email (f.)/mail (inv.) *e-mail*
  mandare un'email/una mail *to send an e-mail*
enorme *enormous*
entrambi/e *both (of them)*
entrare *to come in*
entusiasticamente *enthusiastically*
erba (f.) *grass*
erboristeria (f.) *herbalist's shop*
ereditare *to inherit*
esagerare *to exaggerate, to go too far*
esagerato *exaggerated*
esame (m.) *exam*
escursione (f.) *hike, excursion*
  fare un'escursione *to go hiking*
esistere *to exist*
esperienza (f.) *experience*
esperto/a (m./f.) *expert*
essere *to be*
  C'è ... *There is ...*
  C'è il sole. *It's sunny.*

C'è nebbia. *It's foggy.*
C'è un temporale. *It's stormy.*
C'è vento. *It's windy.*
Ci sono … *There are …*
Di chi è … ? *Whose … is it ?*
Di chi sono … ? *Whose … are they?*
È di … *It belongs to …*
È l'una di notte. *It's 1:00 a.m.*
È nuvoloso. *It's cloudy.*
È ora di … *It's time to …*
essere bocciato *to fail*
essere d'accordo *to agree*
essere impauriti *to be afraid of*
essere in anticipo *to be early*
essere in cerca di … *to be looking for …*
essere in orario *to be on time*
essere in ritardo *to be late*
essere in sovrappeso *to be overweight*
essere nel bisogno *to need*
essere puntuale *to be on time*
essere promosso *to pass*
Sono di … *I'm from …*
estate (f.) *summer*
  d'estate *in the summer*
estero *foreign*
  all'estero *abroad*
  viaggiare all'estero *to travel abroad*
età (f./f/ pl.) *age*
euro (m. sg./pl.) *euro*
Europa (f.) *Europe*
europeo *European*
extra (inv.) *extra*

F

fa *ago*
  due giorni fa *two days ago*
  un mese fa *a month ago*
fabbrica (f.) *factory*
faccia (f.) *face*
facile *easy*
falegname (m.) *carpenter*
falso *false*
fame (f.) *hunger*
  avere fame *to be hungry*
famiglia (f.) *family*
  famiglia numerosa *large family*
famoso *famous*
fantastico (m.)/fantastici (m. pl.) *fantastic*

fare *to do, to make, to be*
  Che tempo fa? *What's the weather like?*
  Fa bello. *It's beautiful. (weather)*
  Fa brutto *It's bad. (weather)*
  Fa caldo. *It's hot.*
  Fa freddo. *It's cold.*
  Fammi vedere. *Let me see.*
  fare amicizia *to make friends*
  fare attenzione *to pay attention*
  fare bella figura *to make a good impression*
  fare colazione *to have breakfast*
  fare giardinaggio *to do gardening*
  fare ginnastica *to exercise*
  fare ginnastica aerobica *to do aerobics*
  fare il bagno *to take a bath*
  fare il bucato *to do the laundry*
  fare il campeggio *to go camping*
  fare il footing *to jog*
  fare il trasloco *to move (to a new house)*
  fare la doccia *to take a shower*
  fare il bucato *to do the laundry*
  fare la spesa/le spese *to go shopping, to do grocery shopping*
  fare le valige *to pack (a suitcase)*
  fare pari *to draw, to tie*
  fare paura *to be scary*
  fare rumore *to make noise*
  fare spese *to shop*
  fare sport *to practice sports*
  fare testa o croce *to flip a coin*
  fare un'escursione *to go hiking*
  fare un giro *to go for a walk/ride*
  fare un giro a piedi *to go for a walk*
  fare un pisolino *to take a nap*
  fare un viaggio *to take a trip*
  fare una domanda *to ask a question*
  fare una foto/fotografia *to take a picture*
  fare una gita *to take a trip*
  fare una passeggiata *to take a walk*
  fare una pausa *to take a break*
  fare una vacanza *to go on a vacation*
  fare vedere *to show*
farmacia (f.) *drugstore, pharmacy*
farsi *to get, to become*
  farsi la barba *to shave*
  farsi una bella dormita *to take a nice long nap*
  farsi una bella mangiata *to have a nice big meal*

fatto (m.) *fact*
fattore (m.) *factor*
favola (f.) *fairy tale*
favore (m.) *favor*
  Per favore. *Please.*
fax (m. sg./pl.) *fax machine*
febbraio (m.) *February*
febbre (f.) *fever*
  avere la febbre *to have a fever*
fegato (m.) *liver*
felice *happy*
femmina (f.) *female*
ferie (f. pl.) *vacation*
  in ferie *on vacation*
fermarsi *to stop*
ferro (m.) *iron (metal)*
  ferro da stiro *iron (appliance)*
festa (f.) *party, holiday*
  Buone feste. *Happy holidays.*
  dare una festa *to have a party*
fettina (f.) *thin slice*
fettuccine (f. pl.) *fettuccine*
fiaba (f.) *fairy tale*
fianco (m.) *hip*
fidanzato *engaged*
fidanzato/a (m./f.) *fiancé(e)*
fiera (f.) *trade fair*
figlia (f.) *daughter*
  figlia di mia moglie (di mio
    marito) *stepdaughter*
figlio (m.) *son*
  figlio di mia moglie (di mio marito) *stepson*
figura (f.) *figure, illustration*
  fare bella figura *to make a good impression*
file (m.) *file*
  allegare un file *to attach a file*
  aprire un file *to open a file*
  chiudere un file *to close a file*
  inviare un file *to send a file*
film (m. sg./pl.) *movie, film*
  film d'azione *action movies*
finalista (m./f.) *finalist*
finalmente *finally*
finché *until*
fine settimana (m. sg./pl.) *weekend*
finestra (f.) *window*
finire *to finish*
  finire di ... *to finish ... ing*

per finire *to end/finish*
fino (a) *up to, until, till*
  fino a tardi *until late*
  fino in fondo *until the end*
fiore (m.) *flower*
Firenze (f.) *Florence*
fisso *fixed, permanent*
  lavoro (m.) fisso *steady job*
fiume (m.) *river*
follia (f.) *folly*
fondo *bottom*
  di fondo *long distance*
  fino in fondo *until the end*
  in fondo a ... *the bottom/end of ...*
  sci (m.) di fondo *cross-country skiing*
footing (m.) *jogging*
  fare il footing *to jog*
foresta (f.) *forest*
forma (f.) *form, shape*
  in ottima forma *in great shape*
formaggio (m.) *cheese*
formazione (f.) *training, education*
forno (m.) *oven*
  forno a microonde *microwave oven*
  maiale (m.) al forno *roast pork*
forse *maybe, perhaps*
forte (adjective) *strong*
forte (adverb) *loudly*
fortuna (f.) *luck*
  Buona fortuna. *Good luck.*
fortunato *lucky*
foto (f. sg./pl.) *photograph*
  fare una foto *to take a picture*
fotografia (f.) *photograph, photography*
  fare una fotografia *to take a picture*
foulard (m.) *scarf (square)*
fra *between, among, in*
  fra ... e ... *between ... and ...*
  fra mezz'ora *in half an hour*
  fra tre quarti d'ora *in forty-five minutes*
fragola (f.) *strawberry*
francamente *frankly*
francese *French*
fratello (m.) *brother*
frattempo *meantime*
  nel frattempo *in the meantime*
freddo (m.) *cold*
  avere freddo *to be cold*

Fa freddo. *It's cold.*
frequentare *to attend*
fresco *fresh*
fretta (f.) *hurry*
  avere fretta *to be in a hurry*
  in fretta *in a hurry, quickly*
frigorifero (m.) (frigo) *refrigerator*
fronte (f.) *forehead*
  di fronte *opposite*
  di fronte a... *facing... , in front of...*
frullatore (m.) *blender*
frutta (f.) *fruit*
  frutta fresca *fresh fruit*
fucsia (inv.) *fuchsia*
fulmine (m.) *lightning*
fungo (m.) *mushroom*
fuori *outside*
  fuori città *out of town*
futbol (m.) *football*
  futbol americano *American football*

G

gabinetto *toilet*
galleria (f.) *gallery*
gamba (f.) *leg*
  in gamba *talented* (colloquial)
gamberetto (m.) *shrimp*
gambero (m.) *shrimp, crawfish*
gara (f.) *event*
garage (m. sg./pl.) *garage*
gas (m. sg./pl.) *gas*
  cucina (f.) a gas *gas stove*
gelato (m.) *ice cream*
generale *general*
genetico (m.)/genetici (m. pl.) *genetic*
genitore (m.)/genitrice (f.)/genitori (pl.) *parent*
gennaio (m.) *January*
gente (f.) *people*
gentile *kind*
Germania (f.) *Germany*
ghiaccio (m.) *ice*
hockey (m.) su ghiaccio *ice hockey*
già *already*
giacca (f.) *jacket*
giaccone (m.) *coat (above the knees)*
giallo *yellow*
giardinaggio (m.) *gardening*
fare giardinaggio *to do gardening*

giardino (m.) *garden*
ginnastica (f.) *gymnastics*
  fare ginnastica *to exercise*
  fare ginnastica aerobica *to do aerobics*
  scarpe (f. pl.) da ginnastica *sneakers*
ginocchio (m.) *knee*
  ginocchia (f. pl.)/ginocchi (m. pl.) *knees*
giocare *to play*
  giocare a carte *to play cards*
  giocare a tennis *to play tennis*
giocatore/trice (m./f.) *player*
giornale (m.) *newspaper*
giornale radio (m.) *news (on the radio)*
giornalista (m./f.) *journalist*
giornata (f.) *day*
  Buona giornata. *Have a good day.*
  giornata piena *full/busy day*
giorno (m.) *day*
  Buon giorno. *Good morning.*
  due giorni fa *two days ago*
  fra qualche giorno *in a few days*
  pochi giorni *a few days*
  tutti i giorni *every day*
giovane *young*
giovedì (m. sg./pl.) *Thursday*
girare *to turn*
giro (m.) *circle, tour*
  fare un giro *to go for a walk/ride*
  fare un giro a piedi *to go for a walk*
  in giro per la casa *around the home*
  in giro per la città *around town*
gita (f.) *day trip, short trip*
  fare una gita *to take a trip*
giugno (m.) *June*
giusto (adjective) *right, correct*
giusto (adverb) *exactly, correctly*
gli *the* (m. pl.) *(in front of s + consonant, z, ps, gn, in front of vowels); to him, to it, to them* (indirect object pronoun)
gnomo (m.) *gnome*
gomito (m.) *elbow*
gonna (f.) *skirt*
grado (m.) *degree*
grande *big*
  grande magazzino (m.) *department store*
grandinare *to hail*
  Grandina. *It's hailing.*
grasso (adjective) *fat*

grasso (m.) *fat*
grattugiare *to grate*
grave *serious*
Grazie. *Thank you.*
  Grazie mille. *Thanks a lot.*
  Molto bene, grazie. *Very well, thanks.*
Grecia (f.) *Greece*
greco *Greek*
grigio *gray*
griglia (f.) *grill*
  pesce (m.) alla griglia *grilled fish*
grosso *large, thick*
gruppo (m.) *group, band (music)*
  gruppi (pl.) inglesi *British bands*
guadagnare *to earn*
guancia (f.) *cheek*
guanti (m. pl.) *gloves*
guardare *to watch, to look at*
  guardare la tivù/tele/televisione *to watch television*
  guardare lo sport in/alla televisione *to watch sports on TV*
guida (f.) *guide*
guidare *to drive*

H

hobby (m./m. pl) *hobby*
hockey (m.) *hockey*
  hockey su ghiaccio *ice hockey*
hotel (m. sg./pl.) *hotel*

I

i *the* (m. pl.) (in front of consonants)
idea (f.) *idea*
  nessuna idea *no idea*
idraulico/a (m./f.) *plumber*
ieri *yesterday*
  ieri sera *last night*
igienico *hygienic*
  carta (f.) igienica *toilet paper*
il *the* (m. sg.) (in front of a consonant)
immaginare *to imagine*
imparare *to learn*
impaurire *to scare*
  essere impauriti da *to be afraid of*
impegnato *busy*
impegno (m.) *obligation, engagement*
imperfetto (m.) *imperfect*

impiegato/a (m./f.) *employee, clerk*
importante *important*
imprenditore (m.) *businessman*
imprenditrice (f.) *businesswoman*
improvvisamente *suddenly*
in *in, at, to, on, by*
  in centro *downtown, to/in the city*
  in gamba *talented* (colloquial)
  in giro per la casa *around the home*
  in giro per la città *around town*
  in vacanza *on vacation*
incontrare *to meet (a person casually)*
incontrarsi *to meet each other*
incrocio (m.) *intersection*
indagine (f.) *study, research*
indeciso *undecided*
indicare *to show, to indicate*
indirizzo (m.) *address*
indossare *to wear*
infarto (m.) *heart attack*
infatti *in fact*
infermiere/a (m./f.) *nurse*
influenza (f.) *influence*
informatica (f.) *computer science*
informatico (adjective) *computer*
ingegnere (m.) *engineer*
inglese *English*
  gruppi (m. pl.) inglesi *British bands (music)*
inglese (m.) *English (language)*
ingrassare *to gain weight*
ingrediente (m.) *ingredient*
ingresso (m.) *hall*
innamorato *in love*
inoltrare *to forward*
inoltre *besides, moreover*
insalata (f.) *salad*
  insalata mista *mixed salad*
insegnante (m./f.) *teacher*
insegnare *to teach*
insieme *together*
  insieme a te *(together) with you*
insistere *to insist*
insonnolito *sleepy*
intellettivo *intellectual*
  quoziente (m.) intellettivo *intelligence quotient (IQ)*
intelligente *intelligent*
interessante *interesting*

interessantissimo *very interesting*
interessare *to interest*
interesse (m.) *interest*
internet (m.) *internet*
intero *whole, entire*
interrompere *to interrupt*
intervallo (m.) *intermission*
intervista (f.) *interview*
   interviste (pl.) alla televisione *talk show*
intestino (m.) *intestine*
intorno *around*
   intorno a mezzanotte *around midnight*
   intorno al mondo *around the world*
invecchiare *to grow old*
invece *instead*
invernale (adjective) *winter*
inverno (m.) *winter*
   d'inverno *in winter*
inviare *to send*
   inviare un file/documento *to send a file/ document*
invitare *to invite*
io *I*
iscrivere *to enroll*
isola (f.) *island*
istituto (m.) *institute*
   istituto tecnico *professional school*
istruzione (f.) *education*
Italia (f.) *Italy*
italiano *Italian*

L

l' *the* (m. sg./f. sg.) (in front of a vowel)
la *the* (f. sg.) (in front of a consonant); *her, it* (direct object pronoun)
La *you* (sg. fml.) (direct object pronoun)
lago (m.) *lake*
   al lago *at the lake*
lampada (f.) *lamp*
lampeggiare *to flash*
lampione (m.) *lamp post*
lampo (m.) *lightning*
lana (f.) *wool*
lasagne (f. pl.) *lasagna*
lasciare *to leave, to let*
latinoamericano *Latin American*
latte (m.) *milk*
lattina (f.) *can*

lattuga (f.) *lettuce*
laurea (f.) *degree, university degree*
laurearsi *to graduate*
lavabiancheria (f.) *washing machine*
lavabo (m.) *sink (wash basin)*
lavanderia (f.) *laundry*
lavandino (m.) *sink (kitchen)*
lavapiatti (f.) *dishwasher*
lavare *to wash*
   lavare i piatti *to do the dishes*
lavarsi *to wash oneself*
lavastoviglie (f.) *dishwasher*
lavatrice (f.) *washing machine*
lavorare *to work*
lavoro (m.) *job, work*
   Che lavoro fai? *What do you do?*
   colloquio (m.) di lavoro *job interview*
   lavoro fisso *steady job*
   lavoro part-time *part-time job*
   lavoro temporaneo *summer job*
   per lavoro *on business*
le *the* (f. pl.) (in front of consonants and vowels); *them* (f.) (direct object pronoun); *to her, to it* (indirect object pronoun)
Le *to you* (sg. fml.) (indirect object pronoun)
leggere *to read*
leggero *light*
legno (m.) *wood*
   di legno *wooden*
lei *she* (subject pronoun); *her, it* (direct object, disjunctive pronoun)
   a lei *to her, to it* (indirect object, disjunctive pronoun)
Lei *you* (sg. fml.) (subject pronoun); *you* (sg. fml.) (direct object, disjunctive pronoun)
   a Lei *to you* (sg. fml.) (indirect object, disjunctive pronoun)
lentamente *slowly*
lenzuolo (m.) *bed sheet*
   lenzuola (f. pl.) *bed sheets*
lettera (f.) *letter*
letteratura (f.) *literature*
letto (m.) *bed*
   camera (f.) da letto *bedroom*
   letto matrimoniale *double bed*
   stanza (f.) da letto *bedroom*
lettore (m.) *reader, player*
   lettore cd *CD-ROM drive*

lettore cd-rom *CD-ROM drive*
lettore di cd *CD player*
lezione (f.) *lesson*
li *them* (m.) (direct object pronoun)
lì *there*
  lì vicino *near there*
libero *free*
  tempo (m.) libero *free time*
libreria (f.) *bookstore, bookcase (in a house or office)*
libro (m.) *book*
  libro (di testo) *textbook*
liceo (m.) *high school*
lingua (f.) *language, tongue*
  lingua straniera *foreign language*
lino (m.) *linen*
  di lino *made out of linen*
lista (f.) *list*
  lista dei vini *wine list*
litro (m.) *liter*
livello (m.) *level*
lo *the* (m. sg.) (in front of s + consonant, z, ps, gn); *him, it* (direct object pronoun)
  Lo so. *I know.*
  Non lo so. *I don't know.*
lontano (adjective) *distant*
lontano (adverb) *far*
loro *they* (subject pronoun); *them* (direct object, disjunctive pronoun)
  a loro *to them* (indirect object, disjunctive pronoun)
Loro *you* (pl. fml.) (subject pronoun)
loro (inv.) *their*
lotteria (f.) *lottery*
luglio (m.) *July*
lui *he* (subject pronoun); *him, it* (direct object, disjunctive pronoun)
  a lui *to him, to it* (indirect object, disjunctive pronoun)
luna (f.) *moon*
lunedì (m. sg./pl.) *Monday*
  il lunedì *on Mondays*
lungo (adjective) *long*
lungo (preposition) *along*
luogo (m.) *place*
lupo (m.) *wolf*
  In bocca al lupo! *Break a leg! (lit. In the mouth of the wolf!)*

Crepi il lupo. *Thank you. (In response to In bocca al lupo! Lit. May the wolf die.)*

M

ma *but*
  Ma come! *How's it possible!/How can this be!*
macchina (f.) *car, machine*
  in macchina *by car*
  macchina del caffè *espresso machine*
  macchina fotografica *camera*
macelleria (f.) *butcher shop*
madre (f.) *mother*
  marito (m.) di mia madre *stepfather*
maestro/a (m./f.) *teacher (nursery school and elementary school)*
magari *I wish, perhaps*
magazzino (m.) *warehouse*
  grande magazzino *department store*
maggio (m.) *May*
maggiore *older, elder*
maglietta (f.) *T-shirt*
maglioncino (m.) *light sweater*
maglione (m.) *sweater*
Magro *thin*
mai *ever, never (in negative sentences)*
  Mai! *Never!*
  mai più *never again*
maiale (m.) *pork*
  braciola (f.) di maiale *pork chop*
  maiale al forno *roast pork*
malato *sick*
malattia (f.) *disease*
male *badly*
  avere male a … *to have a pain in …*
  Fa male. *It hurts.*
mamma (f.) *mom*
manca (f.) *left (hand)*
  Manca un quarto alle quattro. *It's 3:45.*
mancia (f.) *tip*
mancino *left-handed*
mandare *to send*
  mandare un'email *to send an e-mail*
mangiare *to eat*
  farsi una bella mangiata *to have a nice big meal*
mano (f.)/mani (f. pl.) *hand*
manzo (m.) *beef*
mappa (f.) *map*

maratona (f.) *marathon*
marciapiede (m.) *sidewalk*
mare (m.) *sea, seaside*
  al mare *at the beach*
marito (m.) *husband*
  figlia (f.) di mia moglie (di mio
    marito) *stepdaughter*
  figlio (m.) di mia moglie (di mio
    marito) *stepson*
  marito di mia madre *stepfather*
marrone *brown*
martedì (m. sg./pl.) *Tuesday*
marzo (m.) *March*
maschio (m.) *male*
matematica (f.) *math*
materia (f.) *subject*
matrimoniale *matrimonial*
  camera (f.) matrimoniale *double room (one
    queen-size bed)*
  letto (m.) matrimoniale *double bed*
matrimonio (m.) *wedding*
mattina (f.) *morning*
  di mattina *in the morning, from 4 to 11 a.m.*
  Sono le undici e un quarto di mattina.
    It's 11:15 a.m.
  tutte le mattine *every morning*
maturità (f.) *high school degree*
me *me* (direct object, disjunctive pronoun)
  a me *to me* (indirect object, disjunctive pronoun)
meccanico (m.)/meccanici (m. pl.) *mechanic*
media (f.) *average*
medicina (f.) *medicine*
medico (m.) *medical doctor*
meglio (adverb) *better, the best*
  Va meglio. *It's better.*
meglio (inv.) *better*
mela (f.) *apple*
melanzana (f.) *eggplant*
melone (m.) *melon*
memoria (f.) *memory*
meno *less*
  a meno che ... non *unless ...*
  meno ... di/che *less ... than*
  Sono le quattro meno un quarto. *It's 3:45.*
mento (m.) *chin*
mentre *while*
menù (m.) *menu*
meraviglioso *wonderful, marvelous*

mercato (m.) *market*
mercoledì (m. sg./pl.) *Wednesday*
mescolare *to mix*
mese (m.) *month*
  mese prossimo *next month*
  un mese fa *a month ago*
messaggio (m.) *message*
  messaggio immediato *instant message*
messinscena (f.) *production (theater)*
mettersi *to put on*
  Si mette ... *He/She wears/puts on ...*
metrò (m. in Milan/f. in Rome) *subway, metro*
metro (m.) *meter*
mettere *to put*
  mettere in ordine *to put things away*
  metterci *to take (time)*
mezzanotte (f.) *midnight*
  È mezzanotte. *It's midnight.*
  intorno a mezzanotte *around midnight*
mezzo *half, half hour*
  alle sette e mezza *at seven thirty (7:30)*
  due ore e mezzo *two and a half hours*
  fra mezz'ora *in half an hour*
  mezze stagioni *half seasons (spring and fall)*
mezzo (m.) *means*
  mezzo di trasporto *means of transportation*
mezzogiorno (m.) *noon*
  È mezzogiorno. *It's noon.*
mi *me* (direct object pronoun); *to me* (indirect
  object pronoun)
  Mi chiamo ... *My name is ...*
  Mi dispiace. *I'm sorry.*
  Mi piace/piacciono ... (sg./pl.) *I like ...*
microonda (f.) *microwave*
  forno (m.) a microonde *microwave oven*
miele (m.) *honey*
migliore (adjective) *better, the best*
Milano (f.) *Milan*
miliardo (m.)/miliardi (m. pl.) *billion*
milione (m.)/milioni (m. pl.) *million*
  un milione di dollari *a million dollars*
mille (m.)/mila (m. pl.) *thousand*
  duemila *two thousand*
  Grazie mille. *Thanks a lot.*
  mille cose (f. pl.) *tons of things,
    a thousand things*
minerale *mineral*
  acqua (f.) minerale *mineral water*

acqua minerale naturale *still mineral water*
acqua minerale frizzante *sparkling*
   mineral water
minestra (f.) *soup*
minore *younger*
minuto (m.) *minute*
   tra cinque minuti *in five minutes*
mio *my*
   figlia (f.) di mia moglie (di mio
      marito) *stepdaughter*
   figlio (m.) di mia moglie (di mio
      marito) *stepson*
   marito (m.) di mia madre *stepfather*
   (la mia) ragazza (f.) *(my) girlfriend*
   (il mio) ragazzo (m.) *(my) boyfriend*
   moglie (f.) di mio padre *stepmother*
   Piacere mio. *Pleased to meet you, too.*
misto *mixed*
   affettati (m. pl.) misti *mixed cold cuts*
   insalata (f.) mista *mixed salad*
misura (f.) *size (shirts)*
misurare *to measure*
mobili (m. pl.) *furniture*
moda (f.) *fashion*
   sfilata (f.) di moda *fashion show*
modello/a (m./f.) *model (fashion)*
modem (m.) *modem*
moderno *modern*
   arte moderna *modern art*
modo (m.) *way, manner*
   il modo in cui … *the way in which …*
moglie (f.) *wife*
molto (adjective) *much, many, a lot of*
   molto tempo *long time*
molto (adverb) *very*
   Molto bene, grazie. *Very well, thanks.*
   Molto piacere! *Very pleased to meet you!*
molto/a (m./f.) (noun) *much, many, a lot*
momento (m.) *moment*
   in questo momento *right now*
   Un momento. *Wait a second.*
mondo (m.) *world*
   del mondo *in the world*
   intorno al mondo *around the world*
monitor (m.) *monitor, screen*
montagna (f.) *mountain*
   camminare in montagna *to go hiking*
   in montagna *to the mountains*

monumento (m.) *monument*
moquette (f.) *carpet (wall-to-wall)*
morire *to die*
moschea (f.) *mosque*
mostra (f.) *exhibition*
mostrare *to show*
motivo (m.) *reason*
   il motivo per cui … *the reason why …*
moto (f. sg./pl.) *motorbike*
motocicletta (f.) *motorbike*
mouse (m.) (computer) *mouse*
municipio (m.) *city hall, municipal building*
muovere *to move*
muratore/trice (m./f.) *construction worker*
muro (m.) *wall*
muscolo (m.) *muscle*
museo (m.) *museum*
musica (f.) *music*
   musica classica *classical music*
   musica pop *pop music*
musicista (m./f.) *musician*
mutande (f. pl.) *boxers*
mutandine (f. pl.) *underpants (women's)*

N

Napoli (f.) *Naples*
nascere *to be born*
nascita (f.) *birth*
naso (m.) *nose*
natale *native*
   città (f.) natale *hometown*
Natale (m.) *Christmas*
   Buon Natale. *Merry Christmas.*
natura (f.) *nature*
naturale *natural*
   acqua (f.) minerale naturale *still mineral water*
ne *about it/them, of it/them*
   Ce ne sono tre. *There are three of them.*
neanche *not even*
nebbia (f.) *fog*
   C'è nebbia. *It's foggy.*
necessario *necessary*
negozio (m.) *store*
   negozio di abbigliamento *clothing store*
   negozio di alimentari *grocery store*
   negozio di elettronica *electronics store*
   negozio di scarpe *shoe store*
nemmeno *not even*

nero *black*

nervoso *nervous*

nessuno *no*

   nessuna idea *no idea*

nessuno/a (m./f.) *none, nobody*

neve (f.) *snow*

nevicare *to snow*

   Nevica. *It's snowing.*

niente *nothing*

   niente di buono da mangiare *nothing good
   to eat*

nipote (m./f.) *nephew, niece, grandson,
   granddaughter*

no *no*

nocivo *harmful*

noi *we* (subject pronoun); *us* (direct object,
   disjunctive pronoun)

   a noi *to us* (indirect object, disjunctive pronoun)

noioso *boring*

nome (m.) *name*

non *not*

   Non c'è di che. *Don't mention it.*

   Non lo so. *I don't know.*

nonna (f.) *grandmother*

nonno (m.) *grandfather*

nono *ninth*

normale *normal*

normalmente *normally*

norvegese (m./f.) *Norwegian*

nostro *our*

notare *to notice*

notizie (f. pl.) *news*

notte (f.) *night*

   Buona notte. *Good night.*

   di notte *at night, from midnight to 3 a.m.*

   È l'una di notte. *It's 1:00 a.m.*

novanta *ninety*

nove *nine*

novembre (m.) *November*

nubile (f.) *single (woman)*

nulla *nothing*

numero (m.) *number, size (shoes)*

numeroso *numerous, large (family)*

   famiglia (f.) numerosa *large family*

nuotare *to swim*

nuoto (m.) *swimming*

nuovo *new*

   di nuovo *again*

nuvola (f.) *cloud*

nuvoloso *cloudy*

   È nuvoloso. *It's cloudy.*

O

O *or*

occhiali (m. pl.) *eyeglasses*

   occhiali da sole *sunglasses*

occhio (m.) *eye*

occupato *busy*

oceano (m.) *ocean*

offrire *to offer*

oggi *today*

ogni *each, every*

   in ogni caso *in any event*

   ogni volta *every time*

ognuno/a (m./f.) *everyone*

olio (m.) *oil*

oliva (f.) *olive*

ombrello (m.) *umbrella*

omeopatia (f.) *homeopathy*

omeopatico (m.)/omeopatici (m.
   pl.) *homeopathic*

opera (f.) *work, opera*

   opere d'arte *works of art*

operaio/a (m./f.) *worker*

opuscolo (m.) *brochure*

ora (f.) *hour*

   Che ora è?/Che ore sono? *What time is it?*

   due ore e mezzo *two and a half hours*

   È ora di … *It's time to …*

   fra mezz'ora *in half an hour*

orario (m.) *time*

   essere in orario *to be on time*

   orario continuato *open all day*

   orario ridotto *shorter working hours*

ordinare *to order*

ordine (m.) *order*

   mettere in ordine *to put things away*

orecchini (m. pl.) *earrings*

orecchio (m.) *ear*

   orecchi (m. pl.)/orecchie (f. pl.) *ears*

organizzare *to organize*

   viaggio (m.) organizzato *guided tour*

ormai *by now, almost*

orologio (m.) *watch*

orto (m.) *vegetable garden, orchard*

ospedale (m.) *hospital*

ospite (m./f.) *guest (male and female)*
osso (m.) *bone*
  ossa (f. pl.) *bones*
ossobuco (m.) *osso buco*
ostello (m.) *youth hostel*
ottanta *eighty*
ottavo *eighth*
ottimo *excellent*
  in ottima forma *in great shape*
otto *eight*
ottobre (m.) *October*
ovvio *obvious*

P

padre (m.) *father*
  moglie (f.) di mio padre *stepmother*
paese (m.) *town (small), village*
paesino (m.) *village (small)*
pagare *to pay*
  pagare il conto (dell'hotel) *to check out*
pagina (f.) *page*
  pagina web *webpage*
paio (m.) *pair*
  paio di scarpe *pair of shoes*
palazzina (f.) *(4-5 story) apartment building*
palazzo (m.) *palace, mansion, apartment building*
palestra (f.) *gym(nasium), health club*
palla (f.) *ball*
  palla a volo *volleyball*
pallacanestro (f.) *basketball*
pallone (m.) *ball*
pancetta (f.) *bacon*
pancia (f.) *stomach (below the waist), belly*
pane (m.) *bread*
panino (m.) *sandwich*
panorama (m.) *panorama*
pantaloni (m. pl.) *pants*
papà (m.) *dad*
parcheggiare *to park*
parco (m.) *park*
  parco giochi *playground*
parecchio (adjective) *a lot of, several*
parecchio/a (m./f.) (noun) *a lot, several*
parente (m./f.) *relative*
parete (f.) *wall*
pari (inv.) *equal, same*
  fare pari *to draw, to tie*

Parigi (f.) *Paris*
parlare *to speak*
  parlare cinese *to speak Chinese*
parmigiano (m.) *Parmesan cheese*
parolaccia (f.) *bad word*
parte (f.) *part*
partecipare *to participate*
partire *to leave*
  a partire da ... *starting from ...*
partita (f.) *game*
part-time *part-time*
  lavoro (m.) part-time *part-time job*
passaporto (m.) *passport*
passare *to pass*
passato (m.) *past (tense)*
  passato prossimo *present perfect (grammar)*
passeggiata (f.) *walk*
  Buona passeggiata. *Enjoy your walk./Have a good walk.*
  fare una passeggiata *to take a walk*
passione (f.) *passion*
  passione per ... *passion for ...*
pasta (f.) *pasta*
pasticceria (f.) *bakery*
patata (f.) *potato*
patto (m.) *condition*
  a patto che ... *provided that ...*
paura (f.) *fear*
  avere paura (di) *to be afraid (of)*
  fare paura *to be scary*
pausa (f.) *break*
  fare una pausa *to take a break*
pavimento (m.) *floor (inside a house or apartment)*
paziente (m./f.) *patient*
pazienza (f.) *patience*
peccato (m.) *sin*
  Peccato! *Too bad!*
pediatra (m./f.) *pediatrician*
pelle (f.) *skin, leather*
  di pelle *made out of leather*
penne (f. pl.) *penne (pasta)*
pensare *to think*
  pensare a ... *to think about ... (something/somebody)*
  pensare di ... *to think about ... (doing somehing)*
pensionato/a (m./f.) *retired*

pentirsi *to repent, to regret*
pentola (f.) *pan, pot*
pepe (m.) *pepper (spice)*
peperone (m.) *pepper (vegetable)*
per *for, through, by*
　detersivo (m.) per i piatti *dishwashing detergent*
　detersivo (m.) per il bucato *laundry detergent*
　in giro per la casa *around the house*
　in giro per la città *around town*
　passione per ... *passion for ...*
　per caso *by any chance*
　per contorno *as a side dish*
　Per favore. *Please.*
　per lavoro *on business*
　per le sette *by seven (o'clock)*
　pronto per ... *ready to ...*
pera (f.) *pear*
perché *why, because*
perdere *to lose*
　perdere tempo *to waste time*
perfetto *perfect*
pericoloso *dangerous*
periferia (f.) *suburbs*
periferico *suburban*
periodo (m.) *period*
　in questo periodo *in this period, currently*
permettere *to allow*
permettersi *to allow, to afford*
però *however, but*
persona (f.) *person*
　di persona *in person*
　persona sportiva *athletic person*
　persone (pl.) *people*
pesca (f.) *peach*
pesce (m.) *fish*
　pesce alla griglia *grilled fish*
petto (m.) *chest*
pezzo (m.) *piece*
piacere *to be pleasing (to someone)*
　Mi piace/piacciono ... (sg./pl.) *I like ...*
　Piacere. *Pleased to meet you.*
　Piacere mio. *Pleased to meet you, too.*
　Molto piacere! *Very pleased to meet you!*
piacevole *pleasant*
pianeta (m.) *planet*
pianista (m./f.) *pianist*
piano (adjective) *smooth, simple*

piano (adverb) *slowly, softly*
piano (m.) *floor*
　piano terra *ground floor*
　primo piano *first floor (second floor in the U.S.)*
pianoforte (m.) *piano*
　suonare il pianoforte *to play the piano*
pianta (f.) *plant*
piantare *to plant*
pianterreno *ground floor*
piantina (f.) *map*
piatto (m.) *plate, dish*
　detersivo (m.) per i piatti *dishwashing detergent*
　lavare i piatti *to do the dishes*
　primo (piatto) *first course*
　secondo (piatto) *main course*
piazza (f.) *square*
piccolo *small*
piede (m.) *foot*
　a piedi *on foot*
　fare un giro a piedi *to go for a walk*
pieno *full*
　a pieno tempo *full-time*
　giornata (f.) piena *full day*
pietra (f.) *stone*
pigiama (m.) *pajamas*
pioggia (f.) *rain*
piovere *to rain*
　Piove. *It's raining.*
pisolino (m.) *nap*
　fare un pisolino *to take a nap*
più *more*
　mai più *never again*
　non ... più *no longer, no more*
　più ... di/che *more/-er ... than*
piuttosto *rather*
plastica (f.) *plastic*
　di plastica *made from plastic*
plurale (m.) *plural*
poco (adjective) *little, few*
　pochi giorni *a few days*
poco/a (m./f.) (noun) *little, few*
　un poco/un po' *a little*
poema (m.) *poem*
poi *then*
　E poi? *And then?*
poker (m. sg./pl.) *poker*

poliziotto (m.) *policeman*
pollice (m.) *thumb*
pollo (m.) *chicken*
polmone (m.) *lung*
polso (m.) *wrist*
pomeriggio (m.) *afternoon*
  Buon pomeriggio. *Good afternoon. (from 1 p.m. to 6 p.m.)*
  di pomeriggio *in the afternoon*
pomodoro (m.) *tomato*
pop (inv.) *pop*
  musica (f.) pop *pop music*
porta (f.) *door*
portare *to carry, to take, to wear*
porto (m.) *harbor*
posate (f. pl.) *silverware*
possessivo *possessive*
possibile *possible*
posta (f.) *mail*
  posta elettronica *e-mail*
postale (adjective) *mail*
  ufficio postale *post office*
posto (m.) *place*
potere *can, to be able to*
  Posso … ? *May I … ?/Can I … ?*
pranzo (m.) *lunch*
  sala (f.) da pranzo *dining room*
praticare *to play*
  praticare uno sport *to play a sport*
prato (m.) *meadow*
preferire *to prefer*
Prego. *You're welcome.*
prendere *to take, to have (food and drink)*
  Tu cosa prendi? *What are you having?*
prenotare *to reserve*
prenotazione (f.) *reservation*
preoccupare *to worry*
  Sono preoccupato. *I'm worried.*
preparare *to prepare*
prepararsi *to get ready*
preposizione (f.) *preposition*
presentare *to present, to introduce*
presentazione (f.) *introduction*
presente (adjective) *present*
  congiuntivo (m.) presente *present subjunctive*
pressione (f.) *pressure*
presso *at, with*
presto *soon, early*

A presto. *See you soon.*
prezzo (m.) *price*
prima *sooner, in advance*
  prima che … , prima di … *before …*
  prima di tutto *first of all*
primavera (f.) *spring*
  in primavera *in the spring*
primo *first*
  per primo *as first course*
  primo (piatto) (m.) *first course*
  primo piano *first floor (second floor in the U.S.)*
primogenito/a (m./f.) *first-born*
privato *private*
probabile *likely*
probabilmente *probably*
problema (m.) *problem*
prodotto (m.) *product*
professionale *professional*
professore/essa (m./f.) *professor*
profondamente *deep*
profumo (m.) *perfume*
progettare *to plan*
programma (m.) *program*
proibire *to prohibit*
promettere *to promise*
  promettere di … *to promise to … (do something)*
promuovere *to promote*
  essere promosso *to pass (an exam)*
pronome (m.) *pronoun*
pronto *ready, fast*
  pronto per … *ready to …*
  pronto soccorso (m.) *emergency room*
proposito (m.) *intention*
  a proposito *by the way*
proprio *exactly, just, really*
prossimo *next, close*
  mese (m.) prossimo *next month*
  passato (m.) prossimo *present perfect (grammar)*
  prossima settimana (f.) *next week*
  trapassato (m.) prossimo *past perfect (grammar)*
provare *to try, to try on*
provincia (f.) *province*
psichiatra (m./f.) *psychiatrist*
psicologo (m./f.) *psychologist*

pubblicare *to publish*
pulire *to clean*
pulirsi *to clean oneself*
pulito *clean*
pullman (m.) *tour bus*
puntuale *punctual*
  essere puntuale *to be on time*
purché *provided that*
purtroppo *unfortunately*

Q

quaderno (m.) *notebook*
quadro (m.) *painting, picture*
qualche *a few, some*
  fra qualche giorno *in a few days*
  qualche volta *sometimes*
qualcosa *something, anything*
  qualcosa da bere *something to drink*
  qualcosa di bello da fare *anything*
    interesting/cool to do
qualcuno *someone, anyone*
quale *which*
qualsiasi *any*
qualunque *any*
quando *when*
quanto *how many, how much*
  Da quanto tempo … ? *How long has it been*
    since … ?
  Quanti anni hai? *How old are you?*
  Quanto costa? *How much does it cost?*
  tanto … quanto *as much/many … as*
quaranta *forty*
  Sono le tre e quarantacinque. *It's 3:45.*
quartiere (m.) *neighborhood*
quarto *fourth*
quarto (m.) *quarter*
  fra tre quarti d'ora *in forty-five minutes*
  Manca un quarto alle quattro. *It's 3:45.*
  Sono le quattro meno un quarto. *It's 3:45.*
  Sono le tre e tre quarti. *It's 3:45.*
  Sono le undici e un quarto di mattina. *It's*
    11:15 a.m.
quasi *almost*
quattordici *fourteen*
quattro *four*
  Manca un quarto alle quattro. *It's 3:45.*
  Sono le quattro. *It's four (o'clock).*
  Sono le quattro meno un quarto. *It's 3:45.*

quello *that*
questo *this*
  in questo momento *right now*
  in questo periodo *in this period, currently*
  questa sera *this evening*
  questa settimana *this week*
qui *here*
  qui vicino *nearby*
quindi *therefore, so*
quindici *fifteen*
  Sono le tre e quindici. *It's 3:15.*
quinto *fifth*
quotidiano *daily*
  vita (f.) **quotidiana** *everyday life*
quoziente (m.) *quotient*
  quoziente intellettivo *intelligence quotient*
    (IQ)

R

raccogliere *to pick up*
raccontare *to tell*
radersi *to shave*
ragazza (f.) *girl (from 14 to 35 years old)*
  la mia ragazza (f.) *my girlfriend*
ragazzina (f.) *girl (from 11 to 13 years old)*
ragazzino (m.) *boy (from 11 to 13 years old)*
ragazzo (m.) *boy (from 14 to 35 years old)*
  il mio ragazzo *my boyfriend*
raggiungere *to reach*
ragione (f.) *reason*
  avere ragione *to be right*
  la ragione per cui … *the reason why …*
ragù (m. sg./pl.) *meat sauce*
raramente *rarely*
rasoio (m.) *razor*
ravioli (m. pl.) *ravioli*
reception (f. sg./pl.) *reception desk*
regalo (m.) *gift*
reggiseno (m.) *bra*
regista (m./f.) *movie director*
registrarsi (all'hotel) *to check in*
regolarmente *regularly*
rene (m.) *kidney*
residenza (f.) *residence*
respirare *to breathe*
restare *to stay*
ricco *rich*
ricercatore/trice (m./f.) *researcher, scientist*

ricetta (f.) *recipe*
ricevere *to receive*
ricordare *to remember*
  ricordarsi di … *to remember to … (do something)*
ridotto *reduced*
  orario (m.) ridotto *shorter working hours*
riecco *here again*
  Rieccoci ! *Here we are again !*
riempirsi *to fill*
  riempirsi di … *to fill up with …*
rilassarsi *to relax*
rimanere *to remain*
rinascimentale (adjective) *Renaissance*
Rinascimento (m.) *Renaissance*
riposo (m.) *rest*
  Buon riposo. *Have a good rest.*
riso (m.) *rice*
rispettivamente *respectively*
rispondere *to reply*
rispondere (a) *to answer*
  rispondere al telefono *to answer the phone*
ristorante (m.) *restaurant*
ritardo (m.) *delay*
  essere in ritardo *to be late*
ritornare *to return, to go back*
riunione (f.) *meeting*
  sala (f.) delle riunioni *meeting room*
riuscire *to manage, to be able*
  riuscire a … *to manage to … , to be able to …*
rivista (f.) *magazine, journal*
roba (f.) *stuff*
  un sacco di roba *a bunch/lot of stuff*
roccia (f.) *rock*
Roma (f.) *Rome*
romantico (m.)/ romantici (m. pl.) *romantic*
romanzo (m.) *novel*
  romanzi (m. pl.) contemporanei *contemporary novels*
rompere *to break*
rosa (inv.) *pink*
rosolare *to sauté, to brown*
rosso *red*
  vino (m.) rosso *red wine*
rumore (m.) *noise*
  fare rumore *to make noise*
rumoroso *noisy*
rurale *rural*

S

sabato (m.) *Saturday*
sabbia (f.) *sand*
sacco (m.) *bag*
  un sacco di … *a lot of …*
  un sacco di roba *a bunch/lot of stuff*
sala (f.) *room*
  sala da pranzo *dining room*
  sala delle riunioni *meeting room*
salario (m.) *salary*
salato *expensive*
sale (m.) *salt*
salone (m.) *living room*
saltare *to jump*
  saltare la corda *to jump rope*
salutarsi *to greet each other*
salute (f.) *health*
saluto (m.) *greeting*
salvare *to save*
  salvare un documento *to save a document*
Salve. *Hello.*
sangue (m.) *blood*
sano *healthy*
sapere *to know (a fact), to know how*
  Lo so. *I know.*
  Non lo so. *I don't know.*
saponetta (f.) *soap (bar)*
sapore (m.) *taste, flavor*
Sardegna (f.) *Sardinia*
sbattere *to beat*
sbucciare *to peel*
scaffale (m.) *shelf*
  scaffale (dei libri) *book shelf*
scala (f.) *stairs, staircase*
scarpe (f. pl.) *shoes*
  negozio (m.) di scarpe *shoe store*
  paio (m.) di scarpe *pair of shoes*
  scarpe da ginnastica *sneakers*
  scarpe da tennis *tennis shoes, sneakers*
scatola (f.) *box, carton*
scegliere *to choose*
scelta (f.) *choice*
scheda (f.) *report card*
schedario (m.) *file cabinet*
schermo (m.) *monitor, screen*
schiena (f.) *back*
sci (m.)/sci (m., pl.) *skiing*

sci alpino *alpine skiing*
sci di fondo *cross-country skiing*
sciare *to ski*
sciarpa (f.) *scarf (long)*
scodella (f.) *bowl (small, for one person)*
scolare *to drain*
scolastico (m.)/scolastici (m. pl.) *scholastic*
scopa (f.) *broom*
scorso *last*
  anno (m.) scorso *last year*
  settimana (f.) scorsa *last week*
scrittore/trice (m./f.) *writer*
scrivania (f.) *desk*
scrivere *to write*
scultura (f.) *sculpture*
scuola (f.) *school*
  scuola superiore *high school*
scusare *to excuse*
  Scusa. *Excuse me. (infml.)*
  (Mi) scusi. *Excuse me. (sg. fml.)*
  Scusami. *I'm sorry.*
se *if*
sé *himself, herself, itself, oneself*
secco *dry*
secondo *second*
  di secondo *as main course*
  secondo (piatto) (m.) *main course*
secondo (preposition) *according to*
secondogenito/a (m./f.) *second-born*
sedere (m.) *behind*
sedia (f.) *chair*
sedici *sixteen*
segretario/a (m./f.) *secretary*
seguire *to follow*
sei *six*
selvaggio *wild*
semaforo (m.) *street light, traffic light*
sembrare *to seem*
seminterrato (m.) *basement*
sempre *always*
  sempre diritto *straight ahead*
seno (m.) *breast*
sentire *to hear*
sentirsi *to feel*
Mi sento bene. *I am well.*
  sentirsi di ... *to feel like ...*
senza *without*
  senza che ... *without ...*

sera (f.) *evening*
  Buona sera. *Good evening. (from 6 to 11 p.m.)*
  di sera *in the evening*
  ieri sera *last night*
  questa sera *this evening*
  vestito (m.) da sera *evening gown*
serata (f.) *evening*
  Buona serata. *Have a good evening.*
servire *to serve*
servizio (m.) *bathroom*
sessanta *sixty*
sesto *sixth*
seta (f.) *silk*
  di seta *made of silk*
sete (f.) *thirst*
  avere sete *to be thirsty*
settanta *seventy*
sette *seven*
  alle sette e mezza *at seven thirty (7:30)*
  per le sette *by seven (o'clock)*
  Siamo in sette. *There are seven of us.*
settembre (m.) *September*
settimana (f.) *week*
  due volte alla settimana *twice a week*
  fine settimana (m. sg./pl.) *weekend*
  prossima settimana *next week*
  questa settimana *this week*
  settimana scorsa *last week*
settimo *seventh*
sfilata (f.) *parade, march*
  sfilata di moda *fashion show*
shampo (m.) *shampoo*
si *one, they, people (impersonal pronoun)*
sì *yes*
sia ... che *as/so ... as, both ... and*
Sicilia (f.) *Sicily*
sicuro *sure*
signora (f.) *Mrs., lady*
signore (m.) *Mr., gentleman*
silenzioso *silent*
simile *similar*
simpatico *friendly, nice*
sindaco (m.) *mayor*
sinfonia (f.) *symphony*
singolo *single*
  camera (f.) singola *single room (one twin bed)*
sinistra (f.) *left*
  (a) sinistra *on the left, to the left*

sintomo (m.) *symptom*
sistema (m.) *system*
sito (m.) *site*
  sito web *website*
slip (m. pl.) *underpants (men's)*
smettere *to quit, to stop*
  smettere di ... *to quit/stop ... ing*
smog (m.) *smog*
sneakers (m. pl.) *sneakers*
soccorso (m.) *aid, rescue*
  pronto soccorso *emergency room*
sociale *social*
soddisfatto *satisfied*
sofà (m.) *sofa, couch*
soffitto (m.) *ceiling*
soggiorno (m.) *living room*
soldi (m. pl.) *money*
sole (m.) *sun*
  C'è il sole. *It's sunny.*
solito *usual*
  del solito *than usual*
  di solito *usually*
solo *alone, lonely, only, just*
soltanto *only*
sonno (m.) *sleep*
  avere sonno *to be sleepy*
sopracciglio (m.) *eyebrow*
  sopracciglia (f. pl.) *eyebrows*
  soprattutto *above all*
sorella (f.) *sister*
sorprendere *to surprise*
sorpresa (f.) *surprise*
  Che sorpresa! *What a surprise!*
sostanza (f.) *substance*
sostituto/a (m./f.) *substitute*
sottile *thin*
sotto *under*
sottopiano (m.) *basement*
sovrappeso (m. sg./pl.) *overweight*
  essere in sovrappeso *to be overweight*
spaghetti (m. pl.) *spaghetti*
spalla (f.) *shoulder*
spazioso *spacious*
specchio (m.) *mirror*
spedire *to send*
spendere *to spend*
sperare *to hope*
  sperare di ... *to hope to ...*

spesa (f.) *shopping*
  fare la spesa/le spese *to go shopping, to do grocery shopping*
  fare spese *to shop*
spesso *often*
spettacolo (m.) *performance, play (theater)*
spezzatino (m.) *stew*
spiaggia (f.) *beach*
splendere *to shine*
sporco *dirty*
sport (m. sg./pl.) *sport*
  guardare lo sport in/alla televisione *to watch sports on TV*
  fare sport *to practice sports*
  praticare uno sport *to play a sport*
sportivo *athletic, casual*
  persona (f.) sportiva *athletic person*
sposarsi *to get married*
  Si sposa. *He/She is getting married.*
  sposarsi con ... *to marry ... (someone)*
sposato *married*
spumante (m.) *sparkling wine*
spuntino (m.) *snack*
squadra (f.) *team*
squisito *exquisite, delicious*
stadio (m.) *stadium*
staff (m.) *staff*
stage (m. sg./pl.) *internship*
stagione (f.) *season*
  mezze stagioni *half seasons (spring and fall)*
stagno (m.) *pond*
stampante (f.) *printer*
stanco *tired*
stanza (f.) *room, chatroom*
  stanza da letto *bedroom*
stare *to stay, to be feeling, to be*
  Come mi sta? *How do I look?*
  Come sta? *How are you doing* (sg. fml.)*?/How is he?*
  Come stai? *How are you doing* (infml.)*?*
  stare per ... *to be about to ...*
stasera *this evening, tonight*
stato (m.) *state*
  stato civile *marital status*
stazione (f.) *station*
  stazione (dei treni) *train station*
stella (f.) *star*
stereo (m. sg./pl.) *stereo*

stesso *same*
  allo stesso tempo *at the same time*
stimolante *exciting*
stomaco (m.) *stomach (above the waist)*
storia (f.) *story, history*
  storie (pl.) d'amore *love stories*
strada (f.) *street, road*
straniero *foreign*
  lingua (f.) straniera *foreign language*
  turisti (m./f. pl.) stranieri *foreign tourists*
strano *strange*
stressante *stressful*
stressato *stressed, under stress*
studente/essa (m./f.) *student*
  studente universitario *university student*
studiare *to study*
studio (m.) *study, office*
su *on, upon, over, about*
subito *immediately*
succedere *to happen*
succo (m.) *juice*
suo *his, her, its*
Suo *your* (sg. fml.)
suocera (f.) *mother-in-law*
suocero (m.) *father-in-law*
suonare *to play (an instrument), to ring (a bell)*
  suonare il pianoforte *to play the piano*
superiore *superior, higher*
  scuola (f.) superiore *high school*
supermercato (m.) *supermarket*
svegliarsi *to wake up*
svelto *fast*

T

taglia (f.) *size (dresses, pants)*
tagliare *to cut, to slice*
tagliatelle (f. pl.) *tagliatelle (pasta)*
tailleur (m. sg./pl.) *suit (women's)*
  tailleur pantalone *pant suit*
tanto (adjective) *so much, so many, a lot of*
  tanto ... quanto *as much/many ... as*
tanto (adverb) *so, so much, very*
  Tanto vale ... *(One) might as well ...*
tanto/a (m./f.) (noun) *so much, so many*
tappetino (m.) *mouse pad*
tappeto (m.) *carpet, rug*
tardi *late*
  fino a tardi *until late*

tassista (m./f.) *taxi driver*
tastiera (f.) *keyboard*
tavolo (m.) *table*
taxi (m.) *taxi*
tazza (f.) *cup*
te *you* (sg. infml.) (direct object, disjunctive pronoun)
  a te *to you* (sg. infml.) (indirect object, disjunctive
    pronoun)
tè (m.) *tea*
teatro (m.) *theater*
tecnico *technical*
  istituto (m.) tecnico *professional school*
teenager (m./f. sg./pl.) *teenager*
tele (f.) *television*
  guardare la tele *to watch television*
telefonare *to telephone*
telefonarsi *to call each other*
telefonino (m.) *cell phone*
telefono (m.) *telephone*
  rispondere al telefono *to answer the phone*
telegiornale (m.) *news (on TV)*
telegramma (m.) *telegram*
televisione (f.) *television*
  guardare la televisione *to watch television*
  guardare lo sport in/alla televisione *to
    watch sports on TV*
  interviste (f. pl.) alla televisione *talk show*
televisore (m.) *television*
temperatura (f.) *temperature*
tempio (m.) *temple*
tempo (m.) *time, weather*
  a tempo pieno *full-time*
  avere tempo *to have time*
  Che tempo fa? *What's the weather like?*
  Da quanto tempo ... ? *How long has it been
    since ... ?*
  molto tempo *long time*
  perdere tempo *to waste time*
  tempo libero *free time*
temporale (m.) *storm*
  C'è un temporale. *It's stormy.*
temporaneo *temporary*
  lavoro (m.) temporaneo *summer job*
tenda (f.) *curtain*
tendere *to have a tendency*
tendine (m.) *tendon*
tennis (m. sg./pl.) *tennis*
  giocare a tennis *to play tennis*

Glossary

scarpe (f. pl.) da tennis *tennis shoes, sneakers*
televisivo (adjective) *television*
  trasmissione (f.) televisiva *television program*
terme (f. pl.) *spa*
terra (f.) *land*
terra (inv.) *ground*
piano (m.) terra *ground floor*
terribile *terrible*
terrina (f.) *bowl*
terzo *third*
terzogenito/a *third-born*
tesi (f.)/tesi (f., pl.) *thesis*
test (m.) *test*
testa (f.) *head*
  fare testa o croce *to flip a coin*
TG (m.) *news (on TV)*
ti *you* (sg. infml.) (direct object pronoun); *to you* (sg. infml.) (indirect object pronoun)
tipo (m.) *type, kind*
tirare *to draw*
  Tira vento. *It's windy.*
titolo (m.) *title*
tivù (f.) *television*
  guardare la tivù *to watch television*
tornare *to return, to go back*
torre (f.) *tower*
torta (f.) *cake*
tortellini (m. pl.) *tortellini*
torto (m.) *fault*
  avere torto *to be wrong*
tra *between, among, in*
  tra... e... *between... and...*
  tra cinque minuti *in five minutes*
tradizionale *traditional*
traffico (m.) *traffic*
tranquillizzare *to calm down*
trapassato (m.) prossimo *past perfect*
trasferirsi *to move, to transfer*
traslocare *to move (to a new house)*
trasloco (m.) *move, removal*
  fare il trasloco *to move (to a new house)*
trasmissione (f.) *program*
  trasmissione televisiva *television program*
trasparente *transparent*
trasporto (m.) *transportation*
  mezzo (m.) di trasporto *means of transportation*
trattoria (f.) *family style restaurant*

tre *three*
  fra tre quarti d'ora *in forty-five minutes*
  Sono le tre. *It's three (o'clock).*
  Sono le tre e quarantacinque. *It's 3:45.*
  Sono le tre e tre quarti. *It's 3:45.*
tredici *thirteen*
treno (m.) *train*
  in treno *train station*
  stazione (f.) (dei treni) *by train*
trenta *thirty*
  Sono le tre e trenta. *It's 3:30.*
triste *sad*
troppo *too (much/many)*
troppo/a (m./f.) *too much, too many*
trovare *to find*
  andare a trovare *to go visit*
  venire a trovare *to come visit*
tu *you* (sg. infml.) (subject pronoun)
tuo *your* (sg. infml.)
tuonare *to thunder*
tuono (m.) *thunder*
tuorlo (m.) *yolk*
turista (m./f.) *tourist*
  turisti (pl.) stranieri *foreign tourists*
tutto *all*
  a tutti i costi *at all costs*
  di tutti *of all*
  prima di tutto *first of all*
  tutte le mattine *every morning*
  tutti gli altri *everyone else*
  tutti gli anni *every year*
  tutti i giorni *every day*

U

ubriaco *drunk*
ufficio (m.) *office*
  in ufficio *in the office*
  ufficio postale *post office*
ultimo *last, final*
un (m.)/uno (m. in front of s + consonant, z, ps, gn)/una (f.)/un' (m./f. in front of a vowel) *a, one*
  È l'una di notte. *It's 1:00 a.m.*
undicesimo *eleventh*
undici *eleven*
  Sono le undici e un quarto di mattina. *It's 11:15 a.m.*
università (f. sg./pl.) *university*
universitario (adjective) *university*

studente (m.) universitario *university student*
uno *one*
uomo (m.)/uomini (m. pl.) *man*
  abito da uomo *men's suit*
  uomo d'affari *businessman*
uovo (m.) *egg*
  uova (f. pl.) *eggs*
uragano (m.) *hurricane*
urbano *urban*
usare *to use*
uscire *to go out*
utile *useful*
  Posso esserLe utile? *How can I help you?/Can I assist you?* (sg. fml.)
uva (f.) *grapes*
  un grappolo d'uva *a bunch of grapes*

V

vacanza (f.) *vacation, holiday*
  fare una vacanza *to go on vacation*
  in vacanza *on vacation*
vagamente *vaguely*
valere *to be worth*
  Tanto vale … *(One) might as well …*
valigia (f.) *suitcase*
  fare le valige/valigie *to pack*
varietà (f.) *variety*
  varietà di scelta *variety of choices*
vasca (f.) *tub*
  vasca (da bagno) *bath tub*
vecchio *old*
vedere *to see, to meet (a person)*
  Fammi vedere. *Let me see.*
  fare vedere *to show*
  visto che … *given that … /since …*
vedersi *to see each other*
vela (f.) *sail*
  andare in barca a vela *to sail*
vela (f.) *sailing*
velluto (m.) *velvet*
  di velluto a coste *made out of corduroy*
  velluto a coste *corduroy*
veloce *fast, quick*
velocemente *quickly*
venditore (m.) *salesman*
venditrice (f.) *saleswoman*
venerdì (m. sg./pl.) *Friday*
Venezia (f.) *Venice*

venire *to come*
  venire a trovare *to come visit*
venti *twenty*
ventidue *twenty-two*
ventilatore (m.) *fan*
ventiquattro *twenty-four*
ventitré *twenty-three*
vento (m.) *wind*
  C'è vento. *It's windy.*
  Tira vento. *It's windy.*
ventre (m.) *stomach (below the waist)*
ventuno *twenty-one*
veramente *actually, really*
verde *green*
verdura (f.) *vegetable*
vergine (f.) *virgin*
verità (f. sg./pl.) *truth*
vero *true, right*
versare *to pour*
versione (f.) *version*
vestirsi *to get dressed*
vestito (m.) *dress*
  vestito da sera *evening gown*
veterinario/a (m./f.) *veterinarian*
vi *you* (pl.) (direct object pronoun); *to you* (pl.) (indirect object pronoun)
via (f.) *street, way, path*
viaggiare *to travel*
  viaggiare all'estero *to travel abroad*
viaggio (m.) *travel, trip*
  Buon viaggio. *Have a good trip.*
  fare un viaggio *to take a trip*
  viaggio organizzato *guided tour*
viale (m.) *avenue, path*
vicino *near*
  lì vicino *near there*
  qui vicino *nearby*
  vicino a … *near …*
video (m.) *monitor, screen*
villetta (f.) *small house*
vincere *to win*
vino (m.) *wine*
  lista (f.) dei vini *wine list*
  vino bianco *white wine*
  vino rosso *red wine*
viola (inv.) *purple*
visitare *to visit, to go sightseeing*
vista (f.) *view*

Glossary

vita (f.) *life, waist*
  da una vita *for a very long time, since always*
  vita quotidiana *everyday life*
vitello (m.) *veal*
vivere *to live*
  vivere a ... *to live in ...*
voglia (f.) *wish, desire*
  avere voglia di ... *to feel like ...*
voi *you* (pl.) (subject pronoun); *you* (pl.) (direct object, disjunctive pronoun)
  a voi *to you* (pl.) (indirect object, disjunctive pronoun)
volentieri *gladly*
volere *to want*
  Ti voglio bene. *I care about you./I love you.*
  volerci *to take (time)*
  Vorrei ... *I would like ...*
volta (f.) *time*
  a volte *sometimes*
  due volte alla settimana *twice a week*
  ogni volta *every time*
  qualche volta *sometimes*
voltare *to turn*
vostro *your* (pl.)
votazione (f.) *grade*
voto (m.) *grade*
vuoto *empty*

W

water (m.) *toilet*
web log (blog) (m.) *web log (blog)*
web page (f.) *webpage*
weekend (m. sg./pl.) *weekend*

Z

zaino (m.) *backpack*
zero *zero*
zia (f.) *aunt*
zio (m.)/zii (m., pl.) *uncle*
zoo (m.)/zoo (m., pl.) *zoo*
zucchero (m.) *sugar*
zucchino (m.) *zucchini*

English-Italian

A

a *un/uno* (in front of s + consonant, z, ps, gn)/*una*
  a lot *parecchio/a* (m./f.), *molto/a* (m./f.) (noun)
  a lot of *tanto, parecchio, molto, un sacco di*
  a lot of stuff *un sacco di roba*
a.m. *di mattina, di notte*
  It's 11:15 a.m. *Sono le undici e un quarto di mattina.*
  It's 1:00 a.m. *È l'una di notte.*
ability *capacità* (f., pl. *capacità*)
able (to be) *riuscire, potere*
  able to ... (to be) *riuscire a ...*
about *circa, su*
  about it *ci, ne*
  about them *ne*
  I'll think about it. *Ci penserò.*
about to ... (to be) *stare per ...*
above all *soprattutto*
abroad *all'estero*
  travel abroad *viaggiare all'estero*
absolutely *assolutamente*
absorb (to) *assorbire*
abundant *abbondante*
accept (to) *accettare*
accessory *accessorio* (m.)
accommodating *accomodante*
accommodation *alloggio* (m.)
accompany (to) *accompagnare*
according to ... *secondo ...*
action *azione* (f.)
  action movies *film* (m. pl.) *d'azione*
activity *attività* (f., pl. *attività*)
actor *attore* (m.)
actress *attrice* (f.)
actually *veramente*
add (to) *aggiungere*
address *indirizzo* (m.)
adjective *aggettivo* (m.)
adorable *adorabile*
adult *adulto/a* (m./f.)
advance *anticipo* (m.)
  in advance *prima*
advice *consiglio* (m.)
  ask for advice (to) *chiedere (un) consiglio*
aerobic *aerobico*

afford (to) *permettersi*
afraid (to be) *avere paura*
  afraid of (to be) *avere paura di/essere impauriti da*
after *dopo*
afternoon *pomeriggio* (m.)
  Good afternoon. (from 1 p.m. to 6 p.m.) *Buon pomeriggio.*
  in the afternoon *di pomeriggio*
again *ancora, di nuovo*
  never again *mai più*
age *età* (f., pl. *età*)
agency *agenzia* (f.)
ago *fa*
  a month ago *un mese fa*
  two days ago *due giorni fa*
agree (to) *essere d'accordo*
agreed *d'accordo*
agreement *accordo* (m.)
ahead *avanti*
  Go ahead. *Va' avanti.*
aid *soccorso* (m.)
air *aria* (f.)
  air conditioning *aria condizionata*
airplane *aereo* (m.)
  by plane *in aereo*
airport *aeroporto* (m.)
all *tutto*
  above all *soprattutto*
  All right. *Va bene.*
  at all costs *a tutti i costi*
  first of all *prima di tutto*
  not ... at all *non ... affatto*
  of all *di tutti*
  open all day *orario* (m.) *continuato*
allow (to) *permettere, permettersi*
almost *quasi, ormai*
alone *solo*
along *lungo*
alpine *alpino*
  alpine skiing *sci* (m.) *alpino*
already *già*
also *anche*
alternate (to) *alternare*
although *benché*
always *sempre*
American *americano*
  American football *futbol americano* (m.)

among *fra, tra*
amusing *divertente*
ancient *antico*
and *e* (ed before a vowel)
  ... and you? (fml.) *... e Lei?*
  ... and you? (infml.) *... e tu?*
animal *animale* (m.)
ankle *caviglia* (f.)
anniversary *anniversario* (m.)
  Happy anniversary. *Buon anniversario.*
another *un altro/un'altra*
answer (to) *rispondere (a)*
  answer the phone (to) *rispondere al telefono*
anti-stress *antistress* (m., pl. *antistress*)
any *qualsiasi, qualunque, di + definite article*
anyone *chiunque, qualcuno*
anything *qualcosa*
  anything interesting/cool to do *qualcosa di bello da fare*
apartment *appartamento* (m.), *alloggio* (m.)
  apartment building *condominio* (m., pl.: *condomini*)
  apartment building (4-5 story building) *palazzo* (m.), *palazzina* (f.)
aperitif *aperitivo* (m.)
appetite *appetito* (m.)
appetizer *antipasto* (m.)
apple *mela* (f.)
appointment *appuntamento* (m.)
appropriate *adatto*
apricot *albicocca* (f.)
  apricot tree *albicocco* (m.)
April *aprile* (m.)
Arab *arabo*
archeological *archeologico* (m. pl *archeologici*)
architect *architetto* (m.)
arm *braccio* (m.)
arms *braccia* (f. pl.)
aroma *aroma* (m.)
around *attorno, intorno*
  around ... *attorno a ...*
  around midnight *intorno a mezzanotte*
  around the home/house *in giro per la casa*
  around the world *intorno al mondo*
  around town *in giro per la città*
arrive (to) *arrivare*
art *arte* (f.)
  modern art *arte moderna*

article *articolo* (m.)
artist *artista* (m./f.)
as *come*
  as a side dish *di/per contorno*
  as first course *per primo*
  as main course *di secondo*
  as many/much … as *tanto … quanto*
  as/so … as *così … come, sia … che*
  (One) might as well … *Tanto vale …*
ask (to), ask for (to) *chiedere*
  ask a question (to) *fare una domanda*
  ask for advice (to) *chiedere (un) consiglio*
assistant *assistente* (m./f.)
astronaut *astronauta* (m./f.)
at *a, da, in, presso*
  at all costs *a tutti i costi*
  at home *a casa*
  at least *almeno*
  at night, from midnight to 3 a.m *di notte*
  at seven thirty (7:30) *alle sette e mezza*
  at the beach *al mare*
  at the lake *al lago*
  at the same time *allo stesso tempo*
  not … at all *non … affatto*
athlete *atleta* (m./f.)
athletic *sportivo*
  athletic person *persona* (f.) *sportiva*
attach (to) *attaccare*
  attach (a file) (to) *allegare un file/documento*
attachment *allegato* (m.)
attend (to) *frequentare*
attention *attenzione* (f.)
  pay attention (to) *fare attenzione*
  Pay attention! *Sta' attento!*
attentive *attento*
August *agosto* (m.)
aunt *zia* (f.)
author *autore/trice* (m./f.)
availability *disponibilità* (f.)
available *disponibile*
avenue *viale* (m.)
average *media* (f.)
avocado *avocado* (m., pl. *avocado*)

B

baby *bambino/a* (m./f.)
back *schiena* (f.)
  go back (to) *ritornare, tornare*

back yard *cortile* (m.)
backpack *zaino* (m.)
bacon *pancetta* (f.)
bad *cattivo*
  It's bad. (weather) *Fa brutto.*
  Not bad. *Così, così.*
  Too bad! *Peccato!*
bad word *parolaccia* (f.)
badly *male*
bag *sacco* (m.), *borsa* (f.)
baked pork *maiale* (m.) *al forno*
bakery *pasticceria* (f.)
ball *palla* (f.), *pallone* (m.)
banana *banana* (f.)
band (music) *gruppo* (m.)
  British bands *gruppi* (pl.) *inglesi*
bandage *benda* (f.), *cerotto* (m.)
bank *banca* (f.)
banker *banchiere/a* (m./f.)
barbeque *alla brace*
baroque *barocco* (m.)
baseball *baseball* (m.)
basement *seminterrato* (m.), *sottopiano* (m.)
basil *basilico* (m.)
basketball *basket* (m.), *pallacanestro* (f.)
bath gel *bagnoschiuma* (m.), *docciaschiuma* (m.)
bath tub *vasca* (f.) *(da bagno)*
  take a bath (to) *fare il bagno*
bathing trunks/suit *costume* (m.) *da bagno*
bathroom *bagno* (m.), *servizio* (m.)
be (to) *essere, fare, stare*
beach *spiaggia* (f.)
beard *barba* (f.)
beat (to) *sbattere*
beautiful *bello*
  How beautiful! *Che bello!*
  It's beautiful. (weather) *Fa bello.*
  very beautiful *bellissimo*
  What a beautiful dish! *Che bel piatto!*
because *perché*
become (to) *diventare, farsi*
bed *letto* (m.)
  bed sheet *lenzuolo* (m.)
  bed sheets *lenzuola* (f. pl.)
  double bed *letto matrimoniale*
bedroom *camera* (f.), *camera da letto, stanza* (f.) *da letto*
beef *manzo* (m.)

beefsteak *bistecca* (f.)
beer *birra* (f.)
before *avanti*
  before ... *prima che ... , prima di ...*
begin (to) *cominciare*
  begin to ... (to) *cominciare a ...*
behind (n.) *sedere* (m.)
  behind (adv.) *dietro*
beige *beige* (inv.)
believe (to) *credere*
belly *pancia* (f.)
belong (It belongs to ...) *È di ...*
belt *cintura* (f.)
besides *inoltre*
best (the) *migliore, meglio*
better *meglio* (inv.), *migliore, meglio*
  It's better. *Va meglio.*
between *fra, tra*
  between ... and ... *fra ... e ... /tra ... e ...*
bicycle *bicicletta* (f.)
  ride a bike (to) *andare in bicicletta*
big *grande*
  have a nice big meal (to) *farsi una bella mangiata*
bike *bici (f., pl. bici)*
biking *ciclismo* (m.)
bikini *bichini* (m.)
bill *conto* (m.)
billiards *biliardo* (m.)
billion *miliardo (pl. miliardi)*
biology *biologia* (f.)
birth *nascita* (f.)
birthday *compleanno* (m.)
  Happy birthday. *Buon compleanno.*
bitter *amaro*
bitterly *amaramente*
black *nero*
bleach *candeggina* (f.)
blender *frullatore* (m.)
blog *blog* (m.)
blood *sangue* (m.)
blouse *camicetta* (f.)
blue *blu* (inv.)
board *asse* (f.)
  ironing board *asse da stiro*
boat *barca* (f.)
boil (to) *bollire*
bone *osso* (m.)

bones *ossa* (f. pl.)
book *libro* (m.)
bookcase (in a house or office) *libreria* (f.)
bookstore *libreria* (f.)
bored (to get bored) *annoiarsi*
boring *noioso*
born (to be) *nascere*
  first-born *primogenito/a* (m./f.)
  second-born *secondogenito/a* (m./f.)
  third-born *terzogenito/a*
boss *capo/a* (m./f.)
both (of them) *entrambi/e*
  both ... and *sia ... che*
bottle *bottiglia* (f.)
bottom *fondo*
  the bottom of ... *in fondo a ...*
boutique *boutique* (f.)
bowl *ciotola* (f.), *terrina* (f.)
  bowl (small, for one person) *scodella* (f.)
box *scatola* (f.)
boxers *mutande* (f. pl.)
boy (from 11 to 13 years old) *ragazzino* (m.)
  boy (from 14 to 35 years old) *ragazzo* (m.)
boyfriend *ragazzo* (m.)
  my boyfriend *il mio ragazzo*
bra *reggiseno* (m.)
bracelet *braccialetto* (m.)
brain *cervello* (m.)
bread *pane* (m.)
break *pausa* (f.)
  take a break (to) *fare una pausa*
break (to) *rompere*
  Break a leg! (lit. In the mouth of the wolf!) *In bocca al lupo!*
  Thank you. (lit. May the wolf die.) *Crepi il lupo. (in response to In bocca al lupo!)*
breakfast *colazione* (f.)
  have breakfast (to) *fare colazione*
breast *seno* (m.)
breathe (to) *respirare*
broccoli *broccolo* (m.)
brochure *opuscolo* (m.)
broom *scopa* (f.)
brother *fratello* (m.)
brown *marrone*
brown (to) *rosolare*
bruschetta *bruschetta* (f.)
building *edificio* (m.)

Glossary

bus *autobus* (m.)
  tour bus *pullman* (m.)
business *affari* (m. pl.), *business* (m., pl.),
  commercio (m.)
  on business *per lavoro*
businessman *imprenditore* (m.), *uomo* (m.)
  d'affari
businesswoman *imprenditrice* (f.), *donna* (f.)
  d'affari
busy *impegnato, occupato*
  busy day *giornata* (f.) *piena*
but *ma, però*
butcher shop *macelleria* (f.)
butter *burro* (m.)
buy (to) *comprare*
by *per, in, a*
  by any chance *per caso*
  by car *in macchina*
  by now *ormai*
  by plane *in aereo*
  by seven (o'clock) *per le sette*
  by the way *a proposito*
  by train *in treno*
Bye-bye! *Ciao ciao!*

C

cabinet *camera* (f.)
  medicine cabinet *armadietto* (m.)
cable *cavo* (m.)
  cable (dsl) *cavo adsi*
café *bar* (m.)
cake *torta* (f.)
call (to) *chiamare, telefonare*
  call each other (on the phone) (to) *telefonarsi*
calm down (to) *tranquillizzare*
camera *macchina fotografica*
camping *campeggio* (m.)
  go camping (to) *fare il campeggio*
can *potere*
  Can I ... ? *Posso ... ?*
  How can this be! *Ma come!*
can (noun) *lattina* (f.)
cappuccino *cappuccino* (m.)
car *automobile* (f.), *macchina* (f.)
  by car *in macchina*
card *carta* (f.)
  credit card *carta di credito*
  play cards (to) *giocare a carte*

careful *attento*
  Be careful! *Sta' attento!*
carpenter *falegname* (m.)
carpet *tappeto* (m.)
  carpet (wall-to-wall) *moquette* (f.)
carrot *carota* (f.)
carry (to) *portare*
carton *scatola* (f.)
case *caso* (m.)
  in any case *comunque*
cashmere *cachemire* (m.)
  made out of cashmere *di cachemire*
cask *botte* (f.)
casual *sportivo*
CD-ROM *cd rom* (m.)
CD-ROM drive *lettore cd, lettore cd-rom*
ceiling *soffitto* (m.)
celebrate (to) *celebrare*
cell phone *cellulare* (m.), *telefonino* (m.)
center *centro* (m.)
  information center *centro informazioni*
centimeter *centimetro* (m.)
ceremony *cerimonia* (f.)
certain (ones) *certo/a* (m./f.)
certainly *certamente*
chair *sedia* (f.)
champion *campione/essa* (m./f.)
chance *caso* (m.)
  by any chance *per caso*
change (to) *cambiare*
channel *canale* (m.)
  flip channels (to) *cambiare canale*
chatroom *chatroom* (f.)
check *conto* (m.)
check (to) *controllare*
check in (to) *registrarsi (all'hotel)*
check out (to) *pagare il conto (dell'hotel)*
cheek *guancia* (f.)
cheese *formaggio* (m.)
chemical *chimico* (m. pl *chimici*)
chemistry *chimica* (f.)
chest *petto* (m.)
chicken *pollo* (m.)
child (from 0 to 10 years old) *bambino/a* (m./f.)
chin *mento* (m.)
China *Cina* (f.)
Chinese (language) *cinese* (m.)
  speak Chinese (to) *parlare cinese*

choice *scelta* (f.)
  variety of choices *varietà* (f.) *di scelta*
choose (to) *scegliere*
chop *braciola* (f.)
  pork chop *braciola di maiale*
Christmas *Natale* (m.)
  Merry Christmas. *Buon Natale.*
church *chiesa* (f.)
circle *giro* (m.)
circus *circo* (m.)
citizenship *cittadinanza* (f.)
city *città (f., pl. città)*
  in/to the city *in centro*
city hall *municipio* (m.)
civil *civile*
claim (to) *affermare*
classical *classico (m. pl. classici)*
  classical music *musica* (f.) *classica*
classroom, class *classe* (f.)
clean *pulito*
clean (to) *pulire*
  clean oneself (to) *pulirsi*
clear *chiaro*
clearly *chiaro, chiaramente*
clerk *impiegato/a* (m./f.)
climate *clima* (m.)
close *prossimo*
close (to) *chiudere*
  close a file (to) *chiudere un documento/file*
closet *armadio* (m.)
clothing *abbigliamento* (m.)
  clothing store *negozio* (m.) *di abbigliamento*
cloud *nuvola* (f.)
cloudy *nuvoloso*
  It's cloudy. *È nuvoloso.*
club *club (m., pl. club), discoteca* (f.)
coach *allenatore/trice* (m./f.)
coast *costa* (f.)
coat (above the knees) *giaccone* (m.)
  coat (to the knees or longer) *cappotto* (m.)
coffee *caffè (m., pl. caffè)*
coffee maker (stovetop) *caffettiera* (f.)
coffee shop *caffetteria* (f.), *caffè (m., pl. caffè)*
cold (noun) *freddo* (m.)
cold (to be) *avere freddo*
  It's cold. *Fa freddo.*
colleague *collega* (m./f.)
cologne *colonia* (f.)

come (to) *venire*
  come in (to) *entrare*
  come visit (to) *venire a trovare*
comedy *commedia* (f.)
comfortable *comodo*
command (to) *comandare*
commerce *commercio* (m.)
common *comune* (m.)
community *comunità (f., pl. comunità)*
company *compagnia* (f.)
competence *competenza* (f.)
complete (to) *compiere*
completely *affatto*
compliment *complimento* (m.)
computer *computer (m., pl computer);*
  informatico (adjective)
  computer science *informatica* (f.)
concert *concerto* (m.)
condition *patto* (m.), *condizione* (f.)
conditioning *condizionato*
confess (to) *confessare*
Congratulations! *Complimenti!*
construction worker *muratore/trice* (m./f.)
contemporary *contemporaneo*
  contemporary novels *romanzi* (m. pl.)
    contemporanei
continue (to) *continuare*
conversation *colloquio* (m.)
convince (to) *convincere*
  convince to … (to) *convincere a …*
convinced *convinto*
cook (to) *cucinare, cuocere*
cooking *cottura* (f.)
coordinate (to) *coordinare*
corduroy *velluto a coste*
  made out of corduroy *di velluto a coste*
correct *giusto*
correctly *giusto*
cost *costo* (m.)
  at all costs *a tutti i costi*
cost (to) *costare*
  How much does it cost? *Quanto costa?*
costume *costume* (m.)
cotton *cotone* (m.)
couch *divano* (m.), *sofà* (m.)
count (to) *contare*
country *campagna* (f.)
  to the country *in campagna*

countryside *campagna* (f.)
couple *coppia* (f.)
course *corso* (m.)
  as first course *per primo*
  as main course *di secondo*
  first course *primo (piatto)* (m.)
  main course *secondo (piatto)* (m.)
courtyard *cortile* (m.)
cousin *cugino/a* (m./f.)
cream *crema* (f.)
  shaving cream *crema da barba*
credit *credito* (m.)
  credit card *carta* (f.) *di credito*
cross-country skiing *sci* (m.) *di fondo*
crowded *affollato*
cucumber *cetriolo* (m.)
culture *cultura* (f.)
cup *tazza* (f.)
cupboard *credenza* (f.)
cure (to) *curare*
current *attuale*
currently *in questo periodo*
curtain *tenda* (f.)
customer *cliente* (m./f.)
cut (to) *tagliare*
cute *carino*

D

dad *papà* (m.)
  stay-at-home dad *casalingo* (m.)
daily *quotidiano*
dance *ballo* (m.)
dance (to) *ballare*
dangerous *pericoloso*
data *dati* (m. pl.)
date *data* (f.)
daughter *figlia* (f.)
day *giorno* (m.), *giornata* (f.), *data* (f.)
  a few day *pochi giorni* (m. pl.)
  a full day, a busy day *giornata* (f.) *piena*
  day trip *gita* (f.)
  every day *tutti i giorni*
  Have a good day. *Buona giornata.*
  in a few days *fra qualche giorno*
  open all day *orario* (m.) *continuato*
  two days ago *due giorni fa*
December *dicembre* (m.)
decide (to) *decidere*

decide to … (to) *decidere di …*
deep *profondamente*
degree *grado* (m.), *laurea* (f.)
  high school degree *maturità* (f.)
  university degree *laurea* (f.)
delay *ritardo* (m.)
delete (to) *cancellare, eliminare*
delicious *delizioso, squisito*
dentist *dentista* (m./f.)
deodorant *deodorante* (m.)
department store *grande magazzino* (m.)
depressed *depresso*
describe (to) *descrivere*
desert *deserto* (m.)
desire *voglia* (f.)
desire (to) *desiderare*
desk *scrivania* (f.)
dessert *dolce* (m.)
destroy (to) *distruggere*
detergent *detersivo* (m.)
  dishwashing detergent *detersivo per i piatti*
  laundry detergent *detersivo per il bucato*
determine (to) *determinare*
die (to) *morire*
difference *differenza* (f.)
different *diverso*
difficult *difficile*
dining room *sala* (f.) *da pranzo*
dinner *cena* (f.)
  Enjoy your dinner./Have a good
    dinner. *Buona cena.*
diploma *diploma* (m.)
director *direttore* (m.)
  movie director *regista* (m./f.)
dirty *sporco*
disco *discoteca* (f.)
disease *malattia* (f.)
dish *piatto* (m.)
do the dishes (to) *lavare i piatti*
  What a beautiful dish! *Che bel piatto!*
dishwasher *lavapiatti* (f.), *lavastoviglie* (f.)
dishwashing detergent *detersivo* (m.) *per i
piatti*
displease (to) *dispiacere*
distant *lontano*
divorce … (someone) (to) *divorziarsi da …*
  get a divorce (to) *divorziarsi*
do (to) *fare*

do aerobics (to) *fare ginnastica aerobica*
do gardening (to) *fare giardinaggio*
do grocery shopping (to) *fare la spesa/le spese*
do the dishes (to) *lavare i piatti*
do the laundry (to) *fare il bucato*
How are you doing (fml.)? *Come sta?*
How are you doing (infml.)? *Come stai?*
things to do *cose* (f. pl.) *da fare*
What do you do? *Che lavoro fai?*
doctor *dottore/essa* (m./f.)
document *documento* (m.)
  save a document (to) *salvare un documento*
documentary *documentario* (m.)
dollar *dollaro* (m.)
  a million dollars *un milione di dollari*
door *porta* (f.)
double *doppio*
  double bed *letto* (m.) *matrimoniale*
  double room (one queen-size bed) *camera* (f.) *matrimoniale*
  double room (two twin-size beds) *camera* (f.) *doppia*
doubt (to) *dubitare*
downtown *in centro*
drain (to) *scolare*
drama *dramma* (m.)
draw (to) *tirare, fare pari*
drawer *cassetto* (m.)
dress *vestito* (m.), *abito* (m.)
dressed (to get dressed) *vestirsi*
drink *bevanda* (f.)
drink (to) *bere*
  something to drink *qualcosa da bere*
drive (to) *guidare*
drugstore *farmacia* (f.)
drunk *ubriaco*
dry *secco*
due *dovuto*
  due to … *dovuto a …*
DVD player *dvd* (m.)

E

each *ciascuno, ogni*
  each one *ciascuno/a* (m./f.)
ear *orecchio* (m.)
  ears *orecchi/orecchie* (m. pl./f. pl.)
early *presto*

early (to be) *essere in anticipo*
earn (to) *guadagnare*
earrings *orecchini* (m. pl.)
easy *facile*
eat (to) *mangiare*
  eat-in kitchen *cucina* (f.) *abitabile*
  nothing good to eat *niente di buono da mangiare*
economics *economia* (f.)
education *istruzione* (f.)
egg *uovo* (m.)
  eggs *uova* (f. pl.)
eggplant *melanzana* (f.)
eight *otto*
eighteen *diciotto*
eighth *ottavo*
eighty *ottanta*
elbow *gomito* (m.)
elder *maggiore*
electric *elettrico*
electrician *elettricista* (m.)
electrocardiogram *elettrocardiogramma* (m.)
electronics *elettronica* (f.)
  electronics store *negozio* (m.) *di elettronica*
elegant *elegante*
elegantly *elegantemente*
elementary *elementare*
  the first grade at elementary school *la prima elementare*
eleven *undici*
  It's 11:15 a.m. *Sono le undici e un quarto di mattina.*
eleventh *undicesimo*
e-mail *email, mail (f., pl. email, mail), posta* (f.) *elettronica*
  send an e-mail (to) *mandare un'email/una mail*
emergency room *pronto soccorso* (m.)
employee *impiegato/a* (m./f.)
empty *vuoto*
end (to) *per finire*
engaged *fidanzato*
engagement *impegno* (m.)
engineer *ingegnere* (m.)
English *inglese*
  British bands (music) *gruppi* (m. pl.) *inglesi*
English (language) *inglese* (m.)
enjoy oneself (to) *divertirsi*

Enjoy your dinner. *Buona cena.*
Enjoy your meal. *Buon appetito.*
Enjoy your walk. *Buona passeggiata.*
enormous *enorme*
enough *abbastanza*
  enough (to be) *bastare*
  That's enough! *Basta così!*
enroll (to) *iscrivere*
enthusiastically *entusiasticamente*
entire *intero*
equal *pari* (inv.)
espresso machine *macchina* (f.) *del caffè*
euro *euro* (m., pl. *euro*)
Europe *Europa* (f.)
European *europeo*
evening *sera* (f.), *serata* (f.)
  evening gown *vestito* (m.) *da sera*
  Good evening (from 6 to 11 p.m.). *Buona
    sera.*
  Have a good evening. *Buona serata.*
  in the evening *di sera*
  this evening *questa sera*
event *gara* (f.)
  in any event *in ogni caso*
ever *mai*
every *ogni*
  every day *tutti i giorni*
  every morning *tutte le mattine*
  every time *ogni volta*
  every year *tutti gli anni*
everyday life *vita* (f.) *quotidiana*
everyone *ognuno/a* (m./f.)
  everyone else *tutti gli altri*
exactly *giusto, proprio*
exaggerate (to) *esagerare*
exaggerated *esagerato*
exam *esame* (m.)
  fail (an exam) (to) *essere bocciato*
excellent *eccellente, ottimo*
exceptional *eccezionale*
exciting *stimolante*
excursion *escursione* (f.)
excuse (to) *scusare*
  Excuse me. (fml.) *(Mi) scusi.*
  Excuse me. (infml.) *Scusa.*
exercise (to) *fare ginnastica*
exhibition *mostra* (f.)
exist (to) *esistere*

expensive *caro, costoso, salato*
experience *esperienza* (f.)
expert *esperto/a* (m./f.)
exquisite *squisito*
extra *extra* (inv.)
eye *occhio* (m.)
eyebrow *sopracciglio* (m.)
  eyebrows *sopracciglia* (f. pl.)
eyeglasses *occhiali* (m. pl.)
eyelash *ciglio* (m.)
  eyelashes *ciglia* (f. pl.)

F

face *faccia* (f.)
facing... *di fronte a...*
fact *fatto* (m.)
  in fact *infatti*
factor *fattore* (m.)
factory *fabbrica* (f.)
fail (an exam) (to) *essere bocciato*
fairly *abbastanza*
fairy tale *favola* (f.), *fiaba* (f.)
fall *autunno* (m.)
  in the fall *in/d'autunno*
fall (to) *cadere*
  fall asleep (to) *addormentarsi*
false *falso*
family *famiglia* (f.)
  family style restaurant *trattoria* (f.)
  large family *famiglia numerosa*
famous *famoso*
fan *ventilatore* (m.)
fantastic *fantastico* (m. pl. *fantastici*)
far *lontano* (adverb)
  go too far (to) *esagerare*
farmer *contadino/a* (m./f.)
fashion *moda* (f.)
  fashion show *sfilata* (f.) *di moda*
fast *svelto, veloce, affrettato, pronto* (adjective);
  veloce (adverb)
fat *grasso* (m.) *(noun); grasso* (adjective)
father *padre* (m.)
father-in-law *suocero* (m.)
fault *torto* (m.)
favor *favore* (m.)
fax machine *fax* (m., pl. *fax*)
fear *paura* (f.)
February *febbraio* (m.)

feel (to) *sentirsi*
  feel like ... (to) *sentirsi di ... /avere voglia di ...*
  feeling (to be) *stare*
female *femmina* (f.)
fettuccine *fettuccine* (f. pl.)
fever *febbre* (f.)
  have a fever (to) *avere la febbre*
few *poco/a* (m./f.) (noun); *poco* (adjective)
  a few *alcuni/e* (noun); *qualche, certo* (adjective)
  a few days *pochi giorni* (m. pl.)
  in a few days *fra qualche giorno*
fiancé(e) *fidanzato/a* (m./f.)
field *campo* (m.)
fifteen *quindici*
  It's 11:15 a.m. *Sono le undici e un quarto di mattina.*
  It's 3:15. *Sono le tre e quindici.*
fifth *quinto*
fifty *cinquanta*
figure *figura* (f.)
file *documento* (m.), *file* (m.), *cartella* (f.)
  attach a file (to) *allegare un documento/file*
  close a file (to) *chiudere un documento/file*
  open a file (to) *aprire un documento/file*
  send a file (to) *inviare un documento/file*
file cabinet *schedario* (m.)
fill (to) *riempire*
  fill up with ... (to) *riempirsi di ...*
film *film (m., pl. film)*
final *ultimo*
finalist *finalista* (m./f.)
finally *finalmente*
find (to) *trovare*
Fine, thanks. *(Sto) bene, grazie.*
finger *dito* (m.)
fingers *dita* (f. pl.)
finish (to) *finire*
  finish ... ing (to) *finire di ...*
  to finish *per finire*
first *primo*
  as first course *per primo*
  first course *primo (piatto)* (m.)
  first floor (second floor in the U.S.) *primo piano* (m.)
  first of all *prima di tutto*
  first-born *primogenito/a* (m./f.)
  the first grade at elementary school *la*

prima elementare
fish *pesce* (m.)
  grilled fish *pesce alla griglia*
five *cinque*
  in five minutes *tra cinque minuti*
fixed *fisso*
flash (to) *lampeggiare*
flavor *sapore* (m.)
flip a coin (to) *fare testa o croce*
flip channels (to) *cambiare canale*
floor *piano* (m.)
  floor (inside a house or apartment) *pavimento* (m.)
  first floor (second floor in the U.S.) *primo piano*
  ground floor *pianterreno* (m.), *piano terra*
Florence *Firenze* (f.)
flower *fiore* (m.)
fog *nebbia* (f.)
  It's foggy. *C'è nebbia.*
follow (to) *seguire*
folly *follia* (f.)
food *cibo* (m.)
foot *piede* (m.)
  on foot *a piedi*
football *futbol* (m.)
  American football *futbol americano*
for *per, da*
  ask for (to) *chiedere*
  be looking for ... (to) *essere in cerca di ...*
  for a very long time *da una vita*
  go for a ride (to) *fare un giro*
  go for a walk (to) *fare un giro/fare un giro a piedi*
  look for (to) *cercare*
  passion for ... *passione per ...*
  wait for (to) *aspettare*
forehead *fronte* (f.)
foreign *straniero, estero*
  foreign language *lingua* (f.) *straniera*
  foreign tourists *turisti* (m./f. pl.) *stranieri*
forest *foresta* (f.)
forget (to) *dimenticare*
  forget to ... (do something) (to) *dimenticare di ...*
form *forma* (f.)
forty *quaranta*
  from 10:45 a.m. to 3:00 p.m. *dalle undici meno*

un quarto alle tre
in forty-five minutes *fra tre quarti d'ora*
It's 3:45. *Sono le tre e quarantacinque./Sono le tre e tre quarti./Sono le quattro meno un quarto./Manca un quarto alle quattro.*
forward *avanti*
forward (to) *inoltrare*
four *quattro*
It's four (o'clock). *Sono le quattro.*
fourteen *quattordici*
fourth *quarto*
frankly *francamente*
free *libero*
free time *tempo* (m.) *libero*
French *francese*
fresh *fresco*
fresh fruit *frutta* (f.) *fresca*
Friday *venerdì* (m., pl.)
from Monday to Friday *dal lunedì al venerdì*
friend *amico* (m.)/*amici* (m., pl.)
friendly *simpatico*
friendship *amicizia* (f.)
From *da, di*
from ... to ... (time periods) *dalle ... alle ...*
from Monday to Friday *dal lunedì al venerdì*
from 10:45 a.m. to 3:00 p.m. *dalle undici meno un quarto alle tre*
I'm from ... *Sono di ...*
starting from ... *a partire da ...*
Where are you from? (fml.)/Where is he/she from? *Di dov'è?*
Where are you from? (infml.) *Di dove sei?*
fruit *frutta* (f.)
fresh fruit *frutta fresca*
fuchsia *fucsia* (inv.)
full *pieno*
a full day *giornata* (f.) *piena*
full-time *a tempo pieno*
fun (to have fun) *divertirsi*
funny *divertente*
furniture *mobili* (m. pl.)

G

gain weight (to) *ingrassare*
gallery *galleria* (f.)
game *partita* (f.)
garage *garage* (m., pl.)
garden *giardino* (m.)

gardening *giardinaggio* (m.)
do gardening (to) *fare giardinaggio*
gas *gas* (m., pl. *gas*)
general *generale*
genetic *genetico* (m. pl. *genetici*)
gentleman *signore* (m.)
Germany *Germania* (f.)
get (to) *farsi*
get a divorce (to) *divorziarsi*
get bored (to) *annoiarsi*
get dressed (to) *vestirsi*
get married (to) *sposarsi*
get nervous (to) *agitarsi*
get ready (to) *prepararsi*
get up (to) *alzarsi*
gift *regalo* (m.)
girl (from 11 to 13 years old) *ragazzina* (f.)
girl (from 14 to 35 years old) *ragazza* (f.)
girlfriend *ragazza* (f.)
my girlfriend *la mia ragazza*
give (to) *dare*
given that ... *visto che ...*
gladly *volentieri*
glass *bicchiere* (m.)
gloves *guanti* (m. pl.)
gnome *gnomo* (m.)
go (to) *andare*
go ... ing (to) *andare a ...*
Go ahead. *Va' avanti.*
go back (to) *ritornare, tornare*
go camping (to) *fare il campeggio*
go for a ride (to) *fare un giro*
go for a walk (to) *fare un giro/fare un giro a piedi*
go hiking (to) *fare un'escursione/camminare in montagna*
go on a vacation (to) *fare una vacanza*
go out (to) *uscire*
go shopping (to) *fare la spesa/le spese*
go sightseeing (to) *visitare*
Go there. *Vacci.*
go too far (to) *esagerare*
go visit (to) *andare a trovare*
How's it going? *Come va?*
Let's go there. *Andiamoci.*
good *buono* (buon before masculine nouns except when they begin with s followed by another consonant, or with z)

Good afternoon. (from 1 p.m. to 6 p.m.) *Buon pomeriggio.*
Good evening. *Buona sera.*
Good luck. *Buona fortuna.*
Good morning. *Buon giorno.*
Good night. *Buona notte.*
Good-bye (infml.) *Arrivederci./Ciao.*
Good-bye (fml.) *ArriverderLa.*
Have a good day. *Buona giornata.*
Have a good dinner. *Buona cena.*
Have a good evening. *Buona serata.*
Have a good rest. *Buon riposo.*
Have a good trip. *Buon viaggio.*
Have a good walk. *Buona passeggiata.*
make a good impression (to) *fare bella figura*
nothing good to eat *niente di buono da mangiare*
grade *votazione* (f.), *voto* (m.)
the first grade at elementary school *la prima elementare*
graduate (to) *laurearsi*
granddaughter *nipote* (m./f.)
grandfather *nonno* (m.)
grandmother *nonna* (f.)
grandson *nipote* (m./f.)
grapes *uva* (f.)
a bunch of grapes *un grappolo* (m.) *d'uva*
grass *erba* (f.)
grate (to) *grattugiare*
Greece *Grecia* (f.)
Greek *greco*
green *verde*
greet each other (to) *salutarsi*
greeting *saluto* (m.)
gray *grigio*
grill *griglia* (f.)
grilled/barbequed *alla brace*
grilled fish *pesce* (m.) *alla griglia*
grilled/barbequed meat *carne alla brace*
groceries *alimentari* (m. pl.)
do grocery shopping (to) *fare la spesa/le spese*
grocery store *negozio* (m.) *di alimentari*
ground (adjective) *terra* (inv.)
ground floor *piano* (m.) *terra, pianterreno*
group *gruppo* (m.)
grow (to) *coltivare, crescere*
grow old (to) *invecchiare*

guest *ospite* (m./f.)
guide *guida* (f.)
guided tour *viaggio* (m.) *organizzato*
guitar *chitarra* (f.)
gym(nasium) *palestra* (f.)
gymnastics *ginnastica* (f.)

H

habitable *abitabile*
hail (to) *grandinare*
It's hailing. *Grandina.*
hair *capelli* (m. pl.)
half, half hour *mezzo, mezz'ora*
half seasons (spring and fall) *mezze stagioni* (f. pl.)
in half an hour *fra mezz'ora*
two and a half hours *due ore e mezzo*
hall *ingresso* (m.)
hand *mano* (f., pl. *mani*)
happen (to) *succedere*
happy *contento, felice*
Happy anniversary. *Buon anniversario.*
Happy birthday. *Buon compleanno.*
Happy holidays. *Buone feste.*
happy to … *contento di …*
harbor *porto* (m.)
harmful *nocivo*
hat *cappello* (m.)
have (to) *avere*
have (food and drink) (to) *prendere*
Have a good day. *Buona giornata.*
Have a good dinner. *Buona cena.*
Have a good evening. *Buona serata.*
Have a good rest. *Buon riposo.*
Have a good trip. *Buon viaggio.*
Have a good walk. *Buona passeggiata.*
have a nice big meal (to) *farsi una bella mangiata*
have a tendency (to) *tendere*
have breakfast (to) *fare colazione*
have fun (to) *divertirsi*
have to (to) *dovere*
he (subject pronoun) *lui*
he/she who (relative pronoun) *chi*
head *testa* (f.)
health *salute* (f.)
health club *palestra* (f.)
healthy *sano*

hear (to) *sentire*
heart *cuore* (m.)
heart attack *infarto* (m.)
heat *caldo* (m.)
Hello. *Salve./Ciao.*
help *aiuto* (m.)
help (to) *aiutare*
  help ... ing (to) *aiutare a ...*
  help each other (to) *aiutarsi*
  How can I help you? (fml.) *Posso esserLe*
    utile?
her (direct object pronoun) *la*
  her (direct object, disjunctive pronoun) *lei*
  to her (indirect object pronoun) *le*
  to her (indirect object, disjunctive pronoun) *A lei*
  her (possessive) *suo/sua/suoi/sue, di lei*
  His/Her name is ... *Si chiama ...*
herbalist's shop *erboristeria* (f.)
here *ecco, qui, ci*
  here again *riecco*
  Here is ... *Ecco ...*
  Here we are again! *Rieccoci!*
herself *sé*
Hi. *Ciao.*
high school *liceo* (m.), *scuola* (f.) *superiore*
high school degree *maturità* (f.)
higher *superiore*
hike *escursione* (f.)
  go hiking (to) *fare un'escursione/camminare*
    in montagna
hill *collina* (f.)
him (direct object pronoun) *lo*
  him (direct object, disjunctive pronoun) *lui*
  to him (indirect object pronoun) *gli*
  to him (indirect object, disjunctive pronoun) *a lui*
himself *sé*
hip *fianco* (m.)
his *suo/sua/suoi/sue, di lui*
  His/Her name is ... *Si chiama ...*
history *storia* (f.)
hobby *hobby* (m., pl)
hockey *hockey* (m.)
  ice hockey *hockey su ghiaccio*
holiday *festa* (f.), *vacanza* (f.)
  Happy holidays. *Buone feste.*
home *casa* (f.)
  around the home *in giro per la casa*
  at home *a casa*

stay-at-home dad *casalingo* (m.)
stay-at-home mom *casalinga* (f.)
homeopathic *omeopatico (m. pl. omeopatici)*
homeopathy *omeopatia* (f.)
hometown *città* (f.) *natale*
honey *miele* (m.)
hope (to) *sperare*
  hope to ... (to) *sperare di ...*
hospital *ospedale* (m.)
hot (to be) *avere caldo*
  It's hot. *Fa caldo.*
hotel *albergo* (m.), *hotel* (m., pl. *hotel*)
hour *ora* (f.)
  half hour *mezzo*
  in half an hour *fra mezz'ora*
  shorter working hours *orario* (m.) *ridotto*
  two and a half hours *due ore e mezzo*
house *casa* (f.)
  around the house *in giro per la casa*
  small house *villetta* (f.)
how *come*
  how (exclamation) *che*
  How are you doing? (fml.) *Come sta?*
  How are you doing? (infml.) *Come stai?*
  How can I help you? (fml.) *Posso esserLe*
    utile?
  How do I look? *Come mi sta?*
  How is ... ?/How are ... ? *Com'è?/Come*
    sono?
  How long has it been since ... ? *Da quanto*
    tempo ... ?
  how many/much *quanto*
  How much does it cost? *Quanto costa?*
  How nice!/How beautiful! *Che bello!*
  How old are you? (infml.) *Quanti anni hai?*
  How's it going? *Come va?*
  How's it possible!/How can this be! *Ma*
    come!
  know how (to) *sapere*
however *però*
hug (to) *abbracciarsi*
hundred *cento*
hunger *fame* (f.)
hungry (to be) *avere fame*
hurricane *uragano* (m.)
hurry *fretta* (f.)
  in a hurry *in fretta*
  in a hurry (to be) *avere fretta*

husband *marito* (m.)
hygienic *igienico*

I

I *io*
ice *ghiaccio* (m.)
ice cream *gelato* (m.)
ice hockey *hockey* (m.) *su ghiaccio*
idea *idea* (f.)
  no idea *nessuna idea*
if *se*
ill *ammalato*
illustration *figura* (f.)
imagine (to) *immaginare*
immediately *subito*
imperfect *imperfetto* (m.)
important *importante*
impression (to make a good impression) *fare bella figura*
in *fra, tra, in, a*
  check in (to) *registrarsi (all'hotel)*
  come in (to) *entrare*
  in a few days *fra qualche giorno*
  in a hurry *in fretta*
  in advance *prima*
  in any case *comunque*
  in any event *in ogni caso*
  in fact *infatti*
  in five minutes *tra cinque minuti*
  in forty-five minutes *fra tre quarti d'ora*
  in front *davanti*
  in front of … *davanti a … /di fronte a …*
  in great shape *in ottima forma*
  in half an hour *fra mezz'ora*
  in love *innamorato/a*
  in order that *affinché*
  in person *di persona*
  in the afternoon, from 1 to 5 p.m. *di pomeriggio*
  in the city *in centro*
  in the evening, from 6 to 11 p.m. *di sera*
  in the fall *in/d'autunno*
  in the meantime *nel frattempo*
  in the morning, from 4 to 11 a.m. *di mattina*
  in the office *in ufficio*
  in the spring *in primavera*
  in the style of *a + definite article*
  in the summer *d'estate*
  in the world *del mondo*
  in this period *in questo periodo*
  in winter *d'inverno*
  live in … (to) *vivere a …*
  the way in which … *il modo in cui …*
indicate (to) *indicare*
influence *influenza* (f.)
ingredient *ingrediente* (m.)
inherit (to) *ereditare*
insist (to) *insistere*
instead *invece*
institute *istituto* (m.)
intellectual *intellettivo*
intelligence quotient (IQ) *quoziente* (m.) *intellettivo*
intelligent *intelligente*
intention *proposito* (m.)
interest *interesse* (m.)
interest (to) *interessare*
interesting *interessante*
  anything interesting/cool to do *qualcosa di bello da fare*
  very interesting *interessantissimo*
intermission *intervallo* (m.)
internet *internet* (m.)
internship *stage (m., pl stage)*
interrupt (to) *interrompere*
intersection *incrocio* (m.)
interview *colloquio* (m.), *intervista* (f.)
  job interview *colloquio di lavoro*
intestine *intestino* (m.)
introduce (to) *presentare*
introduction *presentazione* (f.)
invite (to) *invitare*
iron *ferro* (m.) *(metal), ferro da stiro (appliance)*
ironing board *asse* (f.) *da stiro*
island *isola* (f.)
it (direct object pronoun) *lo* (m.), *la* (f.)
  it (direct object, disjunctive pronoun) *lui* (m.), *lei* (f.)
  to it (indirect object pronoun) *gli* (m.), *le* (f.)
  to it (indirect object, disjunctive pronoun) *a lui* (m.), *a lei* (f.)
  about it *ci, ne*
  How long has it been since … ? *Da quanto tempo … ?*
  It hurts. *Fa male.*
  It's bad. (weather) *Fa brutto.*

It's beautiful. (weather) *Fa bello.*
It's better. *Va meglio.*
It's cloudy. *È nuvoloso.*
It's cold. *Fa freddo.*
It's 11:15 a.m. *Sono le undici e un quarto di mattina.*
It's foggy. *C'è nebbia.*
It's four (o'clock). *Sono le quattro.*
It's hailing. *Grandina.*
It's hot. *Fa caldo.*
It's midnight. *È mezzanotte.*
It's noon. *È mezzogiorno.*
It's 1:00 a.m. *È l'una di notte.*
It's raining. *Piove.*
It's snowing. *Nevica.*
It's stormy. *C'è un temporale.*
It's sunny. *C'è il sole.*
It's three (o'clock). *Sono le tre.*
It's 3:15. *Sono le tre e quindici.*
It's 3:45. *Sono le tre e quarantacinque./Sono le tre e tre quarti./Sono le quattro meno un quarto./Manca un quarto alle quattro.*
It's 3:30. *Sono le tre e trenta.*
It's time to … *È ora di …*
It's two (o'clock). *Sono le due.*
It's windy. *C'è vento./Tira vento.*
of it, on it *ci, ne*
What time is it? *Che ora è?/Che ore sono?*
Italian *italiano*
Italy *Italia* (f.)
its *suo/sua/suoi/sue*
itself *sé*

J

jacket *giacca* (f.)
January *gennaio* (m.)
jeans *blue jeans* (m. pl.)
job *lavoro* (m.)
  job interview *colloquio* (m.) *di lavoro*
  part-time job *lavoro part-time*
  steady job *lavoro fisso*
  summer job *lavoro temporaneo*
jog (to) *fare il footing*
jogging *footing* (m.)
joke *barzelletta* (f.)
journal *rivista* (f.)
journalist *giornalista* (m./f.)
juice *succo* (m.)

July *luglio* (m.)
jump (to) *saltare*
  jump rope (to) *saltare la corda*
June *giugno* (m.)
just *appena, proprio, solo*

K

keyboard *tastiera* (f.)
kidney *rene* (m.)
kilo *chilo* (m.)
kilometer *chilometro*
kind (adjective) *gentile*
kind (noun) *tipo* (m.)
kiss (to) *baciarsi*
kitchen *cucina* (f.)
  eat-in kitchen *cucina abitabile*
knee *ginocchio* (m.)
  knees *ginocchia/ginocchi* (f./m. pl.)
knife *coltello* (m.)
know (to) *sapere (a fact, how), conoscere (a person)*
  I know. *Lo so.*
  I don't know. *Non lo so.*
  know each other (to) *conoscersi*

L

lady *signora*
lake *lago* (m.)
  at the lake *al lago*
lamp *lampada* (f.)
lamp post *lampione* (m.)
land *terra* (f.)
language *lingua* (f.)
  foreign language *lingua straniera*
large *grosso; numeroso (family)*
  large dinner *cena* (f.) *abbondante*
  large family *famiglia* (f.) *numerosa*
lasagna *lasagne* (f. pl.)
last *scorso, ultimo*
  last night *ieri sera*
  last week *settimana* (f.) *scorsa*
  last year *anno* (m.) *scorso*
last (to) *durare*
late *tardi*
  late (to be) *essere in ritardo*
until late *fino a tardi*
Latin American *latinoamericano*
laundry *bucato* (m.), *lavanderia* (f.)

do the laundry (to) *fare il bucato*
laundry detergent *detersivo* (m.) *per il bucato*
lawyer *avvocato* (m.)
learn (to) *apprendere, imparare*
leather *pelle* (f.)
　made out of leather *di pelle*
leave (to) *partire, lasciare*
left *sinistra* (f.)
　left (hand) *manca* (f.)
　on/to the left *(a) sinistra*
left-handed *mancino*
leg *gamba* (f.)
　Break a leg! (lit. In the mouth of the
　　wolf!) *In bocca al lupo!*
　Thank you. (lit. May the wolf die.) *Crepi il*
　　lupo. (in response to In bocca al lupo!)
less *meno*
　less ... than *meno ... di/che*
lesson *lezione* (f.)
let (to) *lasciare*
　Let me see. *Fammi vedere.*
　Let's go there. *Andiamoci.*
letter *lettera* (f.)
lettuce *lattuga* (f.)
level *livello* (m.)
library *biblioteca* (f.)
lie *bugia* (f.)
life *vita* (f.)
　everyday life *vita quotidiana*
light *leggero*
　light sweater *maglioncino* (m.)
lightning *lampo* (m.), *fulmine* (m.)
like (to) *piacere, amare*
　I like ... *Mi piace/piacciono ...* (sg./pl.)
　I would like ... *Vorrei ...*
likely *probabile*
linen *lino* (m.)
　made out of linen *di lino*
list *lista* (f.)
　wine list *lista dei vini*
listen to (to) *ascoltare*
liter *litro* (m.)
literature *letteratura* (f.)
little *poco/a* (m./f.) (noun); *poco* (adjective)
　a little *un poco/un po'*
live (to) *vivere, abitare*
　live in ... (to) *vivere a ...*
liver *fegato* (m.)

living room *salone* (m.), *soggiorno* (m.)
lobster *aragosta* (f.)
lonely *solo*
long *lungo*
　for a very long time *da una vita*
　How long has it been since ... ? *Da quanto*
　　tempo ... ?
　long distance *di fondo*
　long time *molto tempo*
　take a nice long nap (to) *farsi una bella*
　　dormita
look at (to) *guardare*
　How do I look? *Come mi sta?*
look for (to) *cercare*
　looking for ... (to be) *essere in cerca di ...*
lose (to) *perdere*
　lose weight (to) *dimagrire*
lottery *lotteria* (f.)
loudly *forte* (adverb)
Love *amore* (m.)
　in love *innamorato/a*
　love stories *storie* (f. pl.) *d'amore*
love (to) *amare*
　I love you. *Ti voglio bene. Ti amo.*
low *basso*
luck *fortuna* (f.)
　Good luck. *Buona fortuna.*
lucky *beato, fortunato*
　Lucky you. *Beati voi.* (pl.)
　Lucky you! *Beato te!*
lunch *pranzo* (m.)
lung *polmone* (m.)

M

machine *macchina* (f.)
magazine *rivista* (f.)
mail *posta* (f.) (noun); *postale* (adjective)
　e-mail *posta elettronica*
　send an e-mail (to) *mandare un'email/una*
　　mail
main course *secondo (piatto)* (m.)
　as main course *di secondo*
make (to) *fare*
　made from plastic *di plastica*
　made out of cashmere *di cachemire*
　made out of corduroy *di velluto a coste*
　made out of leather *di pelle*
　made out of linen *di lino*

made out of silk *di seta*
make a good impression (to) *fare bella figura*
make friends (to) *fare amicizia*
make noise (to) *fare rumore*
male *maschio* (m.)
man *uomo* (m.)/*uomini* (pl.)
  men's suit *abito da uomo*
manage (to) *riuscire*
  manage to ... (to) *riuscire a ...*
manner *modo* (m.)
many *molto* (adjective); *molto/a* (m./f.) (noun)
  as many ... as *tanto ... quanto*
  how many *quanto*
  so many *tanto* (adjective); *tanto/a* (m./f.) (noun)
  too many *troppo* (adjective); *troppo/a* (m./f.)
    (noun)
map *cartina* (f.), *mappa* (f.), *piantina* (f.)
marathon *maratona* (f.)
March *marzo* (m.)
march *sfilata* (f.)
marital status *stato civile*
market *mercato* (m.)
married *sposato/a*
marry ... (someone) (to) *sposarsi con ...*
  get married (to) *sposarsi*
  He/She is getting married. *Si sposa.*
marvelous *meraviglioso*
math *matematica* (f.)
matrimonial *matrimoniale*
May *maggio* (m.)
May I ... ? *Posso ... ?*
maybe *forse*
mayor *sindaco* (m.)
me (direct object pronoun) *mi*
  me (direct object, disjunctive pronoun) *me*
  to me (indirect object pronoun) *mi*
  to me (indirect object, disjunctive pronoun) *a me*
meadow *prato* (m.)
means *mezzo* (m.)
  means of transportation *mezzo di trasporto*
meantime *frattempo*
  in the meantime *nel frattempo*
measure (to) *misurare*
Meat *carne* (f.)
  grilled/barbecued meat *carne alla brace*
  meat sauce *ragù* (m., pl.)
  sliced cold meat *affettato* (m.)
mechanic *meccanico* (m.)/*meccanici* (pl.)

medical doctor *medico* (m.)
medicine *medicina* (f.)
  medicine cabinet *armadietto* (m.)
meet (to) *vedere* (a person), *incontrare* (a person
  casually), *conoscere* (a person for the first time)
  meet each other (to) *incontrarsi*
  Pleased to meet you. *Piacere.*
  Pleased to meet you, too. *Piacere mio.*
  Very pleased to meet you! *Molto piacere!*
meeting *riunione* (f.)
  meeting room *sala* (f.) *delle riunioni*
melon *melone* (m.)
memory *memoria* (f.)
menu *menù* (m.)
Merry Christmas. *Buon Natale.*
message *messaggio* (m.)
  instant message *messaggio immediato*
meter *metro* (m.)
metro, subway *metrò* (m. in Milan/f. in Rome)
microwave *microonda* (f.)
  microwave oven *forno* (m.) *a microonde*
midnight *mezzanotte* (f.)
  around midnight *intorno a mezzanotte*
  It's midnight. *È mezzanotte.*
Might as well ... *Tanto vale ...*
Milan *Milano* (f.)
milk *latte* (m.)
million *milione* (m.)/*milioni* (pl.)
  a million dollars *milione di dollari*
mineral *minerale*
  mineral water *acqua* (f.) *minerale*
  still mineral water *acqua minerale naturale*
  sparkling mineral water *acqua minerale
    frizzante*
minute *minuto* (m.)
  in five minutes *tra cinque minuti*
  in forty-five minutes *fra tre quarti d'ora*
mirror *specchio* (m.)
mix (to) *mescolare*
mixed *misto*
  mixed cold cuts *affettati* (m. pl.) *misti*
  mixed salad *insalata* (f.) *mista*
model (fashion) *modello/a* (m./f.)
modem *modem* (m.)
modern *moderno*
  modern art *arte* (f.) *moderna*
mom *mamma* (f.)
  stay-at-home mom *casalinga* (f.)

moment *momento* (m.)
Monday *lunedì* (m., pl.)
  from Monday to Friday *dal lunedì al venerdì*
  on Mondays *il lunedì*
money *denaro* (m.), *soldi* (m. pl.)
monitor *monitor* (m.), *schermo* (m.), *video* (m.)
month *mese* (m.)
  a month ago *un mese fa*
  next month *mese prossimo*
monument *monumento* (m.)
moon *luna* (f.)
more *più*
  more/-er … than *più … di/che*
  no more *non … più*
moreover *inoltre*
morning *mattina* (f.)
  every morning *tutte le mattine*
  Good morning. *Buon giorno.*
  in the morning, from 4 to 11 a.m. *di mattina*
mosque *moschea* (f.)
mother *madre* (f.)
mother-in-law *suocera* (f.)
motorbike *motocicletta* (f.), *moto* (f., pl.)
mountain *montagna* (f.)
  to the mountains *in montagna*
mouse *mouse* (m.) *(computer)*
mouse pad *tappetino* (m.)
mouth *bocca* (f.)
move (to) *muovere, trasferirsi*
  move (to a new house) (to) *traslocare, fare il trasloco*
movie *film* (m., pl.)
  action movies *film d'azione*
  movie director *regista* (m./f.)
  movie theater *cinema* (m., pl.: cinema)
Mr. *signore* (m.)
Mrs. *signora* (f.)
much *molto* (adjective); *molto/a* (m./f.) (noun)
  as much … as *tanto … quanto*
  how much *quanto*
  How much does it cost? *Quanto costa?*
  so much *tanto* (adjective); *tanto/a* (m./f.) (noun), *tanto* (adverb)
  too much *troppo* (adjective); *troppo/a* (m./f.) (noun)
municipal building *municipio* (m.)
muscle *muscolo* (m.)
museum *museo* (m.)

mushroom *fungo* (m.)
music *musica* (f.)
  classical music *musica classica*
  pop music *musica pop*
musician *musicista* (m./f.)
must *dovere*
my *mio/mia/miei/mie*
  My name is … *Mi chiamo …*

N

name *nome* (m.)
  His/Her name is … *Si chiama …*
  My name is … *Mi chiamo …*
named (to be) *chiamarsi*
nap *pisolino* (m.)
  take a nap (to) *fare un pisolino*
  take a nice long nap (to) *farsi una bella dormita*
Naples *Napoli* (f.)
native *natale*
natural *naturale*
nature *natura* (f.)
naughty *cattivo*
near *vicino*
  near … *vicino a …*
  near there *lì vicino*
nearby *qui vicino*
necessary *necessario*
neck *collo* (m.)
necklace *collana* (f.)
need *bisogno* (m.)
  need (to) *essere nel bisogno*
  need … (to) *avere bisogno di …*
neighborhood *quartiere* (m.)
nephew *nipote* (m./f.)
nervous *nervoso*
  get nervous (to) *agitarsi*
never *mai* (in negative sentences)
  Never! *Mai!*
  never again *mai più*
new *nuovo*
news *notizie* (f. pl.), *giornale radio* (m.) *(on the radio)*, *telegiornale* (m.) *(on TV)*, *TG* (m.) *(on TV)*
newspaper *giornale* (m.)
next *prossimo*
  next month *mese* (m.) *prossimo*
  next week *prossima settimana* (f.)
nice *simpatico, bravo*

have a nice big meal (to) *farsi una bella mangiata*
How nice! *Che bello!*
take a nice long nap (to) *farsi una bella dormita*
niece *nipote* (m./f.)
night *notte* (f.)
at night, from midnight to 3 a.m. *di notte*
Good night. *Buona notte.*
last night *ieri sera*
nine *nove*
nineteen *diciannove*
ninth *nono*
ninety *novanta*
no *no* (adverb); *nessuno* (adjective)
no idea *nessuna idea*
no longer *non ... più*
no more *non ... più*
nobody *nessuno/a* (m./f.)
noise *rumore* (m.)
make noise (to) *fare rumore*
noisy *rumoroso*
none *nessuno/a* (m./f.)
noon *mezzogiorno* (m.)
It's noon. *È mezzogiorno.*
normal *normale*
normally *normalmente*
Norwegian *norvegese* (m./f.)
nose *naso* (m.)
not *non*
not ... at all *non ... affatto*
Not bad. *Così, così.*
not even *neanche, nemmeno*
notebook *quaderno* (m.)
nothing *niente, nulla*
nothing good to eat *niente di buono da mangiare*
notice (to) *notare*
novel *romanzo* (m.)
contemporary novels *romanzi* (pl.) *contemporanei*
November *novembre* (m.)
now *adesso*
by now *ormai*
right now *in questo momento*
number *numero* (m.)
numerous *numeroso*
nurse *infermiere/a* (m./f.)

O

O.K. *d'accordo*
obligation *impegno* (m.)
obvious *ovvio*
ocean *oceano* (m.)
October *ottobre* (m.)
of *di*
first of all *prima di tutto*
means of transportation *mezzo* (m.) *di trasporto*
of all *di tutti*
of it *ci, ne*
of them *ne*
out of town *fuori città*
pair of shoes *paio* (m.) *di scarpe*
speaking of ... *a proposito di ...*
There are seven of us. *Siamo in sette.*
There are three of them. *Ce ne sono tre.*
variety of choices *varietà* (f.) *di scelta*
works of art *opere* (f. pl.) *d'arte*
offer (to) *offrire*
office *ufficio* (m.), *studio* (m.)
in the office *in ufficio*
often *spesso*
oil *olio* (m.)
old *vecchio*
grow old (to) *invecchiare*
How old are you? *Quanti anni hai?*
I am ... years old. *Ho ... anni.*
older *maggiore*
olive *oliva* (f.)
on *in, su*
on business *per lavoro*
on foot *a piedi*
on it *ci*
on Mondays *il lunedì*
on the contrary *anzi*
on the left *a sinistra*
on the right *a destra*
on time (to be) *essere in orario, essere puntuale*
on vacation *in ferie, in vacanza*
one *un/uno* (in front of s + consonant, z, ps, gn)*/una*
one (impersonal pronoun) *si*
one (number) *uno*
It's 1:00 a.m. *È l'una di notte.*
the one who, whoever (relative pronoun) *chi*

oneself *sé*
onion *cipolla* (f.)
only *soltanto, solo*
open *aperto*
  open all day *orario* (m.) *continuato*
open (to) *aprire*
  open a file (to) *aprire un documento/file*
opera *opera* (f.)
opposite *di fronte*
or *o*
orange *arancione* (inv.) *(color); arancia* (f.) *(fruit)*
orchard *orto* (m.)
order *ordine* (m.)
  in order that *affinché*
order (to) *ordinare*
organize (to) *organizzare*
osso buco *ossobuco* (m.)
other *altro*
our *nostro/nostra/nostri/nostre*
out of town *fuori città*
outdoors *all'aperto*
outside *fuori*
oven *forno* (m.)
  microwave oven *forno a microonde*
over *su*
overweight *sovrappeso* (m., pl.)
overweight (to be) *essere in sovrappeso*

P

p.m. *di pomeriggio, di sera*
pack (a suitcase) (to) *fare le valige/valigie*
page *pagina* (f.)
pain *dolore* (m.)
  have a pain in … (to) *avere un dolore a … / avere male a …*
painting *quadro* (m.)
pair *paio* (m.)
  pair of shoes *paio di scarpe*
pajamas *pigiama* (m.)
pan *pentola* (f.)
panorama *panorama* (m.)
pants *pantaloni* (m. pl.)
  pant suit *tailleur* (m.) *pantalone*
paper *carta* (f.)
  toilet paper *carta igienica*
parade *sfilata* (f.)
parent *genitore/trice* (m./f.)
Paris *Parigi* (f.)

park *parco* (m.)
park (to) *parcheggiare*
Parmesan cheese *parmigiano* (m.)
part *parte* (f.)
participate (to) *partecipare*
part-time *part-time*
  part-time job *lavoro* (m.) *part-time*
party *festa* (f.)
  have a party (to) *dare una festa*
pass (an exam) (to) *passare, essere promosso*
passion *passione* (f.)
  passion for … *passione per …*
passport *passaporto* (m.)
past (tense)
  past perfect *passato* (m.)
trapassato (m.) *prossimo*
pasta *pasta* (f.)
path *viale* (m.), *via* (f.)
patience *pazienza* (f.)
patient *paziente* (m./f.)
pay (to) *pagare*
  pay attention (to) *fare attenzione*
  Pay attention! *Sta' attento!*
peach *pesca* (f.)
pear *pera* (f.)
pediatrician *pediatra* (m./f.)
peel (to) *sbucciare*
penne (pasta) *penne* (f. pl.)
penthouse *attico (m., pl. attici)*
people *gente* (f.), *persone* (pl.)
people (impersonal pronoun) *si*
pepper (spice) *pepe* (m.) *(spice); peperone* (m.)
  (vegetable)
perfect *perfetto*
performance *spettacolo* (m.)
perfume *profumo* (m.)
perhaps *magari, forse*
period *periodo* (m.)
  in this period *in questo periodo*
permanent *fisso*
person *persona* (f.)
  athletic person *persona sportiva*
  in person *di persona*
personal information *dati* (m. pl.) *anagrafici*
pharmacy *farmacia* (f.)
photograph *foto* (f., pl.), *fotografia* (f.)
  take a picture (to) *fare una foto/fotografia*
photography *fotografia* (f.)

pianist *pianista* (m./f.)
piano *pianoforte* (m.)
  play the piano (to) *suonare il pianoforte*
pick up (to) *raccogliere*
picture *quadro* (m.) *(painting); foto* (f., pl.),
  fotografia (f.) *(photograph)*
  take a picture (to) *fare una foto/fotografia*
piece *pezzo* (m.)
pillow *cuscino* (m.)
pineapple *ananas (m., plural ananas)*
pink *rosa* (inv.)
place *luogo* (m.), *posto* (m.)
plan (to) *progettare*
planet *pianeta* (m.)
plant *pianta* (f.)
plant (to) *piantare*
plastic *plastica* (f.)
  made from plastic *di plastica*
plate *piatto* (m.)
play (theater) *spettacolo* (m.)
play (to) *giocare (sport, game); praticare (sport);*
  suonare (instrument)
  play a sport (to) *praticare uno sport*
  play cards (to) *giocare a carte*
  play tennis (to) *giocare a tennis*
  play the piano (to) *suonare il pianoforte*
player *giocatore/trice* (m./f.) *(person); lettore*
  (m.) *(machine)*
  CD player *lettore di cd (ci-di)*
  DVD player *dvd* (m.)
playground *parco giochi*
pleasant *piacevole*
Please. *Per favore.*
pleasing (to someone) (to be) *piacere*
  Pleased to meet you. *Piacere.*
  Pleased to meet you, too. *Piacere mio.*
  Very pleased to meet you! *Molto piacere!*
plentiful *abbondante*
plumber *idraulico/a* (m./f.)
plural *plurale* (m.)
poem *poema* (m.)
poker *poker* (m., pl.)
policeman *poliziotto* (m.)
  policewoman *donna* (f.) *poliziotto*
pond *stagno* (m.)
pool *biliardo* (m.)
pop *pop* (inv.)
  pop music *musica* (f.) *pop*

pork *maiale* (m.)
  baked pork *maiale al forno*
  pork chop *braciola* (f.) *di maiale*
possessive *possessivo*
possible *possibile*
  How's it possible! *Ma come!*
post office *ufficio* (m.) *postale*
pot *pentola* (f.)
potato *patata* (f.)
pour (to) *versare*
powder (talcum) *borotalco* (m.)
practice sports (to) *fare sport*
prefer (to) *preferire*
prepare (to) *preparare*
preposition *preposizione* (f.)
present (adjective) *presente*
  present perfect *passato* (m.) *prossimo*
  present subjunctive *congiuntivo* (m.) *presente*
present (to) *presentare*
pressure *pressione* (f.)
pretty *carino*
price *prezzo* (m.)
printer *stampante* (f.)
private *privato*
probably *probabilmente*
problem *problema* (m.)
product *prodotto* (m.)
production (theater) *messinscena* (f.)
professional
professional school *professionale*
istituto (m.) tecnico
professor *professore/essa* (m./f.)
program *trasmissione* (f.), *programma* (m.)
  television program *trasmissione televisiva*
prohibit (to) *proibire*
promise (to) *promettere*
  promise to … (do something)
    (to) *promettere di …*
promote (to) *promuovere*
pronoun *pronome* (m.)
provided that … *a patto che … / a condizione*
  che … / purché
province *provincia* (f.)
psychiatrist *psichiatra* (m./f.)
psychologist *psicologo* (m./f.)
publish (to) *pubblicare*
punctual *puntuale*
purple *viola* (inv.)

purse *borsa* (f.)
put (to) *mettere*
put things away (to) *mettere in ordine*
put on (to) *mettersi*
He/She puts on … (to) *Si mette …*

Q

quarter *quarto* (m.)
question *domanda* (f.)
  ask a question (to) *fare una domanda*
quick *veloce*
quickly *velocemente, in fretta*
quit (to) *smettere*
quit … ing (to) *smettere di …*
quotient *quoziente* (m.)
  intelligence quotient (IQ) *quoziente*
    intellettivo

R

rain *pioggia* (f.)
rain (to) *piovere*
  It's raining. *Piove.*
raise (to) *crescere*
rarely *raramente*
rather *piuttosto*
ravioli *ravioli* (m. pl.)
razor *rasoio* (m.)
reach (to) *raggiungere*
read (to) *leggere*
reader *lettore* (m.)
ready *pronto*
  get ready (to) *prepararsi*
  ready to … *pronto per …*
really *veramente, davvero, proprio*
reason *motivo* (m.), *ragione* (f.)
  the reason why … *il motivo per cui … / la*
    ragione per cui …
receive (to) *ricevere*
reception desk *accettazione* (f.), *reception* (f., pl.)
recipe *ricetta* (f.)
red *rosso*
  red wine *vino* (m.) *rosso*
reduced *ridotto*
refrigerator *frigorifero* (m.) (*frigo*)
regret (to) *pentirsi*
regularly *regolarmente*
reject (to) *bocciare*
relative *parente* (m./f.)

relax (to) *rilassarsi*
remain *rimanere*
remember (to) *ricordare*
  remember to … (do something)
    (to) *ricordarsi di …*
removal *trasloco* (m.)
Renaissance *Rinascimento* (m.) (noun);
  rinascimentale (adjective)
rent (to) *affittare*
repent (to) *pentirsi*
reply (to) *rispondere*
report card *scheda* (f.)
rescue *soccorso* (m.)
research *indagine* (f.)
researcher *ricercatore/trice* (m./f.)
reservation *prenotazione* (f.)
reserve (to) *prenotare*
residence *residenza* (f.)
respectively *rispettivamente*
rest *riposo* (m.)
  Have a good rest. *Buon riposo.*
restaurant *ristorante* (m.)
  family style restaurant *trattoria* (f.)
retired *pensionato/a* (m./f.)
return (to) *ritornare, tornare*
rib *costa* (f.)
rice *riso* (m.)
rich *ricco*
ride a bike (to) *andare in bicicletta*
right *destra* (f.) (noun); *vero, giusto* (adjective)
  on/to the right *(a) destra*
  right (to be) *avere ragione*
  right now *in questo momento*
ring *anello* (m.)
ring (a bell) (to) *suonare*
river *fiume* (m.)
road *strada* (f.)
roast *arrosto*
roast pork *maiale* (m.) *al forno*
rock *roccia* (f.)
romantic *romantico* (m., pl. *romantici*)
Rome *Roma* (f.)
room *sala* (f.), *camera* (f.), *stanza* (f.)
  bedroom *camera* (f.), *camera da letto, stanza*
    (f.) *da letto*
  dining room *sala da pranzo*
  double room (one queen-size bed) *camera*
    matrimoniale

double room (two twin-size beds) *camera doppia*
emergency room *pronto soccorso* (m.)
living room *salone* (m.), *soggiorno* (m.)
meeting room *sala delle riunioni*
single room (one twin bed) *camera singola*
study (room) *studio* (m.)
rope *corda* (f.)
  jump rope (to) *saltare la corda*
rug *tappeto* (m.)
run (to) *correre*
rural *rurale*
rushed *affrettato*

S

sad *triste*
sail *vela* (f.)
sail (to) *andare in barca a vela*
sailing *vela* (f.)
salad *insalata* (f.)
  mixed salad *insalata mista*
salary *salario* (m.)
salesman *venditore* (m.)
saleswoman *venditrice* (f.)
salt *sale* (m.)
same *stesso, pari* (inv.)
  at the same time *allo stesso tempo*
sand *sabbia* (f.)
sandwich *panino* (m.)
Sardinia *Sardegna* (f.)
satisfied *soddisfatto*
Saturday *sabato* (m.)
sauté (to) *rosolare*
save (to) *salvare*
  save a document (to) *salvare un documento*
say (to) *dire*
scare (to) *impaurire*
scarf *sciarpa* (f.) *(long), foulard* (m.) *(square)*
scary (to be) *fare paura*
scholastic *scolastico (m. pl. scolastici)*
school *scuola* (f.)
  high school *liceo* (m.), *scuola* (f.) *superiore*
  professional school *istituto* (m.) *tecnico*
  the first grade at elementary school *la prima elementare*
scientist *ricercatore/trice* (m./f.)
screen *monitor* (m.), *schermo* (m.), *video* (m.)
sculpture *scultura* (f.)

sea *mare* (m.)
seaside *mare* (m.)
season *stagione* (f.)
  half seasons (spring and fall) *mezze stagioni*
second *secondo*
  second-born *secondogenito/a* (m./f.)
secretary *segretario/a* (m./f.)
see (to) *vedere*
  Let me see. *Fammi vedere.*
  see each other (to) *vedersi*
  See you later. *A dopo.*
  See you soon. *A presto.*
seem (to) *sembrare*
send (to) *inviare, mandare, spedire*
  send a file (to) *inviare un documento/file*
  send an e-mail (to) *mandare un'email/una mail*
September *settembre* (m.)
serious *grave*
serve (to) *servire*
set (a table) (to) *apparecchiare*
settings *ambientazione* (f.)
seven *sette*
  at seven thirty (7:30) *alle sette e mezza*
  by seven (o'clock) *per le sette*
  There are seven of us. *Siamo in sette.*
seventeen *diciassette*
seventh *settimo*
seventy *settanta*
several *parecchio* (adjective); *parecchio/a* (m./f.) (noun)
shampoo *shampo* (m.)
shape *forma* (f.)
  in great shape *in ottima forma*
share (to) *condividere, avere in comune*
shave (to) *farsi la barba, radersi*
shaving cream *crema* (f.) *da barba*
she (subject pronoun) *lei*
  he/she who (relative pronoun) *chi*
shelf *scaffale* (m.)
  book shelf *scaffale (dei libri)*
shine (to) *splendere*
shirt *camicia* (f.)
shoes *scarpe* (f. pl.)
  pair of shoes *paio* (m.) *di scarpe*
  shoe store *negozio* (m.) *di scarpe*
  tennis shoes *scarpe da tennis*
shop (to) *fare spese*

shopping *spesa* (f.)
  go shopping (to), do grocery shopping
    (to) *fare la spesa/le spese*
shopping mall *centro acquisti, centro*
  commerciale
short *corto, basso*
  short trip *gita* (f.)
  shorter working hours *orario* (m.) *ridotto*
shoulder *spalla* (f.)
show (to) *mostrare, indicare, fare vedere*
shower *doccia* (f.)
  take a shower (to) *fare la doccia*
shrimp *gambero* (m.), *gamberetto* (m.)
Sicily *Sicilia* (f.)
sick *malato, ammalato*
side dish *contorno* (m.)
  as a side dish *di/per contorno*
sidewalk *marciapiede* (m.)
sightseeing (to go sightseeing) *visitare*
silent *silenzioso*
silk *seta* (f.)
  made out of silk *di seta*
silverware *posate* (f. pl.)
similar *simile*
simple *piano*
sin *peccato* (m.)
since *da*
  How long has it been since … ? *Da quanto*
    tempo … ?
  since … *visto che …*
  since always *da una vita*
sing (to) *cantare*
single *singolo*
  single (man) *celibe* (m.)
  single (woman) *nubile* (f.)
  single room (one twin bed) *camera* (f.)
    singola
sink (kitchen) *lavandino* (m.) *(kitchen); lavabo*
  (m.) *(wash basin)*
sister *sorella* (f.)
site *sito* (m.)
situation *condizione* (f.)
six *sei*
sixteen *sedici*
sixth *sesto*
sixty *sessanta*
size *taglia* (f.) *(dresses, pants), misura* (f.) *(shirts),*
  numero (m.) *(shoes)*

ski (to) *sciare*
skiing *sci* (m., pl.)
  alpine skiing *sci alpino*
  cross-country skiing *sci di fondo*
skillful *bravo*
skin *pelle* (f.)
skirt *gonna* (f.)
sky *cielo* (m.)
sleep *sonno* (m.)
sleep (to) *dormire*
sleepy *insonnolito*
  sleepy (to be) *avere sonno*
slice (to) *affettare, tagliare*
  sliced cold meat *affettato* (m.)
slowly *lentamente, piano*
small *piccolo*
smog *smog* (m.)
smoked *affumicato*
smooth *piano*
snack *spuntino* (m.)
sneakers *scarpe* (f. pl.) *da ginnastica, scarpe da*
  tennis, sneakers (m. pl.)
snow *neve* (f.)
snow (to) *nevicare*
  It's snowing. *Nevica.*
so *così, tanto, allora, quindi*
  I don't think so. *Non credo.*
  so … as *così … come/sia … che*
  so many *tanto/a* (m./f.) (noun); *tanto* (adjective)
  so much *tanto/a* (m./f.) (noun); *tanto* (adjective);
    tanto (adverb)
  So so. *Così, così.*
  so that *affinché*
soap (bar) *saponetta* (f.)
soccer *calcio* (m.)
social *sociale*
socks *calze* (f. pl.)
soda *bibita* (f.)
sofa *sofà* (m.), *divano* (m.)
soft drink *bibita* (f.)
softly *piano*
some *alcuni/e, qualche, certo, di + definite article*
someone *qualcuno*
something *qualcosa*
  something to drink *qualcosa da bere*
sometimes *qualche volta, a volte*
son *figlio* (m.)
song *canzone* (f.)

soon *presto*
  See you soon. *A presto.*
sooner *prima*
Sorry (I'm sorry.) *Mi dispiace./Scusami.*
soup *minestra* (f.)
sour *amaro*
spacious *spazioso, ampio*
spaghetti *spaghetti* (m. pl.)
sparkling wine *spumante* (m.)
spa *terme* (f. pl.)
speak (to) *parlare*
  speak Chinese (to) *parlare cinese*
  speaking of … *a proposito di …*
speech *discorso* (m.)
spend (to) *spendere*
spoon *cucchiaio* (m.)
sport *sport* (m., pl.)
  play a sport (to) *praticare uno sport*
  practice sports (to) *fare sport*
  watch sports on TV (to) *guardare lo sport in/ alla televisione*
spring *primavera* (f.)
  in the spring *in primavera*
square *piazza* (f.)
stadium *stadio* (m.)
staff *staff* (m.)
staircase *scala* (f.)
stairs *scale* (f.)
star *stella* (f.)
starting from … *a partire da …*
state *stato* (m.)
station *stazione* (f.)
  train station *stazione (dei treni)*
stay (to) *restare, stare*
  stay-at-home dad *casalingo* (m.)
  stay-at-home mom *casalinga* (f.)
steady job *lavoro* (m.) *fisso*
stepdaughter *figlia* (f.) *di mia moglie (di mio marito)*
stepfather *marito* (m.) *di mia madre*
stepmother *moglie* (f.) *di mio padre*
stepson *figlio* (m.) *di mia moglie (di mio marito)*
stereo *stereo* (m., pl.)
stew *spezzatino* (m.)
still *ancora*
stomach *stomaco* (m.) *(above the waist);* ventre (m.), *pancia* (f.) *(below the waist)*
stone *pietra* (f.)

stop (to) *fermarsi, smettere*
stop … ing (to) *smettere di …*
store *negozio* (m.)
  clothing store *negozio di abbigliamento*
  department store *grande magazzino* (m.)
  electronics store *negozio di elettronica*
  grocery store *negozio di alimentari*
  shoe store *negozio di scarpe*
storm *temporale* (m.)
  It's stormy. *C'è un temporale.*
story *storia* (f.)
  love stories *storie* (pl.) *d'amore*
stove (electric, gas) *cucina* (f.) *elettrica, cucina* (f.) *a gas*
straight *diritto*
  straight ahead *sempre diritto*
strange *strano*
strawberry *fragola* (f.)
street *strada* (f.), *via* (f.)
street light *semaforo* (m.)
stressed *stressato*
stressful *stressante*
strong *forte*
student *studente/essa* (m./f.)
  university student *studente universitario*
study *indagine* (f.), *studio* (m.) *(room)*
study (to) *studiare*
stuff *roba* (f.)
  a bunch/lot of stuff *un sacco di roba*
subject *materia* (f.)
subjunctive mood (grammar) *congiuntivo* (m.)
  present subjunctive *congiuntivo presente*
substance *sostanza* (f.)
substitute *sostituto/a* (m./f.)
suburban *periferico*
suburbs *periferia* (f.)
subway *metrò* (m. in Milan/f. in Rome)
suddenly *improvvisamente*
sugar *zucchero* (m.)
suit *abito* (m.) *(men's)*, *tailleur* (m., pl.) *(women's)*
  men's suit *abito da uomo*
  pant suit *tailleur pantalone*
suitcase *valigia* (f.)
summer *estate* (f.)
  in the summer *d'estate*
  summer job *lavoro* (m.) *temporaneo*
sun *sole* (m.)
  It's sunny. *C'è il sole.*

Sunday *domenica* (f.)
sunglasses *occhiali da sole*
superior *superiore*
supermarket *supermercato* (m.)
sure *sicuro*
surprise *sorpresa* (f.)
  What a surprise! *Che sorpresa!*
surprise (to) *sorprendere*
sweater *maglione* (m.)
sweet *dolce*
swim (to) *nuotare*
swimming *nuoto* (m.)
symphony *sinfonia* (f.)
symptom *sintomo* (m.)
system *sistema* (m.)

T

table *tavolo* (m.)
tagliatelle (pasta) *tagliatelle* (f. pl.)
tail (of coin) *croce* (f.)
take (to) *portare, prendere*
  take (time) (to) *metterci, volerci*
  take a bath (to) *fare il bagno*
  take a break (to) *fare una pausa*
  take a nap (to) *fare un pisolino*
  take a nice long nap (to) *farsi una bella
    dormita*
  take a picture (to) *fare una foto/fotografia*
  take a shower (to) *fare la doccia*
  take a trip (to) *fare una gita, fare un viaggio*
  take a walk (to) *fare una passeggiata*
take off (to) *decollare*
talented *bravo, con talento; in gamba* (colloquial)
talk *discorso* (m.), *colloquio* (m.)
  talk show *interviste* (f. pl.) *alla televisione*
tall *alto*
taste *sapore* (m.)
taxi *taxi* (m.)
taxi driver *tassista* (m./f.)
tea *tè* (m.)
tea kettle *bollitore* (m.)
teach (to) *insegnare*
teacher *insegnante* (m./f.); *maestro/a* (m./f.)
  (*nursery school and elementary school*)
team *squadra* (f.)
technical *tecnico*
teenager *adolescente* (m./f.), *teenager* (m./f., pl.
  teenager)

telegram *telegramma* (m.)
telephone *telefono* (m.)
  answer the phone (to) *rispondere al telefono*
  cell phone *cellulare* (m.), *telefonino* (m.)
telephone (to) *telefonare, chiamare*
television *televisione* (f.), *tele* (f.), *tivù* (f.),
  televisore (m.) (noun); *televisivo* (adjective)
  television program *trasmissione* (f.) *televisiva*
  watch television (to)) *guardare la
    televisione/tele/ tivù*
  watch sports on TV (to) *guardare lo sport in/
    alla televisione*
tell (to) *raccontare, dire*
temperature *temperatura* (f.)
temple *tempio* (m.)
temporary *temporaneo*
ten *dieci*
  from 10:45 a.m. to 3:00 p.m. *dalle undici meno
    un quarto alle tre*
tendon *tendine* (m.)
tennis *tennis* (m., pl. *tennis*)
  play tennis (to) *giocare a tennis*
  tennis shoes *scarpe* (f. pl.) *da tennis*
tenth *decimo*
terrible *terribile*
test *test* (m.)
textbook *libro (di testo)*
than *di, che*
  less … than *meno … di/che*
  more/-er … than *più … di/che*
  than usual *del solito*
Thank you. *Grazie.*
Fine, thanks. *(Sto) bene, grazie.*
Thanks a lot. *Grazie mille.*
Very well, thanks. *Molto bene, grazie.*
that (conjunction) *che*
that (demonstrative) *quello*
that (relative pronoun) *che*
the *il* (m. sg.) (in front of a consonant); *lo* (m. sg.)
  (in front of s + consonant, z, ps, gn); *l'* (m. sg./f. sg.)
  (in front of a vowel); *la* (f. sg.) (in front of a
  consonant); *i* (m. pl.) (in front of consonants); *gli* (m.
  pl.) (in front of s + consonant, z, ps, gn, in front of
  vowels); *le* (f. pl.) (in front of consonants or vowels)
theater *teatro* (m.)
  movie theater *cinema* (m., pl.)
their *loro* (inv.)
them (direct object pronoun) *li/le* (m./f.)

them (direct object, disjunctive pronoun) *loro*
to them (indirect object pronoun) *gli*
to them (indirect object, disjunctive pronoun) *a loro*
then *poi, allora*
  And then? *E poi?*
there *lì, ci*
  Go there. *Vacci.*
  Let's go there. *Andiamoci.*
  near there *lì vicino*
  There is... *C'è...*
  There are... *Ci sono...*
  There are seven of us. *Siamo in sette.*
  There are three of them. *Ce ne sono tre.*
therefore *dunque, quindi*
thesis *tesi (f., pl. tesi)*
they (subject pronoun) *loro*
  they (impersonal pronoun) *si*
thick *grosso*
thin *magro, sottile*
thin slice *fettina (f.)*
thing *cosa (f.)*
  things to do *cose da fare*
  tons of things, a thousand things *mille cose*
think (to) *pensare*
  I don't think so. *Non credo.*
  I'll think about it. *Ci penserò.*
  think about... (doing somehing)
    (to) *pensare di...*
  think about... (something/somebody)
    (to) *pensare a...*
third *terzo*
  third-born *terzogenito/a*
thirst *sete (f.)*
thirsty (to be) *avere sete*
thirteen *tredici*
thirty *trenta*
  at seven thirty (7:30) *alle sette e mezza*
  It's 3:30. *Sono le tre e trenta.*
this *questo*
  in this period *in questo periodo*
  this evening *questa sera, stasera*
  this week *questa settimana*
thousand *mille (m.), mila (pl.)*
  two thousand *duemila*
three *tre*
  from 10:45 a.m. to 3:00 p.m. *dalle undici meno un quarto alle tre*

It's three (o'clock). *Sono le tre.*
It's 3:15. *Sono le tre e quindici.*
It's 3:45. *Sono le tre e quarantacinque./Sono le tre e tre quarti./Sono le quattro meno un quarto./Manca un quarto alle quattro.*
It's 3:30. *Sono le tre e trenta.*
There are three of them. *Ce ne sono tre.*
through *per*
thumb *pollice (m.)*
thunder *tuono (m.)*
thunder (to) *tuonare*
Thursday *giovedì (m., pl.)*
ticket *biglietto (m.)*
tie *cravatta (f.)*
tie (to) *fare pari*
till *fino (a)*
time *tempo (m.), orario (m.), volta (f.)*
  at the same time *allo stesso tempo*
  every time *ogni volta*
  for a very long time *da una vita*
  free time *tempo libero*
  full-time *a pieno tempo*
  have time (to) *avere tempo*
  It's time to... *È ora di...*
  long time *molto tempo*
  on time (to be) *essere in orario, essere puntuale*
  part-time *part-time*
  part-time job *lavoro part-time*
  waste time (to) *perdere tempo*
  What time is it? *Che ora è?/Che ore sono?*
tip *mancia (f.)*
tired *stanco*
title *titolo (m.)*
to *in, a, da*
  from... to... (time periods) *dalle... alle...*
  from Monday to Friday *dal lunedì al venerdì*
  from 10:45 a.m. to 3:00 p.m. *dalle undici meno un quarto alle tre*
  nothing good to eat *niente di buono da mangiare*
  something to drink *qualcosa da bere*
  things to do *cose (f. pl.) da fare*
  to the city *in centro*
  to the country *in campagna*
  to the left *(a) sinistra*
  to the mountains *in montagna*
  to the right *(a) destra*

today *oggi*
toe (big) *alluce* (m.)
together *insieme*
  (together) with you *insieme a te*
toilet *water* (m.), *gabinetto* (m.)
toilet paper *carta* (f.) *igienica*
tomato *pomodoro* (m.)
tomorrow *domani*
tongue *lingua* (f.)
tonight *stasera*
tons of things *mille cose* (f. pl.)
too *anche*
  Pleased to meet you, too. *Piacere mio.*
too (much/many) *troppo/a* (m./f.) (noun); *troppo*
  (adjective)
  go too far (to) *esagerare*
  Too bad! *Peccato!*
tooth *dente* (m.)
tortellini *tortellini* (m. pl.)
tour *giro* (m.)
  guided tour *viaggio* (m.) *organizzato*
  tour bus *pullman* (m.)
tourist *turista* (m./f.)
  foreign tourists *turisti* (pl.) *stranieri*
towel *asciugamano* (m.)
tower *torre* (f.)
town *cittadina* (f.); *paese* (m.) *(small)*
  around town *in giro per la città*
  hometown *città* (f.) *natale*
  out of town *fuori città*
trade fair *fiera* (f.)
traditional *tradizionale*
traffic *traffico* (m.)
traffic light *semaforo* (m.)
train *treno* (m.)
  by train *in treno*
  train station *stazione* (f.) *(dei treni)*
training *formazione* (f.)
transfer (to) *trasferirsi*
transparent *trasparente*
transportation *trasporto* (m.)
  means of transportation *mezzo* (m.) *di*
    trasporto
travel *viaggio* (m.)
travel (to) *viaggiare*
  travel abroad (to) *viaggiare all'estero*
tread on (to) *calpestare*
treat (to) *curare*

tree *albero* (m.)
trip *viaggio* (m.)
  day trip *gita* (f.)
  Have a good trip. *Buon viaggio.*
  short trip *gita* (f.)
  take a trip (to) *fare un viaggio*
true *vero*
truth *verità* (f., pl.)
try (to) *provare*
  try on (to) *provare*
  try to … (to) *cercare di …*
t-shirt *maglietta* (f.)
tub *vasca* (f.)
  bath tub *vasca (da bagno)*
Tuesday *martedì* (m., pl. *martedì)*
turn (to) *girare, voltare*
twelve *dodici*
twenty *venti*
twenty-four *ventiquattro*
twenty-one *ventuno*
twenty-three *ventitré*
twenty-two *ventidue*
twice a week *due volte alla settimana*
two *due*
  It's two (o'clock). *Sono le due.*
  two and a half hours *due ore e mezzo*
  two days ago *due giorni fa*
  two thousand *duemila*
type *tipo* (m.)

U

ugly *brutto*
umbrella *ombrello* (m.)
uncle *zio (m., pl. zii)*
undecided *indeciso*
under *sotto*
  under stress *stressato*
underpants *slip* (m. pl.) *(men's)*; *mutandine* (f. pl.)
  (women's)
undershirt *canottiera* (f.)
understand (to) *capire*
unemployed *disoccupato/a* (m./f.)
unfortunately *purtroppo*
unfriendly *antipatico*
university *università (f., pl. università)* (noun);
  universitario (adjective)
  university degree *laurea* (f.)
  university student *studente* (m.) *universitario*

unless... *a meno che... non*
until *finché, fino (a)*
  until late *fino a tardi*
  until the end *fino in fondo*
up to *fino (a)*
upon *su*
upset (to) *dispiacere*
urban *urbano*
us (direct object pronoun) *ci*
  us (direct object, disjunctive pronoun) *noi*
  to us (indirect object pronoun) *ci*
  to us (indirect object, disjunctive pronoun) *a noi*
use (to) *usare*
useful *utile*
usual *solito*
  than usual *del solito*
usually *di solito*

V

vacation *ferie* (f. pl.), *vacanza* (f.)
  on vacation *in ferie, in vacanza*
vaguely *vagamente*
variety *varietà* (f.)
  variety of choices *varietà di scelta*
veal *vitello* (m.)
vegetable *verdura* (f.)
vegetable garden *orto* (m.)
velvet *velluto* (m.)
vendor *commerciante* (m./f.)
Venice *Venezia* (f.)
version *versione* (f.)
very *molto, tanto*
  for a very long time *da una vita*
  very beautiful *bellissimo*
  very interesting *interessantissimo*
  Very pleased to meet you! *Molto piacere!*
  Very well! *Benissimo!*
  Very well, thanks. *Molto bene, grazie.*
veterinarian *veterinario/a* (m./f.)
view *vista* (f.)
village *paese* (m.); *paesino* (m.) (small)
virgin *vergine* (f.)
visit (to) *visitare*
  come visit (to) *venire a trovare*
  go visit (to) *andare a trovare*
volleyball *palla* (f.) *a volo*

W

waist *vita* (f.)
wait for (to) *aspettare*
  Wait a second. *Un momento.*
waiter *cameriere* (m.)
waitress *cameriera* (f.)
wake up (to) *svegliarsi*
walk *passeggiata* (f.)
  Enjoy your walk./Have a good walk. *Buona passeggiata.*
  go for a walk (to) *fare un giro/fare un giro a piedi*
  take a walk (to) *fare una passeggiata*
walk (to) *camminare*
wall *parete* (f.), *muro* (m.)
want (to) *volere, desiderare*
wardrobe *armadio* (m.)
warehouse *magazzino* (m.)
wash (to) *lavare*
  wash oneself (to) *lavarsi*
washing machine *lavatrice* (f.), *lavabiancheria* (f.)
waste time (to) *perdere tempo*
watch *orologio* (m.)
watch (to) *guardare*
  Watch out! *Sta' attento!*
  watch sports on TV (to) *guardare lo sport in/alla televisione*
  watch television (to) *guardare la tivù/tele/televisione*
water *acqua* (f.)
  mineral water *acqua minerale*
  still mineral water *acqua minerale naturale*
  sparkling mineral water *acqua minerale frizzante*
way *via* (f.), *modo* (m.)
  by the way *a proposito*
  the way in which... *il modo in cui...*
we (subject pronoun) *noi*
weak *debole*
wear (to) *portare, indossare*
  He/She wears. *Si mette...*
weather *tempo* (m.)
  What's the weather like? *Che tempo fa?*
web log *web log* (m.)
webpage *web page* (f.), *pagina* (f.) *web*
website *sito* (m.) *web*

wedding *matrimonio* (m.)
Wednesday *mercoledì* (m., pl.)
week *settimana* (f.)
  last week *settimana scorsa*
  next week *prossima settimana*
  this week *questa settimana*
  twice a week *due volte alla settimana*
weekend *fine settimana* (m., pl.), *weekend* (m., pl.)
welcome *benvenuto*
  You're welcome. *Prego.*
  Welcome back. *Bentornato.*
well *bene*
  I am well. *Mi sento bene.*
  (One) might as well… *Tanto vale…*
  Very well! *Benissimo!*
  Very well, thanks. *Molto bene, grazie.*
Well… *Beh…*
what *che*
  What? *Che cosa?*
  What a beautiful dish! *Che bel piatto!*
  What a surprise! *Che sorpresa!*
  What are you having? *Tu cosa prendi?*
  What do you do? *Che lavoro fai?*
  What time is it? *Che ora è?/Che ore sono?*
  What's the weather like? *Che tempo fa?*
when *quando*
where *dove*
  Where are you from? (fml.)/Where is he/she
    from? *Di dov'è?*
  Where are you from? (infml.) *Di dove sei?*
  Where is… ?/Where are… ? *Dov'è… ?/
    Dove sono… ?*
which *quale* (question); *cui, che* (relative pronoun)
  the way in which… *il modo in cui…*
while *mentre*
white *bianco*
  white wine *vino* (m.) *bianco*
who *chi* (question); *che* (relative pronoun)
whoever *chi*
whole *intero*
whom *che, cui*
Whose… is it ?/Whose… are they?
  Di chi è… ?/Di chi sono… ?
why *perché*
  the reason why… *il motivo per cui… / la
    ragione per cui…*
wide *ampio*
wife *moglie* (f.)

wild *selvaggio*
win (to) *vincere*
wind *vento* (m.)
  It's windy. *C'è vento./Tira vento.*
window *finestra* (f.)
wine *vino* (m.)
  red wine *vino rosso*
  wine list *lista* (f.) *dei vini*
  white wine *vino bianco*
winter *inverno* (m.) (noun); *invernale* (adjective)
  in winter *d'inverno*
wish *voglia* (f.)
  I wish *magari*
with *con, presso*
  (together) with you *insieme a te*
without *senza*
  without… *senza che…*
wolf *lupo* (m.)
woman *donna* (f.)
  businesswoman *donna d'affari*
  policewoman *donna poliziotto*
  saleswoman *venditrice* (f.)
wonderful *meraviglioso*
  Wonderful! *Benissimo!*
wood *legno* (m.), *bosco* (m.)
wooden *di legno*
wool *lana* (f.)
work *lavoro* (m.), *opera* (f.)
  works of art *opere* (pl.) *d'arte*
work (to) *lavorare*
worker *operaio/a* (m./f.)
  construction worker *muratore/trice* (m./f.)
world *mondo* (m.)
  around the world *intorno al mondo*
  in the world *del mondo*
worry (to) *preoccupare*
  I'm worried. *Sono preoccupato.*
worth (to be) *valere*
wrist *polso* (m.)
write (to) *scrivere*
writer *scrittore/trice* (m./f.)
wrong (to be) *avere torto*

Y

year *anno* (m.)
  every year *tutti gli anni*
  I am… years old. *Ho… anni.*
  last year *anno scorso*

yellow *giallo*
yes *sì*
yesterday *ieri*
yet *ancora*
yolk *tuorlo* (m.)
you (subject pronoun) *Lei* (sg. fml.), *tu* (sg. infml.),
 Loro (pl. fml.), *voi* (pl.)
  you (direct object pronoun) *La* (sg. fml.), *ti* (sg.
  infml.), *vi* (pl.)
  you (direct object, disjunctive pronoun) *Lei* (sg.
  fml.), *te* (sg. infml.), *voi* (pl.)
  to you (indirect object pronoun) *Le* (sg. fml.), *ti*
  (sg. infml.), *vi* (pl.)
  to you (indirect object, disjunctive pronoun) *a Lei*
  (sg. fml.), *a te* (sg. infml.), *a voi* (pl.)
young *giovane*
younger *minore*
your *Suo/Sua/Suoi/Sue* (sg. fml.); *tuo/tua/tuoi/*
 tue (sg. infml.); *Loro/Loro* (pl. fml.); *vostro/*
 vostra/vostri/vostre (pl. infml.)
youth hostel *ostello* (m.)

Z

zero *zero*
zoo *zoo* (m., pl.)
zucchini *zucchino* (m.)